SO-BFE-056

FEDERAL BUDGET AND FISCAL POLICY

FEDERAL BUDGET AND FISCAL POLICY
1789-1958

By LEWIS H. KIMMEL

THE BROOKINGS INSTITUTION
Washington, D. C.

Foreword

IN RECENT decades there has been a revolutionary change in theory and policy in regard to the balancing of the federal budget. Here is a review of the prevailing views that dictated policy from 1789 to the 1930's, and of the remarkable change in attitude that emerged after 1932 and led to the concept of pump priming, compensatory fiscal policy, and the assumption by government of responsibility for economic growth and cyclical stability. In a sense this is an account of the evolution of ideas, events, and policies that have led the American people toward a new conception of governmental responsibility. Only as these changes are seen against the full sweep of our fiscal history can the import of these developments be fully grasped. This account is presented as a contribution to public understanding of this vital aspect of federal policy.

The Institution is indebted to Lewis H. Kimmel for the preparation of this study. Helpful comments and suggestions have been made by John G. Gurley, Bert G. Hickman, Marshall A. Robinson, Walter S. Salant, and Ralph J. Watkins of the Brookings staff, by Gerhard Colm of the National Planning Association, and by Joseph A. Pechman and Herbert Stein of the Committee for Economic Development. A. Evelyn Breck gave helpful assistance in editing the manuscript. Virginia Angel prepared the index. To them the author and the Institution join in expressing their appreciation.

A major portion of the research underlying this volume was conducted in the Library of Congress and the library of the United States Treasury Department. The personnel of the Library of Congress, Isabella S. Diamond, librarian of the

vii

Treasury Department, and Margaret Maltby, librarian of the Brookings Institution, and her assistants generously responded to countless requests promptly and efficiently, thereby greatly facilitating the research. To them the author and the Institution wish to acknowledge their indebtedness and express their gratitude.

This study was undertaken with funds provided in the form of general support by the Ford Foundation. For this invaluable assistance the Institution is especially grateful.

The views expressed in the study are those of the author and should not be regarded as representing the views of those who have read the manuscript, or of the other staff members, officers, or Trustees of the Brookings Institution, nor should they be regarded as reflecting the views of the Ford Foundation.

Robert D. Calkins
President

Contents

Introduction

MODERN FISCAL THEORISTS hold that the federal government has a positive role to play in the economy. They regard the budget as an instrument of economic policy, and consider changes in the level and character of public expenditures from the standpoint of their effects on income and employment. On the other hand, until a few decades ago the federal budget was viewed mainly in terms of money costs. Governmental activities were widely thought to be a burden on the economy. The philosophy of the annually balanced budget enjoyed virtually universal acceptance. A balanced federal budget was believed to be a prerequisite for financial stability and economic growth.

This study traces the evolution of budget and fiscal policy from the beginning of the nation to the present time. The object is to provide the background for an understanding of current budget and fiscal policies. A major portion of the analysis is devoted to the balanced budget philosophy and to the theories and ideas advanced in explanation of the role of government. The change in outlook since the early 1930's, which has been influenced both by circumstances and by developments in fiscal and economic theory, is emphasized in later chapters.

Underlying the analysis is the thought that the great majority of ideas in economics and finance have a time-and-place significance. They are not immutable truths. Yet specific doctrines are often expounded in a manner that suggests neither temporal nor institutional limitations. An appreciation of the environment in which budget and fiscal

1

theories were developed is essential for their understanding. Any theory or idea should be appraised in the light of the conditions prevailing in the society in which it was advanced.

The federal government has operated under a budget, properly so-called, only since 1921—a period embracing about one fifth of our national history. The budget idea, however, was clearly in the minds of leading political and financial leaders as early as the Revolutionary and formative periods. The absence of logical or systematic budget methods during the early years and throughout the nineteenth century should not be construed as a lack of appreciation of the role of public finance.

It is a historical fact that the federal government and the present Constitution owe their existence in part to financial and budgetary considerations. The absence of effective financial powers during the Revolutionary War and under the Articles of Confederation was a major reason for the convention of 1787 that framed the new Constitution. The financial resources available to the Continental Congress during the Revolution were inadequate. The system of requisitioning funds from the several colonies, which was followed under the Articles of Confederation, was plainly unworkable. Though the Congress was a feeble institution from its inception—especially on the financial side—by the mid-1780's it was rapidly approaching complete impotency.[1]

With the ratification of the Constitution, the way was clear for the establishment of a responsible financial system. A first approach to budgeting was authorized by a law providing for the establishment of the Treasury Department enacted in September 1789.[2] Among other provisions, this act required the Secretary of the Treasury "to prepare and

[1] Charles J. Bullock, *The Finances of the United States from 1775 to 1789, with Especial Reference to the Budget* (1895), p. 251.
[2] 1 Stat. 65.

report estimates of the public revenues, and the public expenditures." However, Alexander Hamilton's efforts in the direction of an executive budget were unsuccessful, mainly because of congressional jealousy and existing party divisions. Buck states that

... jealousy between the legislative and executive branches of the government became so intensified that Congress sought executive decentralization in budgetary matters. In this situation the President did not insist upon the exercise of his evident constitutional right to prepare a budget as an administrative proposal, hence the budgetary powers passed to congressional committees. Thus budget making became an exclusively legislative function in the national government and as such it continued for more than a century.[3]

The book of estimates compiled under the supervision of the Secretary of the Treasury was a far cry from an executive budget. These estimates "were not compiled in accordance with any one principle, or in such a way that their significance could be clearly seen. There was no budgetary message; no proper scheme of summary, analytical, and comparative tables." Moreover, "expenditures were not considered in connection with revenues."[4] In the circumstances it is not surprising that a close correspondence between receipts and expenditures was attained only at infrequent intervals and more or less fortuitously.

The federal government relied on customs duties for the bulk of its revenues during most of our history. Customs rates were designed for revenue as well as protection, but it was not the intention of the Congress to adjust these rates annually or periodically with a view to achieving an approximate balance between receipts and expenditures. The abundance

[3] A. E. Buck, *Public Budgeting* (1929), p. 17. See also W. F. Willoughby, *The National Budget System* (1927), pp. 4 ff.

[4] *Ibid.*, p. 9. The budget idea was clearly in the minds of some federal officials and members of Congress from the beginning of the national government. For example, in his entry for January 14, 1790 Senator Maclay of Pennsylvania stated: "This day the 'budget,' as it is called, was opened in the House of Representatives." Edgar S. Maclay, ed., *Journal of William Maclay* (1890), p. 177.

of customs revenues during most of the nineteenth century made it unnecessary to weigh expenditures against revenues and brought about a progressive deterioration of the budget process.[5]

The first important step in the movement that culminated in the federal executive budget was taken in 1910, when President Taft appointed the Commission on Economy and Efficiency. This commission reached the conclusion that a recasting of the system for determining and providing for the financial needs of the government was of paramount importance. One of its first reports was entitled *The Need for a National Budget*.[6] To show how the proposed system might operate, estimates for 1914 in the form of a budget were presented in a separate report.[7] The Congress resented this move, and the report was not even considered by the Appropriations Committee of the House of Representatives to which it was referred.[8]

The work of this commission had enormous educational value. The defects of the existing system (or lack of system) were pointed out, and the merits of a budget system as a corrective were emphasized. "The prestige of the Commission and its strong backing by the President made budgeting an issue of national significance."[9] The commission's efforts did not result in the immediate adoption of a well-organized budget system. The moderate size of federal fiscal requirements and inertia were perhaps the major reasons for setting aside the budget proposal. Almost a decade was to elapse before the movement for an executive budget reached fruition.

The changed fiscal situation following World War I caused renewed interest in the executive budget. The war catapulted

[5] Arthur Smithies, *The Budgetary Process in the United States* (1955), p. 49.

[6] H. Doc. 854, 62 Cong. 2 sess.

[7] S. Doc. 1113, 62 Cong. 3 sess. This report was entitled *Message of the President of the United States Submitting for the Consideration of the Congress a Budget with Supporting Memoranda and Reports.*

[8] For a full account, see Willoughby, *The National Budget System*, pp. 20–23.

[9] Jesse Burkhead, *Government Budgeting* (1956), p. 21.

peacetime federal expenditures to an entirely new order of
magnitude—over $3 billion annually compared with about
$700 million before the war. After World War I interest pay-
ments alone exceeded federal expenditures for all purposes in
the prewar years. For the first time internal revenue taxes
represented a substantial burden. In this situation the
effective control of federal expenditures became a matter of
prime importance. A well-conceived budget system seemed
to many a logical means to this end.

The Budget and Accounting Act was approved by President Harding on June 10, 1921. It gave the President the
authority to prepare and submit an annual budget to the
Congress. It was provided that the budget document should
give complete information regarding the condition of the
Treasury, revenues and expenditures in the last completed
fiscal year, estimates for the current year, and the President's
program for the forthcoming year—including the manner in
which the proposed expenditures should be financed. It was
also provided that a Bureau of the Budget should be established, with the primary function of a service agency of the
President in the preparation of the budget.[10]

From the beginning of the national government, budget
and financial policies were predicated on the belief that an
annually balanced budget was essential in time of peace.[11]
The budget was regarded as balanced when revenues were
at least equal to expenditures. The surpluses and deficits as
officially announced may be misleading, unless one is familiar
with the manner in which they were derived. When is the
budget balanced? has long been regarded as fundamentally

[10] 42 Stat. 20. The legislative history of this measure is fully considered in Willoughby, *The National Budget System*, pp. 25–33. A comprehensive discussion of
federal budgeting since the establishment of the executive budget will be found in
Smithies, *The Budgetary Process in the United States*. A brief discussion of modern
fiscal policy and the budgetary process is presented in Chapter 7. See p. 283.

[11] The federal budgetary record from 1789 to 1958 is summarized in the Appendix.
See p. 313.

an accounting problem; the approach has also been in considerable measure a legal one. Until recent decades virtually no attention was paid to the economic aspects of budgeting. These observations do not imply any criticism of the treatment of specific items by the budget and accounting officers of the government. They are necessarily influenced mainly by the provisions of appropriation acts and other controlling legislation.

CHAPTER I

Budget Policy Before the Civil War

DURING MOST OF OUR national history, the views of federal officials and the public concerning budget policy often were not expressed directly. They are more frequently to be inferred from observations about the public debt. For this reason a substantial portion of this analysis deals with the public debt and debt attitudes.[1] The discussion frequently goes beyond budget and debt policies. The issues inevitably involve the functions of government and attitudes toward federal expenditures.

The discussion relates to budget policy rather than fiscal policy. For the first 140 years of our national history, or until the 1930's, federal budget policy was concerned mainly with the money costs of government and raising the revenues to meet them. In present-day usage fiscal policy has a different connotation. Fiscal policy may be defined as "a policy under which the government uses its expenditure and revenue programs to produce desirable effects and avoid undesirable effects on the national income, production, and employment."[2] It "emphasizes the effects of government expenditure and revenue upon the total economy and argues that

[1] In this study we are concerned with attitudes toward the public debt and debt policy rather than with problems of debt management. The borrowing operations of the Treasury during the period covered by the present chapter are considered in Robert A. Love, *Federal Financing* (1931), Chapters 1–3.

[2] Arthur Smithies, "Federal Budgeting and Fiscal Policy," in *A Survey of Contemporary Economics*, Vol. 1, Howard S. Ellis, ed. (1948), p. 174.

they should be used deliberately and consciously as 'a balancing factor' to secure economic stabilization."[3] At no time prior to the 1930's were public expenditures used deliberately and consciously as a balancing factor; there was little or no evidence of a conscious fiscal policy in the modern sense of the term.

The Formative Years

In the early days of the administration of George Washington (1789–1797), attaining an approximate balance between receipts and expenditures was part of the process by which financial stability was sought. Mainly because of the absence of effective revenue-raising powers, the central government under the Articles of Confederation had been reduced almost to impotency. If the finances of the new nation were to be placed on an even keel, revenues derived through the exercise of the federal taxing power were essential. In line with this objective, a plan for the provision of revenues (import duties) was placed before the House of Representatives in April 1789, the month in which Washington assumed office and about five months before the Treasury Department was established. This measure was enacted on July 4, and an act providing for the regulation and administration of the customs system was approved on July 31.[4]

[3] James A. Maxwell, *Fiscal Policy* (1955), p. 11.

[4] 1 Stat. 24, 29. Largely because of this strong beginning, the accounts for the fiscal period 1789–1791 showed a surplus of $150,000. Total revenues were $4.4 million; all but $19,000 was obtained from customs. *Annual Report of the Secretary of the Treasury on the State of the Finances for the Fiscal Year Ended June 30, 1956*, pp. 318–19. The figures here mentioned seem extremely small by present-day standards. The population in 1790 was only 3.9 millions. The economy was predominantly agricultural. The American people were dependent upon Europe for "ordinary wants of manufactured goods." The beginning of the Industrial Revolution in the United States, during which household industries gave way to the factory system, is placed by Harold U. Faulkner at 1790. *American Economic History* (1931), p. 291.

A major problem that engaged the attention of the new government was the establishment of the federal credit. The leading role was taken by Alexander Hamilton.[5] In the introduction to the "First Report on the Public Credit" dated January 9, 1790, Hamilton referred to the momentous nature of the truth contained in the resolution under which his investigations were conducted—"That an adequate provision for the support of the public credit is a matter of high importance to the honor and prosperity of the United States." In the "Second Report on the Public Credit" (January 16, 1795) he observed that a sound public credit was desirable not solely for governmental reasons. "Public and private credit are closely allied, if not inseparable."[6]

To Hamilton's fertile mind the financial difficulties of the preceding period suggested that the appropriate policy was to assume the state debts and to bring the domestically held public debt into more manageable form. Establishment of the federal credit required, above all else, adequate servicing and management of the outstanding debt. With this objective in mind, both the assumption of the state debts and consolidation of the domestically held public debt were proposed in the "First Report." With the consent of the creditors, the debt should be "remoulded into such a shape as will bring the expenditure of the nation to a level with its income." In modern parlance, Hamilton was proposing that the form of the debt be changed—or that it be funded—with a view to achieving a balanced budget. The latter goal was regarded as of prime importance: "Till this shall be accomplished the finances of the United States will never wear a proper countenance."[7]

The importance of adequate revenues for the success of Hamilton's plans is suggested by the dominant position of

[5] "During Washington's two administrations the United States was governed practically by his [Hamilton's] ideas, if not by his will." Herbert Croly, *The Promise of American Life* (1909), pp. 38–39.

[6] Alexander Hamilton, *Papers on Public Credit, Commerce and Finance*, Samuel McKee, Jr., ed. (1934), pp. 3, 171.

[7] *Ibid.*, p. 35.

interest payments in the federal budget. For the period 1789–1797 interest accounted for more than half of federal expenditures, a larger proportion than in any other era of our history.[8] Covering these payments from current revenues was an important element in the process through which the credit of the United States was established.[9] Hamilton was not greatly concerned by the large proportion of expenditures represented by interest. Though he did not stress the point, within a brief span of years the growth of the country might make an annual interest obligation of a few millions seem a matter of little consequence.

It would be incorrect to interpret Hamilton's expressed desire for an approximate balance between revenues and expenditures as tantamount to espousal of a rigid balanced budget philosophy. On the contrary, his entire analysis conveys the impression that he regarded the public credit as a valuable resource, especially in the event of an emergency. A factor often overlooked is that many of his views had a time-and-place significance. The immediate goals to which his attention was directed were placing the finances of the new government on an orderly basis and establishing the public credit. The merits of Hamilton's analysis and recommendations are in no way minimized by pointing out that the funding and assumption proposals—especially the latter —required the exercise of great skill, if they were to be made palatable to the Congress and to the electorate.

With this objective uppermost in mind, Hamilton was careful to mention that there were certain advantages or benefits in a funded public debt. In "countries in which the national debt is properly funded, and an object of established confidence, it answers most of the purposes of money. Transfers of stock or public debt are there equivalent to payments

---

[8] *Annual Report of the Secretary of the Treasury on the State of the Finances for the Fiscal Year Ended June 30, 1956*, p. 319.

[9] A fairly elaborate schedule of customs duties on wines, distilled spirits, tea, and coffee was proposed in the "First Report." The object of the suggested duties was stated to be "the firm establishment of the public credit." *Papers on Public Credit, Commerce and Finance*, p. 44.

in specie. . . . " Following an elaboration of the specific benefits, Hamilton alluded to the necessity of discharging the foreign-held debt according to the original agreements.[10]

The funding and assumption proposals were combined in a single measure, which was approved in August 1790.[11] Their acceptance was facilitated by the strong moral connotation of indebtedness—both public and private. Only a few years before the Reverend Samuel Wales of Connecticut had pointed out that refusal to pay just public debts was equivalent to taking property without the consent of the owner. The debt held abroad was a matter of special concern. The Reverend Joseph Huntington stated that if we refuse to pay this debt, God will be on the side of the foreigners as they resort to arms to collect their debts.[12]

From a policy standpoint, an important element in Hamilton's thinking was his suggestion in the "Second Report" that the entire debt of the United States—foreign and domestic—be extinguished in not more than 30 years, or by 1825.[13] There is the clear implication that as long as debt was outstanding, a balanced budget should be a primary goal of budget policy and a surplus was highly desirable. This suggestion by Hamilton re-enforces the view that the benefits of a funded public debt, which were discussed at some length, were emphasized in order to gain acceptance of the funding and assumption plans.[14]

---

[10] *Ibid.*, pp. 7 ff.

[11] 1 Stat. 138.

[12] Joseph Dorfman, *The Economic Mind in American Civilization, 1606–1865* (1946), Vol. 1, p. 244. Wales' observations appeared in *The Dangers of Our National Prosperity; and the Way to Avoid Them* (1785), pp. 13–19.

[13] *Papers on Public Credit, Commerce and Finance*, p. 154. The debt was actually extinguished by 1835. It is probable that if the War of 1812 had not intervened, Hamilton's goal would have been achieved. The combined deficits for the four years 1812–1815 amounted to approximately $68 million.

[14] One financial historian has stated categorically that "Hamilton was no believer in the doctrine that a national debt is a national blessing. As soon as the debt was funded, he began to mature measures for paying it." Albert S. Bolles, *Financial History of the United States from 1789 to 1860* (1885), p. 42. Charles J. Bullock has observed that it is not possible to reconcile all of Hamilton's remarks about public credit. *Selected Readings in Public Finance* (1906), p. 498. When one considers the situation at the time the "First Report" was prepared and Hamilton's immediate

Hamilton's views on the federal debt and the budget were neither narrow nor doctrinaire. To a remarkable extent for his period, he was able to distinguish between the use and abuse of credit. In his view the public credit was an intangible asset of enormous value, not only because of possible emergency needs but also because it stood at the very center of the financial system. Its establishment on firm ground was an essential first step if financial institutions were to evolve and grow as the nation progressed.[15]

In 1797 John Adams, a Federalist, succeeded Washington as President. Adams' political theory was not unlike Hamilton's, yet "his views on economic matters were the kind that Hamiltonians labeled 'agrarian.' Adams disliked banks with the note-issue power and public debts and had little enthusiasm for protective tariffs."[16] In his inaugural address he referred to the fact that the sums loaned and debts contracted in time of war "have necessarily become the subject of what have been called funding systems."[17] It was further observed that the "consequences arising from the continual accumulation of public debts in other countries ought to admonish us to be careful to prevent their growth in our own. The national defense must be provided for as well as the support of the Government; but both should be accomplished as much as possible by immediate taxes, and as little as possible by loans."[18]

Adams had heartily approved the funding system and the

objectives, the apparent inconsistency between the alleged benefits of a funded debt and the above policy recommendation in the "Second Report" seems less significant.

[15] "Apart from administration, Hamilton had extraordinary intuition in forecasting with a statesman's imagination the material development of America." Edward Channing, *A History of the United States* (1927), Vol. 4, p. 66.

[16] Dorfman, *The Economic Mind in American Civilization*, Vol. 1, p. 433.

[17] *Funding system* refers to the entire process through which that portion of expenditures not covered by revenues was converted into debt. This process frequently involved the issue of short-term obligations to cover deficits and their conversion later into bonds or other obligations of longer maturity. In the early period *funding system* was often used as equivalent to public debts.

[18] James D. Richardson, ed., *Messages and Papers of the Presidents* (1897), Vol. 1, pp. 243–44. The federal budget showed a surplus in three of the four years of Adams' administration.

assumption of the state debts. His sole objective was the establishment of the public credit, and he was happy to see the obligations of the government rise to par. But in his view the improvement in the federal credit was not attributable mainly to the genius of Hamilton. The policies of the Secretary had been successful because the new government had strength and adequate sources of revenue.[19]

The Jeffersonian Era

The change in administration in 1801, when Thomas Jefferson succeeded John Adams as head of the national government, is of considerable importance for students of finance. There was a fundamental difference of opinion between the two parties with respect to centralization of functions. The Jeffersonians or Republicans looked askance at almost any expansion of federal activity in new directions; the philosophy of Hamilton and other leading Federalists permitted a broader outlook. However, one should not overstate the case. When the opportunity to purchase the Louisiana Territory arose, neither the increase in debt nor any other consideration was allowed to stand in the way of consummation of the transaction.[20] Another difference between the two early parties had to do with the level at which national defense should be supported; there was a sharp difference of opinion concerning the need for a larger Navy.

The new administration continued to favor a balanced

[19] Manning J. Dauer, "The Political Economy of John Adams," *Political Science Quarterly*, Vol. 56 (1941), p. 554.

[20] "The Louisiana Purchase seems to be the one magnificent exception to Jefferson's rule of frugality." Adrienne Koch, *The Philosophy of Thomas Jefferson* (1943), p. 176. The purchase price of the Louisiana Territory was $15 million. Of this amount, $11,250,000 was borrowed at the rate of 6 per cent. The balance of $3,750,-000 was covered from current revenues. Bolles, *Financial History of the United States from 1789 to 1860*, pp. 66–67.

budget and debt reduction.[21] The first change in control from one party to another did not mean a change in these basic policies. Jefferson always believed that the public debt was the first charge on governmental revenues.[22] Perhaps his strongest statement in regard to the public debt is in his second annual message, where he expressed satisfaction concerning the "large and effectual payments toward the discharge of our public debt and the emancipation of our posterity from that mortal canker."[23] Jefferson's attitude toward the public debt was influenced by his conviction that one generation should not be permitted to bind the next one: "the earth belongs always to the living generation." He believed the "living generation" thesis was logically applicable to national debts. If it were necessary to incur public debts, they should be extinguished in something like 20 years.[24]

In a very real sense, Jefferson was the first "economy" president. Several years before assuming the Presidency, he wrote: "I am for a government rigorously frugal and simple, applying all the possible savings of the public revenue to the discharge of the national debt."[25] And on a later occasion: "I place economy among the first and most important of republican virtues, and public debt as the greatest of the dangers to be feared."[26] Developments during the first decade of the new government had not been entirely to his liking. In

[21] Throughout the nineteenth century "balanced budget" was less widely used than in recent decades. Peacetime policy was focused directly on the avoidance of deficits and the prevention of debt increases. The goal was revenues at least equal to expenditures.

[22] Dorfman, *The Economic Mind in American Civilization*, Vol. 1, p. 439.

[23] *Messages and Papers of the Presidents*, Vol. 1, p. 333. The second annual message was dated December 15, 1802.

[24] Dumas Malone, *Jefferson and His Time: Jefferson and the Rights of Man*, Vol. 2 (1951), pp. 179, 291. The strength of Jefferson's conviction is suggested by the observation that every "constitution . . . and every law, naturally expires at the end of 19 years. If it be enforced longer, it is an act of force and not of right."

[25] Letter to Elbridge Gerry, January 26, 1799, *The Writings of Thomas Jefferson* (1854), Vol. 4, p. 268; also in *Jeffersonian Principles*, James Truslow Adams, ed. (1928), p. 7.

[26] Letter to Governor William Plumer of New Hampshire, July 21, 1816, *The Writings of Thomas Jefferson*, Vol. 7, p. 19; also in William Plumer, Jr., *Life of William Plumer* (1857), p. 441.

his first annual message Jefferson questioned whether the federal government had become too complicated and too expensive. He believed a policy of retrenchment was urgently needed. In his view offices and officers may have "multiplied unnecessarily and sometimes injuriously to the service they were meant to promote." Expenditures for both the Army and the Navy were sharply reduced; the construction of several vessels under way in 1801 was actually stopped. The cost of the so-called civil list was also reduced appreciably.[27]

Jefferson was ably seconded by Albert Gallatin, who was easily the leader of his party in the mastery of the principles of political economy, in skill in handling financial details, and in clearness of conviction and intensity of purpose.[28] Gallatin especially disliked having to apply so large a percentage of revenues—about one third in 1805—to the payment of interest. Requirements for interest acted as a bar to the free disposal of the government's resources. The only way "the United States can ultimately obtain the full command of their revenue" is to retire the principal of the debt.[29]

Jefferson believed the activities of the federal government should be held to a minimum. He favored keeping government as close to the people as possible.[30] He envisioned a

[27] *Messages and Papers of the Presidents*, Vol. 1, p. 316. Federal expenditures for 1802 were less than $8 million, or about 30 per cent less than the $10.8 million recorded in 1800. A total as large as that for 1800 was not reached in any year of Jefferson's two administrations. *Annual Report of the Secretary of the Treasury on the State of the Finances for the Fiscal Year Ended June 30, 1956*, p. 319.

[28] Davis R. Dewey, *Financial History of the United States* (1931), p. 119. Gallatin's approach to federal finance has been likened to that of a thrifty businessman. John Spencer Bassett, *The Federalist System 1789–1801* (1906), p. 29.

[29] "It is sufficiently evident that, whilst one-third of the national revenue is necessarily absorbed by the payment of interest, a persevering application of the resources afforded by seasons of peace and prosperity, to the discharge of the principal, in the manner directed by the Legislature, is the only effectual mode by which the United States can ultimately obtain the full command of their revenue, and the free disposal of all their resources." "Report on the Finances: December 1805," in *Reports of the Secretary of the Treasury*, Vol. 1, 1790–1814 (1828), p. 301.

[30] The Jeffersonian philosophy of government was to a large extent a reflection of strong prejudices held by himself and his followers. No prejudice was more deeply ingrained than "the assumption that government was inherently corrupt, oppressive, and malevolent. For centuries ordinary men had looked upon political authority as a tool of the rich, as a means for perpetuating privilege and legalizing

healthy expansion of state and local activities, with a minimum of federal functions. As governor of Virginia, Jefferson
had "advocated a calculated dispersal of functions" and
"favored a government that was mild as well as reasonable."[31] His ideas concerning the functions of the several
strata of government were influenced by his belief that, as
the nation developed, it would remain primarily agricultural.
But his views were by no means rigid. When in 1806 it appeared that the federal government would soon have surplus
revenues that could not be applied to debt reduction without
modifying the terms of contract with the creditors, Jefferson
frankly proposed that the Congress explore the possibilities
of federal appropriations for the "great purposes of the public education, roads, rivers, canals, and such other objects of
public improvement" as may be thought proper.[32] He visualized the need for education at public expense as the new nation evolved. "In long retrospect, Americans have come to
regard him as the chief prophet of public education in the
first half-century of the Union."[33]

Madison to Buchanan

The Presidents who followed Jefferson favored a balanced
peacetime budget, together with the reduction and eventual
elimination of the federal debt. Surplus revenues were
deemed desirable because they made debt reduction possible.
A policy of reducing the debt was not only conducive to a

---

inequality." Clinton Rossiter, "Which Jefferson Do You Quote?" *The Reporter*,
Vol. 13 (Dec. 15, 1955), p. 33.

[31] Malone, *Jefferson and His Time: Jefferson the Virginian*, Vol. 1 (1948), p. 382.

[32] *Messages and Papers of the Presidents*, Vol. 1, pp. 397–98. Jefferson believed a
constitutional amendment would be necessary "because the objects now recommended are not among those enumerated in the Constitution, and to which it
permits the public moneys to be applied."

[33] Malone, *Jefferson and His Time: Jefferson the Virginian*, p. 280.

strong federal credit; as the debt was reduced, public revenues were freed for other purposes.

When James Madison (1809–1817) stated that one of the goals of his administration would be "to liberate the public resources by an honorable discharge of the public debts," he was expressing this philosophy.[34] James Monroe (1817–1825) took a similar position. He visualized effective use of the additional revenues that would be released when the debt was fully retired. After the elimination of the public debt, the government "would be left at liberty . . . to apply such portions of the revenue as may not be necessary for current expenses to such other objects as may be most conducive to the public security and welfare."[35] During the administration of John Quincy Adams (1825–1829), Secretary Richard Rush took special pride in the fact that "large sums have been applied to objects wearing a character neither temporary nor annual"—that is, for capital additions. These expenditures were facilitated by the steady decline in the debt and in interest payments.[36]

To John Quincy Adams a balanced budget was a sound maxim of political economy: "among the maxims of political economy which the stewards of the public moneys should never suffer without urgent necessity to be transcended is that of keeping the expenditures of the year within the limits of its receipts." A year earlier Adams had stated: "It is well for us . . . to be admonished of the necessity of abiding by the maxims of the most vigilant economy, and of resorting

[34] *Messages and Papers of the Presidents*, Vol. 2, pp. 452–53. The phrase "liberate the public resources" reflects the influence of Albert Gallatin who remained as Secretary of the Treasury until April 1813. Gallatin continued to advance his thesis that interest payments were equivalent to a deduction from aggregate receipts. "Report on the Finances: November 1811," in *Reports of the Secretary of the Treasury*, Vol. 1, p. 447.

[35] *Messages and Papers of the Presidents*, Vol. 2, p. 823. "Buoyant enthusiasm and unlimited self-confidence were . . . the characteristic note in the United States during the decade after 1815. . . . The country had found itself." Carl Becker, *The United States: An Experiment in Democracy* (1920), p. 128.

[36] "Report on the Finances: December 1827," in *Reports of the Secretary of the Treasury*, Vol. 2, 1815–1828 (1829), p. 389.

to all honorable and useful expedients for pursuing with steady and inflexible perseverance the total discharge of the debt."[37] Debt reduction was both a duty and an indication of financial capacity, in the opinion of Secretary Rush. "Amongst the highest duties of a nation, is faithfully to keep to its pecuniary engagements, and there need be no better demonstration of its pecuniary ability than when it is seen to pay off with promptitude and punctuality its funded debt."[38]

The pronouncements of Madison, Monroe, John Quincy Adams, and Treasury officials imply that federal revenues were narrowly restricted. One gets the impression they were thinking in terms of a fund that might fluctuate in amount, but that probably would not expand more rapidly than the economy as a whole. The fund approach suggested by phrases such as "liberate the public resources" was in fact quite realistic. Peacetime financial operations were predicated on the belief that customs duties should provide the bulk of the revenues, supplemented by proceeds from the sale of public lands[39] and small amounts of income from other sources. Except in war periods, there was strong resistance to the imposition of internal revenue taxes.[40]

The emphasis on interest payments as a special kind of burden on the public revenues suggests a fairly sophisticated

[37] *Messages and Papers of the Presidents,* Vol. 3, pp. 924, 953.

[38] "Report on the Finances: December 1828," in *Reports of the Secretary of the Treasury,* Vol. 2, p. 439. The views of Madison, Monroe, and John Quincy Adams concerning the public debt were somewhat less rigid than those of Jefferson. For example, Madison found Jefferson's living-generation thesis unacceptable. He believed that debts may be incurred for the benefit of the unborn no less than the living, and that obligations could be rightly inherited along with benefits. Malone, *Jefferson and His Time: Jefferson and the Rights of Man,* p. 291.

[39] There were no *net* receipts from the sale of public lands during the early decades of the federal government. To September 30, 1832 the lands—Louisiana, Florida, and others—had cost $49.7 million and the total revenue received on account of public lands was $38.4 million. *Messages and Papers of the Presidents,* Vol. 3, p. 1282.

[40] The internal taxes imposed during the War of 1812 were continued for several years after the end of hostilities. But strong opposition developed and they were repealed in response to public demand. The movement that led to repeal was in harmony with the Republican Party philosophy of the Jeffersonian era, which held that such taxes were "inquisitorial and inconsistent with democratic freedom, particularly in time of peace." Dewey, *Financial History of the United States,* pp. 119–20

outlook on federal finance. Though the modern concept of a transfer payment did not find expression, the basic idea is implied in official messages and reports. In the thinking of high government officials, federal expenditures requiring the allocation of goods and services to the government were in effect financed from a fund equal to ordinary receipts less interest payments.

To Andrew Jackson (1829–1837) a public debt represented an economic burden, as well as a fiscal one. When he took office, the financial position of the government and prevailing trends suggested that the federal debt would soon be extinguished. After this goal is reached, "our population will be relieved from a considerable portion of its present burthens, and will find not only new motives to patriotic affection, but additional means for the display of individual enterprise."[41]

The nature of the economic burden was spelled out by Samuel D. Ingham, Secretary of the Treasury. Discussing the impending extinguishment of the debt, he observed that the "interest is now paid to capitalists out of the profits of labor; not only will this labor be released from the burden, but the capital, thus thrown out of an unproductive, will seek a productive employment; giving thereby a new impetus to enterprise in agriculture, the arts, commerce, and navigation, at a lower charge for interest than before."[42] This statement embraces the principal economic arguments against public debts advanced during the first half of the nineteenth century: (1) interest on the public debt was a burden on the working classes; (2) interest payments involved a redistribution of income in favor of the well-to-do; and (3) the capital freed from unproductive employment through debt reduction would find its way into productive uses.

Extinguishment of the public debt was regarded by Jack-

---

[41] *Messages and Papers of the Presidents*, Vol. 3, p. 1014. This statement is from the first annual message to the Congress.

[42] "Report on the Finances: December 1829," in *Reports of the Secretary of the Treasury*, Vol. 3, 1829–1836 (1837), p. 17.

son and leading finance officials as desirable on patriotic and moral grounds. In 1831 it appeared that the remaining debt might be retired by the close of his first administration, or by March 1833. "We shall then exhibit the rare example of a great nation, abounding in all the means of happiness and security, altogether free from debt." A year later (December 1832) Jackson again congratulated Congress and the people "on the near approach of that memorable and happy event— the extinction of the public debt of this great and free nation."[43] In the opinion of Secretary Louis McLane, such an example would have a "moral influence . . . throughout the world." It would remove apprehension and inspire "new confidence in our free institutions."[44] When the debt was finally extinguished, Levi Woodbury, Secretary of the Treasury, stated that an "unprecedented spectacle is thus presented to the world."[45]

Jackson's views are of more than ordinary interest to the student of public finance. He is often referred to as a man of the people. His origins were more humble than those of his predecessors, most of whom were of aristocratic lineage. Jackson was a man of limited intellectual attainments. To a large degree his outlook and opinions were a reflection of those of rural and frontier America. The satisfaction expressed both before and after the extinguishment of the debt is understandable, only when one takes into account the view that public debt was not merely a misfortune but also evil and immoral. In his last year in office (December 1836) Jackson said: "The experience of other nations admonished us to hasten the extinguishment of the public debt; but it will be in vain that we have congratulated each other upon the disappearance of this evil if we do not guard against the equally great one of promoting the unnecessary accumula-

---

[43] *Messages and Papers of the Presidents*, Vol. 3, pp. 1118–19, 1160.
[44] "Report on the Finances: December 1831," in *Reports of the Secretary of the Treasury*, Vol. 3, pp. 222–23.
[45] "Report on the Finances: December 1835," *ibid.*, p. 643.

tion of public revenue."[46] This statement was an accurate reflection of public opinion. A public debt should be paid off promptly for it was at once a misfortune and an evil; and revenues markedly in excess of needs could not be condoned.[47]

When Martin Van Buren (1837–1841) became President, it appeared that, in the absence of outstanding debt, getting surplus revenues back into circulation would be a troublesome problem.[48] Unless a workable policy could be devised, the government would be "constantly exposed to great deficiencies or excesses, with all their attendant embarrassments."[49] When the recession of 1837–1838 resulted in a sharp drop in customs revenues and a substantial deficit, surpluses temporarily ceased to be a problem.

Van Buren stressed the financial freedom enjoyed by a nation free of debt. "The creation in time of peace of a debt likely to become permanent is an evil for which there is no equivalent." The federal government should always be "in a condition to discharge with ease and vigor the highest functions should their exercise be required by any sudden conjuncture of public affairs. . . . To this end it is indispensable that its finances should be untrammeled and its resources as far as practicable unencumbered. No circumstance could present greater obstacles to the accomplishment of these vitally important objects than the creation of an onerous national debt." In his last annual message Van Buren al-

[46] *Messages and Papers of the Presidents*, Vol. 4, p. 1459.

[47] See the later discussion at pp. 55–60.

[48] The act of June 23, 1836 providing for the distribution of federal surpluses among the states was at best a makeshift expedient. This act authorized the distribution of the balance in the Treasury on January 1, 1837, after reserving $5 million, among the several states of the Union. 5 Stat. 55. The amount thus available was $37.5 million. Payment in four installments was provided, but the fourth installment was not paid. These distributions took the form of deposits which were callable by the Treasury, but they were not repaid.

Van Buren was the only President who assumed office when the federal government was free of debt. Only the years 1836 and 1837 show no interest payments. A small amount of non-interest-bearing debt was outstanding in these years.

[49] "Report on the Finances: September 1837," in *Reports of the Secretary of the Treasury*, Vol. 4, 1837–1844 (1851), pp. 9–10.

luded to what was then considered an important objection
to public debts. The "tendency of public securities to con-
centrate ultimately in the coffers of foreign stockholders is
one which is every day gathering strength." Another "objection, scarcely less formidable, to the commencement of a
new debt, is its inevitable tendency to increase in magnitude
and to foster national extravagance."[50]

The moderate debt outstanding during the late 1830's and
1840's was regarded as a misfortune. John Tyler (1841–
1845) took the position that "a public debt in time of peace
should be sedulously avoided." When it appeared that the
deficit for 1842 might amount to as much as $14 million, he
observed that the "gravity of the evil calls for a remedy
proportioned to it." The President stated that "relying . . .
on the representatives of a people rendered illustrious among
nations by having paid off its whole debt," he would not
shrink from his responsibility to point out such measures as
would ensure adequate relief.[51]

Though the short-run financial results were frequently
viewed with misgivings, the federal record for the first half
century was considered excellent. From 1789 to 1835 the
Treasury had retired debt in the amount of $257 million and

[50] *Messages and Papers of the Presidents*, Vol. 4, p. 1752; Vol. 5, pp. 1824–25.
The large amount of state debts held abroad was a matter of concern. The interest
on such holdings was then about $12 million annually. Entirely aside from this
financial drain, such holdings afforded foreign holders a pretext to scrutinize the
management of our domestic affairs. A little less than a year before Van Buren's
last annual message, Alexander Trotter had published his *Observations on the
Financial Position and Credit of Such of the States of the North American Union as
Have Contracted Public Debts.* This work was published in London and was dated
December 26, 1839. Trotter estimated the combined debts of the states at $183
million as of 1835. Pp. 350, 406.

[51] *Messages and Papers of the Presidents*, Vol. 5, pp. 1891, 1961. To Tyler the
credit of the federal government was "the very soul of the Government itself—a
principle of vitality without which all its movements are languid and all its operations embarrassed." *Ibid.*, p. 2060.

The patriotic motive was stressed by Secretary Walter Forward. "The honor
of the country, its just self-respect, the pride which every citizen must feel in the
high character of its Government—all these require that the public faith and credit
of that Government should be placed above doubt or question." "Report on the
Finances: December 1842," in *Reports of the Secretary of the Treasury*, Vol. 4, p. 490.

paid $158 million in interest, a total of $415 million. This achievement was hailed by Secretary George M. Bibb in the following encomium:

> The moral power, courage, and capabilities by which a nation in its infancy, loaded with a debt of the revolutionary war of such magnitude, harassed by Indian wars, and encumbered by another debt of the war of 1812, terminated in 1815, discharged those debts faithfully—exhibiting to a gazing and astonished world the example of a nation which had exerted such energies, of a Government without a national debt, with an overflowing Treasury, and without direct taxes, internal duties, and excises—are to be looked for in the genius of the Government, the integrity of those who have been elected to administer it, the good sense, honesty, and enterprise of the citizens, and lastly, though not least, in the beneficent smiles of an all-wise and protecting Providence.[52]

From the official papers of James K. Polk (1845–1849). one gets the impression that the brief period when the federal government was free of debt ranked as a great moment in history. Our country "owes to mankind the permanent example of a nation free from the blighting influence of a public debt." Only a few years before we had "presented to the world the rare and noble spectacle of a great and growing people who had fully discharged every obligation." Polk probably gave more emphasis to the patriotic motive—the strength-among-nations argument—than any earlier President. He believed that the national debts of European monarchies, and especially attempts to rationalize them, were indefensible. "Melancholy is the condition of that people whose government can be sustained only by a system which periodically transfers large amounts from the labors of the many to the coffers of the few."[53]

The goal of a nation again debt-free eluded Polk because of the War with Mexico. But his philosophy remained unchanged. In his last annual message (December 1848), Polk stated that "it is our true policy, and in harmony with the

---

[52] "Report on the Finances: December 1844," *ibid.*, p. 655.
[53] *Messages and Papers of the Presidents*, Vol. 5, pp. 2227, 2252–53.

genius of our institutions, that we should present to the
world the rare spectacle of a great Republic . . . wholly ex-
empt from public indebtedness. This would add still more to
our strength, and give to us a still more commanding position
among the nations of the earth."[54]

The Presidents who served between the War with Mexico
and the Civil War favored debt reduction. Thus, Zachary
Taylor (1849–1850) stated in his inaugural address that one
of the objectives of his administration would be the "speedy
extinguishment of the public debt." The use of surplus
revenues to retire debt was a cardinal principle in the fiscal
philosophy of Franklin Pierce (1853–1857). In 1853 when
the revenue "levied almost insensibly" on the taxpayer was
increasing to a level beyond immediate needs, a two-pronged
policy was suggested: (1) apply the surplus to the discharge
of the public debt so far as it could judiciously be done; and
(2) "devise means for the gradual reduction of the revenue
to the standard of the public exigencies."[55] When James
Buchanan (1857–1861) took office, the financial condition of
the government was "without a parallel in history. No nation
has ever before been embarrassed from too large a surplus in
its treasury." Increased expenditures for "great national objects for which a clear warrant can be found in the Constitution" were suggested. Included were extinguishment of the
public debt, a reasonable increase of the Navy, and improvement of coastal defenses.[56]

The most cogent economic argument offered in support of
balanced budgets in the two decades before the Civil War
was that public borrowing diminishes the capital fund from
which wages are paid. This thesis was advanced in 1848 by
Robert J. Walker, Secretary of the Treasury. "Wages can

---

[54] *Ibid.*, p. 2500.
[55] *Ibid.*, Vol. 6, pp. 2544, 2746–47. Pierce viewed the flow of customs revenues
with enormous satisfaction. "Ours is almost, if not absolutely, the solitary power
of Christendom having a surplus revenue drawn immediately from imposts on
commerce. . . ."
[56] *Ibid.*, Vol. 7, p. 2964.

only be increased in any nation, in the aggregate, by augmenting capital, the fund out of which wages are paid. . . . On the other hand, the destruction or diminution of capital, by destroying or reducing the fund from which labor is paid, must reduce wages."[57]

The role of credit in time of war received increasing attention as the war clouds gathered. A little over two years before the outbreak of hostilities, Buchanan stressed the importance of a reserve of credit power. "In case of war our credit must be our chief resource, at least for the first year, and this would be greatly impaired by having contracted a large debt in time of peace."[58] This of course is a special application of the preservation-of-the-public-credit argument advanced by Alexander Hamilton, among others.

DEPRESSION POLICIES

The question of an appropriate budget policy during a recession or depression was considered by several Presidents. At the time of the recession of 1837–1838 Van Buren's views were set forth at some length in a message to a special session of Congress. Under the adverse conditions then prevailing, the President recommended "caution and forbearance in appropriations." Federal expenditures should be rigidly controlled. The official position was that no circumstance could justify deficits in time of peace. Under no conditions should the citizen look to the government for aid to relieve embarrassments arising from losses by "revulsions" in commerce and credit.

All communities are apt to look to government for too much. Even in our own country, where its powers and duties are so strictly limited, we are prone to do so, especially at periods of

[57] "Report on the Finances: December 1848," in *Reports of the Secretary of the Treasury*, Vol. 6, 1845–1848 (1851), p. 290. Walker adopted a favorite argument of the economists as his own, though no credit is given. See p. 45 of this study.

[58] *Messages and Papers of the Presidents*, Vol. 7, p. 3052.

sudden embarrassment and distress. But this ought not to be. The framers of our excellent Constitution and the people who approved it with calm and sagacious deliberation acted at the time on a sounder principle. They wisely judged that the less government interferes with private pursuits the better for the general prosperity.[59]

In the autumn of 1839 there was a return of financial difficulties. At this juncture Van Buren took a firm stand against both increased taxes and new loans. The struggle against the ruinous practice of supplying the supposed necessities of government by new loans "must be made at the threshold. To make our efforts effective, severe economy is necessary."[60] The foreign-held debt of American states and business concerns, which was estimated at not less than $200 million, was a matter of concern; more than $10 million annually was required to cover the interest. The nation, the President said, should not turn for relief to gigantic banking institutions or splendid, though in many instances profitless, railroads and canals. "It is not by the increase of this debt that relief is to be sought, but in its diminution."[61]

The financial panic and recession of 1857–1858 during Buchanan's administration had sharp repercussions on federal finance. In a special message on finance submitted in June 1858, the President observed: "Adversity teaches useful lessons to nations as well as individuals. The habit of extravagant expenditures, fostered by a large surplus in the Treasury, must now be corrected or the country will be involved in serious financial difficulties." It was apparent that econo-

---

[59] *Ibid.*, Vol. 4, p. 1561.

[60] *Ibid.*, p. 1752. Secretary Levi Woodbury commented on the difficulty of controlling expenditures. "It is difficult in a young, growing, and enterprising community, to restrict public expenditures within reasonable limits." In his opinion, federal expenditures of $20 million for ordinary purposes were more than "sound policy justifies, while the present unusual embarrassment in moneyed affairs shall continue." "Report on the Finances: December 1839," in *Reports of the Secretary of the Treasury*, Vol. 4, p. 238.

[61] *Messages and Papers of the Presidents*, Vol. 4, pp. 1769–70; Edward M. Shepard, *Martin Van Buren* (1899), pp. 370–74.

mies alone would not solve the budget problem, and the President called for additional revenues. Without additional revenue, "the Treasury will be exhausted . . . and the public credit will be seriously impaired. This disgrace must not fall upon the country." Faced with a substantial deficit, Buchanan stated later that it would be a ruinous policy to "go on increasing the national debt to meet the ordinary expenses of the Government."[62]

By late 1858 Buchanan was able to report that the effects of the financial "revulsions" were slowly passing away. The rather pronounced increase in the national debt caused by the recession, together with the unwillingness of Congress to heed the request for revenues, was regarded with disfavor. "It is our true policy to increase our revenue so as to equal our expenditures." Though deficits were incurred during the last two years of Buchanan's administration, he never lost sight of the goal of a balanced budget.[63]

WARTIME POLICIES

Well before the outbreak of the War of 1812, Secretary Albert Gallatin proposed that in the event of war the extraordinary expenses should be covered by borrowings. Under this plan revenues should at least equal the expenses of the peacetime establishment, plus interest on both the existing debt and the debt incurred to carry on the war.[64] Because

[62] *Messages and Papers of the Presidents*, Vol. 7, pp. 3019–20, 3052.

[63] *Ibid.* Requests for additional revenues were repeated in his last two annual messages, but no action commensurate with the requirements was taken. *Ibid.*, pp. 3105, 3181. Bolles states that the credit of the government had been undermined by Buchanan's administration. *Financial History of the United States from 1861 to 1885* (1886), pp. 4–5. The combined deficits for the first three years amounted to $50 million. The deficit for the fiscal year 1861, which included the first four months of Lincoln's administration and the beginning of hostilities, was $25 million. The unsettled political situation, which became explosive in 1860 and early 1861, was doubtless a more important factor than the financial policies of Buchanan's administration.

[64] "Report on the Finances: November 1807," in *Reports of the Secretary of the Treasury*, Vol. 1, p. 360.

of the sharp decline in customs revenues that had been caused by the disruption in foreign trade, it appeared that even this minimum program would require new sources of revenue. Following the outbreak of hostilities, requests for additional revenues were made. They went unheeded until the summer of 1813, when internal taxes designed to yield $5 million were approved. This legislation, together with rate increases approved in 1814, contributed to a marked improvement in the finances during the latter part of the war.[65] In no year, however, did revenues cover as much as half of expenditures. The increase in debt during the four years 1812–1815 was about $68 million.[66]

Budget policy under wartime and postwar conditions received considerable attention during and after the War with Mexico. This war did not have any serious repercussions on federal finance, and the requirements were easily met. Polk regarded the war as a special reason for economy in ordinary expenditures. "Economy in the public expenditures is at all times a high duty which all public functionaries of the Government owe to the people. This duty becomes the more imperative in a period of war, when large and extraordinary expenditures become unavoidable."[67]

After the war limitation of public expenditures to necessary objects and the use of surpluses for debt retirement were recommended by Polk. The errors of the period after the War of 1812 should be avoided. Congress had then authorized large and in some instances unnecessary and extravagant expenditures. The powers of the federal government, he pointed out, had been enlarged, and internal improvements had been federally financed.[68]

---

[65] Dewey, *Financial History of the United States*, pp. 138–42.

[66] The figures for receipts, expenditures, and deficits for these years are shown in the appendix table on p. 316.

[67] *Messages and Papers of the Presidents*, Vol. 6, p. 2348.

[68] *Ibid.*, pp. 2442–43, 2505. A special tribute was accorded to Jackson, whose "stern will and unbending policy" had resulted in a nation free of debt.

The discussion thus far has dealt mainly with broad aspects of budget and debt policy on which there was substantial unanimity of opinion. In contrast, sharp differences developed with respect to internal improvements. Though this controversy was waged primarily on constitutional grounds, the scope of the federal budget was clearly at issue.

INTERNAL IMPROVEMENTS

The reference above implies that Polk believed the federal government had actively promoted internal improvements after the War of 1812. It is true that both Madison and Monroe regarded roads and canals as essential for the development of the nation.[69] Their position on this question was not unlike that of Albert Gallatin who believed that internal improvements would increase and diffuse the national wealth and "strengthen the bonds of union."[70] But neither Madison nor Monroe was willing to approve bills authorizing additional expenditures for internal improvements when their validity seemed questionable. Moreover, the record does not support the charge of extravagance, unless the moderate expenditures on projects such as the Cumberland Road be so construed.

By 1824, when an appropriation of $30,000 for plans and surveys suggested the possibility of a broader program, the internal improvement question had become the center of almost continuous controversy. John Quincy Adams referred to the great importance of roads in his inaugural address (March 1825), and he was criticized for making Monroe's

[69] In 1815 Madison called the attention of the Congress to "the great importance of establishing throughout our country the roads and canals which can best be executed under the national authority." No "objects within the circle of political economy so richly repay the expense bestowed on them; there are none the utility of which is more universally ascertained and acknowledged." *Ibid.*, Vol. 2, p. 552. Similar views were expressed by Monroe on a number of occasions. *Ibid.*, pp. 577, 586–87, 785.

[70] "Report on the Finances: November 1807," in *Reports of the Secretary of the Treasury*, Vol. 1, p. 359.

proposals his own.[71] Appropriations for the Cumberland
Road, other roads, canals, removal of obstructions from
rivers and harbors, and for the erection of lighthouses, bea-
cons, piers, and buoys were strongly defended.[72]

Because of the oratorical flourishes surrounding the discussion of internal improvements, one at times gets the impression that the federal government was spending large sums.
The approximate amounts involved will be helpful in attaining perspective. For 1825 federal expenditures for internal
improvements were placed by Adams at upwards of $1 mil-
lion, not including expenditures for defense works and forti-
fications of about $1.5 million. For the next few years an-
nual expenditures for this purpose were in the range of $3 to
$4 million.[73] Though internal improvements accounted for
approximately one fifth of total federal expenditures, differences in ideology were of greater import than their budgetary
impact.[74]

At the time of Jackson's election, the subject of internal
improvements was at once a leading constitutional, political,
economic, and financial question.[75] Jackson's opposition to

[71] *Messages and Papers of the Presidents*, Vol. 2, p. 864. In a later reference to
the much-disputed appropriation of $30,000 for plans and surveys approved by
Monroe in April 1824, Adams stated that the topographical knowledge gained
more than justified the expenditure. *Ibid.*, Vol. 3, p. 955.

[72] These facilities "may be considered rather as treasures laid up from the contributions of the present age for the benefit of posterity than as unrequited applica-
tions of the accruing revenues of the nation." *Ibid.* In Adams' thinking federal
internal improvements and the public lands were closely linked. The sale of the
lands would provide funds which should be used to build roads, canals, and other
improvements which would aid directly in opening up unsettled areas to civilization. *Memoirs of John Quincy Adams* (1876), Vol. 9, p. 162.

[73] *Messages and Papers of the Presidents*, Vol. 2, p. 870; Vol. 3, p. 955. In the period
1826–1830 an expenditure of $3 to $4 million was a fairly large sum. The price level
was much lower than at the present time. In 1830 the population of the United
States was only 12.9 millions; there were 24 states. Agriculture was by far the most
important economic activity.

[74] The National Republicans of 1828, when Adams was defeated by Jackson,
"represented the Federalist point of view, with the added result of a generation's
schooling." Carl Russell Fish, *The Rise of the Common Man* (1927), p. 167.

[75] The party realignment then in process was influenced in no small degree by
differences of opinion on the internal improvement question. It was chosen deliberately by Jackson, Van Buren, and Thomas Hart Benton, Senator from Missouri, as one of the chief battlegrounds of the evolving Democratic party.

federal expenditures for internal improvements was based on three grounds: (1) there was no constitutional sanction; (2) they would lead to political corruption; and (3) they were conducive to extravagance. When it appeared that surplus revenues would be available after the debt was fully retired, he proposed distribution among the states; the states could use these funds for the desired improvements.[76] In Jackson's opinion even the best-planned and constitutional public works, such as aids to navigation, might lead to extravagance. Van Buren followed in the same tradition. As a Senator, he had spoken strongly against the policy of internal improvements and the "scrambles and combinations" in Congress unavoidably resulting from this question.[77] Van Buren believed that, in the absence of Jackson's firmness, extreme financial embarrassments—perhaps even insolvency— would have been the lot of the federal government.[78]

Polk's objections to federal outlays for internal improvements went much further than is implied by his criticism of developments after the War of 1812. His opposition was completely unrestrained. Strict adherence to clearly granted powers was the only way to avoid recurring collisions between the federal government and the states. In vetoing a rivers and harbors bill, he pointed out that if it were approved, only discretion would remain as a controlling force. It would "produce a disreputable scramble for the public money."[79] To Polk the internal improvement branch of the American system was "a menace to prosperity."[80] It is

[76] *Messages and Papers of the Presidents*, Vol. 3, pp. 1014–15. When Jackson vetoed the Maysville road bill, he based his argument squarely on constitutional doctrine, as expounded by Madison and Monroe. Jackson's position was strengthened by the fact that the proposed road was exclusively within the state of Kentucky and only 60 miles in length. *Ibid.*, p. 1049.

[77] Shepard, *Martin Van Buren*, p. 244.

[78] *Messages and Papers of the Presidents*, Vol. 4, p. 1536; Vol. 5, pp. 1825–26, 1829.

[79] *Ibid.*, p. 2224; Vol. 6, pp. 2311–14.

[80] The elements of the American system, as interpreted by Polk, were a national bank, a protective tariff levied solely for protection, internal improvements, and the distribution of the proceeds from public lands. *Ibid.*, p. 2508. The American system, according to Polk, was patterned after European plans. Not only did

"capable of indefinite enlargement and sufficient to swallow up as many millions annually as could be exacted from the foreign commerce of the country." It was in Polk's opinion a convenient adjunct of the protective tariff. "The operation and necessary effect of the whole system were to encourage large and extravagant expenditures, and theieby to increase the public patronage, and maintain a rich and splendid government at the expense of a taxed and impoverished people."[81]

Those who favored a more active role for the federal government based their case largely on the importance of internal improvements for national growth. From the time he entered the Senate in 1806, Henry Clay took the lead in championing the cause of federal participation in the development of roads, canals, and other improvements. During Monroe's administration he had attacked the President's view that Congress had no constitutional authority to construct roads and canals.[82] He agreed with John Quincy Adams that the federal government should play a more active part in shaping the development of the nation. After the defeat of Adams in 1828, the theory that a federally active administration was needed did not vanish. On the contrary, it remained an essential element in the philosophy of some of the ablest statesmen of the period, including Daniel Webster as well as Henry Clay.

When the Whig party evolved into a potent political force about a decade later, opposition to the strict constructionist view was at the heart of the political creed held by influential members of the new party. A new interpretation of federal powers and responsibilities seemed imminent at the time of

---

Great Britain have a national bank of large capital. She also "had an enormous public debt, and it had become a part of her public policy to regard this as a 'public blessing.' " Britain's restrictive policy concentrated power and wealth in the hands of the few, and Polk would have none of it in his own country. *Ibid.*, p. 2505. The term "American system" dated from the tariff agitation of 1819. It was the title of an anonymous pamphlet attributed to Daniel Raymond published in 1828; this pamphlet was a defense of Henry Clay's tariff program.

[81] *Ibid.*, pp. 2506–07.

[82] Carl Schurz, *Life of Henry Clay* (1892), Vol. 1, pp. 38 ff., 145–46.

William Henry Harrison's election in 1840. But Harrison died after a month in office, and John Tyler (1841–1845) was a strict constructionist.[83] On the issue of internal improvements, his views were the opposite of those of the party leaders in Congress. The arguments of Henry Clay and others who kept this question in the forefront of public discussion continued to enjoy strong backing from the public, especially in frontier and partly developed areas. Transportation and communication were vital if the more remote sections were to be integrated effectively into the Union. When a large expanse of territory such as Texas was acquired, the case for a federally active policy seemed overwhelming.[84]

With the election of Taylor and Fillmore in 1848, the Whig philosophy became dominant. In accordance with a promise in his inaugural address, Zachary Taylor (March 1849–July 1850) recommended appropriations for river and harbor improvements and for "examinations and estimates preparatory to the commencement of such others as the wants of the country, and especially the advance of our population over new districts and the extension of commerce, may render necessary."[85] After Taylor's death Millard Fillmore (1850–1853) made the cause of internal improvements his own.[86]

[83] Tyler's strict constructionist views were well known. He was given second place on the ticket because of "the desire of the Whig political leaders to hold that element by giving it recognition without power." Fish, *The Rise of the Common Man*, p. 170.

[84] The situation with respect to Texas, which was admitted as a state in 1845, has been aptly described by Griffis. The United States "had been the wooing party to get Texas into the Union, and great things had been promised from Washington in the way of internal improvements, besides coast and frontier defense. After the marriage, the wooer failed to fulfil his pledges. The Texans felt they had been wronged, and were irritated and defiant." William Elliot Griffis, *Millard Fillmore* (1915), p. 66.

[85] *Messages and Papers of the Presidents*, Vol. 6, pp. 2544, 2558–59.

[86] In 1850 when Fillmore acceded to the Presidency the population of the United States was 23.2 millions. There were 30 states in the Union. The nation was well along in the third period of the Industrial Revolution, but agriculture "still continued to occupy the chief energies of the people." The "third period, 1840–60, profited from the discovery of the practical use of coal for smelting iron and for steam power." It was marked by "the rise of railroads" and by "the introduction of many new improvements in machinery which quickened the diversified manufacturing enterprises." Faulkner, *American Economic History*, p. 291.

Fillmore's approach to this delicate subject was both diplomatic and closely reasoned. In an unusually felicitous statement, he pointed out that the federal government is a limited government and that "it is at all times an especial duty to guard against any infringement on the just rights of the States." The "beauty of our system of government consists, and its safety and durability must consist, in avoiding mutual collisions and encroachments." Later in the same message Fillmore stated that he entertained no doubt of the authority of Congress to make appropriations for internal improvements. In his opinion this authority was derived chiefly from the commerce clause of the Constitution and the power to lay and collect imposts. Referring to improvements of navigable lakes and rivers, he stated: "The position or sight [site] of the work is necessarily local, but its utility is general."[87]

A basic tenet of Fillmore's philosophy was that "the Government must keep pace with the progress of the people." Among other objectives it should "lend its powerful strength to the improvement of such means of inter-communication as are necessary to promote our internal commerce and strengthen the ties which bind us together as a people."[88] The obligation of the federal government is not to a particular part of the country, but to the whole. To Fillmore and other leading statesmen of his period, including Clay and Webster, the paramount issue before the nation was national growth.[89]

When the Democratic party was returned to power in 1853, opposition to internal improvements remained a leading tenet of party doctrine. Everyone could agree with Pierce that this subject represented "a deep-graven line of division between statesmen of eminent ability and patriotism." Yet his approach was far from conciliatory. His op-

[87] *Messages and Papers of the Presidents*, Vol. 6, pp. 2615–16, 2626–27.
[88] *Ibid.*, p. 2717.
[89] "The view held in common by Clay, Webster, Fillmore, and Lincoln, was that the paramount issue before the nation was not slavery, but national growth." Griffis, *Millard Fillmore*, p. 71.

position to a more liberal construction of federal powers was
so extreme that not even completion of partly completed
projects was favored.[90] Pierce's successor, James Buchanan,
believed that federal powers should not be arbitrarily extended to include expenditures for internal improvements.
"The jarring and collision which would occur from the exercise by two separate governments of jurisdiction over the
same subjects could not fail to produce disastrous consequences." The corrupting and seducing influence exerted by
"the General Government in carrying into effect a system of
internal improvements" was something to be avoided.[91]

Until the time of the Civil War the internal improvement
and tariff questions were closely intertwined. Customs duties
provided the bulk of federal revenues. The rate levels that
could be justified under the tariff-for-revenue-only philosophy were influenced by the scope of the federal budget.
More important, influential elements regarded the protective
feature of the tariff and the stimulation of internal improvements as complementary factors in furthering industrial and
economic growth.

The controversy over the protective tariff was an important feature in the political life of the nation, especially during the two decades after the War of 1812. "On the whole,
from 1816 on, there was applied for some twenty years a continuous policy of protection; for the first eight years with
much moderation, but after 1824 with high duties, and
stringent measures for enforcing them." The young industries argument was the great rallying cry of the protection-
ists.[92]

The tariff controversy differed in one particular from that
on internal improvements. The disputants usually divided on
sectional rather than on party lines. Referring to the situa-

---

[90] *Messages and Papers of the Presidents,* Vol. 6, p. 2751; Vol. 7, pp. 2790–2804.
[91] *Ibid.,* pp. 3134–35.
[92] Frank W. Taussig, *The Tariff History of the United States* (1931), pp. 7, 24, 106.
This early protective movement, in the opinion of Taussig, lost its vigor after 1832.

tion in 1832, one commentator states that the protective
tariff that

> . . . had been in operation for years met with bitter denunciation
> and the deadliest hostility from the southern states, especially
> South Carolina. . . . The American system of protection was
> vigorously assailed, and the assailants as vigorously and promptly
> met. . . . The existing system, by its assailants, was alleged to be
> unconstitutional and legally inoperative, and defended by its
> friends by enumerating the advantages of a protective tariff, and
> reference to the signature of George Washington for its constitu-
> tionality.[93]

At times the tariff seemed to engender more heat than internal improvements and other aspects of the American
system. But it would be easy to exaggerate its importance as
a center of controversy. Attitudes toward protection were
influenced in considerable degree by its bearing on other
questions on which party and sectional differences arose. In
the tariff debates Henry Clay played a leading role. Though
he was an advocate of a protective tariff, he did not favor
extremely high or prohibitive rates. In the opinion of one
observer, he "never claimed for Congress the authority to
extend the manufacturers anything more than incidental
protection under a tariff for revenue."[94] While this may be a
slight understatement, during the period in which Clay
wielded his greatest influence, the productivity of the combined tariff schedules was a matter of first-rate importance.

The public lands question also tied in closely with internal
improvements. The federal government was "the largest
proprietor of land in the nation."[95] Its policies with respect
to the disposition and use of public lands played a prominent
role in the evolution of the economy. Though there were no
net receipts from public lands prior to Jackson's administration, the idea that the proceeds should be set aside as a spe-

---

[93] W. J. Barre, *The Life and Public Services of Millard Fillmore* (1856), p. 184.

[94] Hugh McCulloch, *Men and Measures of a Half Century* (1888), p. 500.

[95] "The Federal Government of the United States is and always has been the
largest proprietor of land in the nation." Marion Clawson and Burnell Held, *The
Federal Lands: Their Use and Management* (1957), p. 15.

cial fund for internal improvements was advanced repeatedly.[96] There was also a close relationship between land policy, the tariff, and industrial development. "The old States . . . saw distinctly the relation of the lands to the tariff. Everything which enhanced the attractiveness of the land, and made it easier to get at it, was just so much force drawing the man who had no land and no capital away from the old States and out of the wages class."[97] To many the "land pull" appeared more important as a wage determinant than any other factor.

Our examination of official statements and attitudes with respect to the federal budget and debt policy has shown that certain key ideas were dominant. First, a low level of public expenditures was believed desirable. The smaller the revenues required, the less was the interference through taxation with the operation of the economy. Second, a balanced federal budget was the minimum goal deemed acceptable in time of peace. When deficits were incurred, they were neither condoned nor rationalized. Third, when federal debt was outstanding, official policy called for its retirement. The latter idea, as previously suggested, served for many years as a unifying principle in the management of the federal finances.

Views of the Economists

Official attitudes toward the budget and the federal debt found strong support in the mainstream of economic thought.

[96] Among the other plans suggested were: (1) the states should seize the lands by virtue of their "sovereignty"; (2) the land should be sold to the states at a nominal price; (3) the land should be sold for what it would bring; and (4) the land should be given to actual settlers. William Graham Sumner, *Andrew Jackson* (1924), pp. 229–30.

[97] *Ibid.*, p. 230.

The pronouncements of the Presidents and other officials often resembled closely the views of leading economists. In the nature of the case, the influence of the economists cannot be determined precisely. However, the catholicity of interests of leading American statesmen and the arguments they advanced suggest that this influence was substantial. Their familiarity with economic ideas was enhanced by the fact that until late in the nineteenth century economics was regarded as a branch of moral philosophy or moral science, a subject in which many of them were well versed.

THE CLASSICAL ECONOMISTS, ADAM SMITH TO JOHN STUART MILL

Adam Smith's *Wealth of Nations*, which was first published in 1776, "set up the first generally acceptable philosophy of free enterprise."[98] In important particulars the policies followed by the new government conformed closely with the views outlined in Smith's classic. The numerous references to this work in historical and economic literature suggest that it had an appreciable influence on American thought. Participants in discussions of the great economic issues of the day were adept at citing the latest literature in Great Britain.[99] This is not to say that with the appearance of the *Wealth of Nations*, the mercantilist philosophy against which it was directed became outmoded. Rather, the infiltration of Smith's ideas was an important step in the process by which the hold of mercantilist conceptions was lessened.

[98] J. M. Clark, "Adam Smith and the Spirit of '76," in *The Spirit of '76 and Other Essays* (1927), p. 71. The *Wealth of Nations* is generally regarded as marking the beginning of classical economics. The fifth edition was published in 1789, the year the government under the Constitution was established.

[99] Dorfman, *The Economic Mind in American Civilization*, Vol. 1, pp. 243, 295. Leading pamphleteers such as George Logan were especially impressed by Smith's work. There were three American printings of the *Wealth of Nations* during the early decades of the new nation: Philadelphia (1789), and Hartford (1811 and 1818). Charles F. Dunbar, "Economic Science in America, 1776–1876," *North American Review*, Vol. 122 (January 1876), p. 134.

Smith's views concerning the necessity of balancing public budgets are nowhere stated in positive terms. However, they are quite evident from his discussion of public expenditures and public debts, especially the latter. A policy of borrowing to meet public expenditures leads to waste, since it relieves the government of the necessity of raising the necessary revenues through taxation. Only borrowing for war purposes is justified. "In this exigency government can have no other resource but in borrowing." But even wartime borrowing has a great disadvantage. Once a nation "foresees the facility of borrowing, it dispenses itself from the duty of saving." The most serious aspect of public borrowing, according to Smith, is that it involves a draft on capital. It reduces the funds or savings available for providing additional capital in productive employments.[100]

Under Smith's system of free enterprise (natural liberty), government has only three main duties: (1) the defense of the country; (2) the administration of justice; and (3) the construction and maintenance of certain public works that would be unprofitable to individuals and private enterprise.[101] His views concerning the role of government were strongly influenced by his opposition to mercantilism. He regarded the pattern of special trading privileges, grants of monopoly, and tariffs that characterized the mercantilist system with extreme disfavor.[102] When Smith castigates governments by saying that they are "always, and without any exception, the greatest spendthrifts in the society,"[103] it is the inefficient

---

[100] Smith, *Wealth of Nations*, Cannan edition (1922), Vol. 2, pp. 395–96, 409–11.

[101] *Ibid.*, pp. 184–85.

[102] Jesse Burkhead, "The Balanced Budget," *Quarterly Journal of Economics*, Vol. 68 (1954), p. 193. "The *Wealth of Nations* summed up and clarified . . . two streams of thought. . . . On the one hand it destroyed the intellectual foundations of the old mercantilism, while on the other it consolidated laissez-faire thought into a system which was destined to shape men's minds and acts for more than a century." Shepard B. Clough and Charles W. Cole, *Economic History of Europe* (1946), p. 364.

[103] *Wealth of Nations*, Vol. 1, p. 328.

and wasteful governments of the mercantilist era he has in mind.[104]

Jean-Baptiste Say, a native of France, played a major role in refining and popularizing the economic ideas expounded by Smith. *A Treatise on Political Economy*, which was first published in 1803, was more popular in the United States than either Smith's *Wealth of Nations* or Ricardo's *Principles* which appeared in 1817.[105] A factor in Say's favor was that he avoided Smith's distinction between "productive" and "unproductive" employments. Neither professors of moral philosophy nor the clergy had been quite willing to accept an exposition in the so-called moral science of political economy that classified them as unproductive.

Say opposed budget deficits and public borrowing because they interfere with the capital expansion necessary for economic growth. To attain a desirable rate of capital expansion, both public and private consumption must be held within bounds. He saw only one possible advantage in a public debt; it provided a suitable investment outlet for small amounts of savings. This advantage accrued only if the amounts involved were spent on objects of permanent benefit such as roads and canals. Unless the latter course were followed, the savings would be squandered. Say recognized that borrowing makes possible the spreading of emergency costs over a number of years. But this advantage was minor, compared with the general tendency of national loans to

---

[104] In Smith's view non-intervention was a general principle rather than an absolute rule. "He was no doctrinaire, and he never forgot that to every rule there are some exceptions." Charles Gide and Charles Rist, *A History of Economic Doctrines*, American edition (Heath), p. 96. J. M. Clark has suggested that if Smith had been alive in 1926, he "would not belittle government nor would he idealize it as the all-sufficient social agency." *The Spirit of '76 and Other Essays*, p. 96.

[105] Say was a friend and correspondent of Thomas Jefferson, who was closely acquainted with the standard literature on political economy. In Jefferson's opinion, Say expressed the same principles as the *Wealth of Nations* and in a "shorter compass and more lucid manner." Dorfman, *The Economic Mind in American Civilization*, Vol. 1, p. 434; Vol. 2, pp. 513–14.

withdraw capital from productive employment and divert it "into the channel of barren consumption."[106]

Say's views concerning the role of government were comparable to those of Adam Smith. He attached considerable importance to the facilitating or complementary aspect of public works, especially in transportation and communications. Public benevolent institutions and public education were classified as separate or independent governmental functions. These and other activities are discussed under "public consumption." The consumption of nations or the governments that represent them occasions a loss of value, and consequently of wealth. It is justifiable only in so far as there results from it some national advantage, equivalent to the sacrifice of value. "The whole skill of government . . . consists in the continual and judicious comparisons of the sacrifice about to be incurred, with the expected benefit to the community." In some places Say's attitude toward government seems rather extreme.[107] However, in his last work—the *Complete Course on Political Economy*—there is "less sharpness against the governing powers."[108] There are numerous digressions on public consumption, public works, education, and national defense.[109]

David Ricardo published his *Principles of Political Economy and Taxation* in 1817. Members of Congress and numerous learned persons were familiar with this work.[110] Ricardo's

[106] Say, *A Treatise on Political Economy*, American edition (1832), pp. 444–47.

[107] *Ibid.*, pp. 378–79, 393, 400, 405.

[108] J. A. Blanqui, *History of Political Economy in Europe*, American edition (1880), p. 452. Say's *Cours Complet d'Economie Politique* was published in six volumes in 1828 and 1829.

[109] "The progress of general wealth had demonstrated to him the utility and even the necessity of the intervention of the government in great enterprises of public utility. He relaxed by degrees the vigor of the exclusive principles which had so long made him reject that powerful intervention." Blanqui, *History of Political Economy in Europe*, p. 532.

[110] Ricardo's influence on American thought concerning public budgets, public debts, and the role of government was perhaps somewhat less than that of Smith or Say. That half of the first American edition was subscribed by government

views concerning governmental budgets are included in his discussion of public expenditures. He favored covering not only ordinary expenditures from revenues, but also extraordinary expenses—if at all possible. It "must not be inferred that I consider the system of borrowing as the best calculated to defray the extraordinary expenses of the State. It is a system which tends to make us less thrifty—to blind us to our real situation."[111] Ricardo emphasized that public borrowing involved a draft on capital. It was in this drawing on the capital fund—including current capital accumulations— that the real burden consists. He was the first economist of eminence to point out clearly that interest payments within a nation are in the nature of a transfer; in the *Principles* he takes the position that there is no particular advantage in retiring the debt.[112]

In the "Funding System" Ricardo stressed the desirability of eliminating the national debt. He proposed that the debt be retired "once for all" through a levy on property, which would be fully paid in two or three years. "Thus, by one great effort, we should get rid of one of the most terrible scourges which was ever invented to afflict a nation; and our commerce would be extended without being subject to all the vexatious delays and interruptions which our present artificial system imposes upon it."[113] In the *Principles* Ricardo had pointed out that a country which has accumulated a large debt "is placed in a most artificial situation," and that "it becomes the interest of every citizen to withdraw his

---

officials and others in advance of publication was attributable mainly to the controversy over the Bank of the United States and Ricardo's eminence as an authority on money and banking. Dorfman, *The Economic Mind in American Civilization*, Vol. 1, p. 369.

[111] P. Sraffa and M. H. Dobb, eds., *The Works and Correspondence of David Ricardo* (1951), Vol. 1, p. 247.

[112] *Ibid.*, p. 246.

[113] *Ibid.*, Vol. 4, p. 197. The views expressed in this essay were doubtless influenced by his opposition to the so-called "funding system," particularly the extravagant claims made in behalf of the sinking fund.

shoulder from the burthen."[114] He feared as a possible consequence of heavy annual taxes to meet debt charges the transfer of capital to other countries. To Ricardo, as to other economists of his era, the growth of capital was of prime importance.

In a speech delivered in Parliament in December 1819, Ricardo started with the premise that wages were determined by the proportion of capital to population, and then stated his conviction that "to augment them, it was important to increase the capital of the country." Instead of following a rational course, England had aggravated the situation. The corn laws had raised the price of grain, import duties enacted by other countries in a spirit of retaliation enhanced the distress, and the national debt tended to cause an exportation of capital. Ricardo's logic pointed to only one conclusion with respect to the debt—it should be paid off.[115]

Ricardo favored low or minimum public expenditures. It is by "the profuse expenditure of Government, and of individuals, and by loans, that the country is impoverished; every measure, therefore, which is calculated to promote public and private economy, will relieve the public distress." Say is quoted with approval; "the very best of all plans of finance is to spend little, and the best of all taxes is that which is least in amount."[116] In Ricardo's analysis, virtually all public policies in the economic field could be "approved or condemned by reference to their effects in increasing or diminishing industrial profits. . . . All taxes were bad because no tax could fail to diminish profits either directly or indirectly through raising wages. The best tax—probably a tax on rent—was that which had the least adverse effect on profits."[117]

---

[114] *Ibid.*, Vol. 1, p. 247.
[115] *Ibid.*, Vol. 5, pp. 32–34.
[116] *Ibid.*, Vol. 1, pp. 242, 246.
[117] Arthur Smithies, "Economic Welfare and Policy," in *Economics and Public Policy*, Brookings Lectures, 1954 (1955), p. 6.

The views of Thomas Robert Malthus concerning governmental budgets and public debts differed appreciably from those of his principal contemporaries and predecessors. Public debts are not the unmitigated evil they are often assumed to be. Recipients of interest on the national debt "contribute powerfully to distribution and demand." Malthus visualized the necessity of an orderly growth of both production and consumption. The assumption that debt reduction and the lower taxes it made possible were economically desirable in all circumstances he regarded as unwarranted. Malthus saw clearly the relation between capital expansion and economic growth. Saving in numerous instances is "a most sacred private duty." But the maximum possible saving is not necessarily the optimum, as some economists seemed to assume. He suggested that on occasion there may be "a greater tendency to parsimony than is consistent with the most effective encouragement to the growth of public wealth."[118]

In his discussion of the role of government and taxation, Malthus adhered closely to the classical tradition. "It may . . . safely be asserted that a propensity to govern too much is a certain indication of ignorance and rashness." Taxes interfere with the normal operation of the economy. They interfere with individual industry and wealth when they are imposed, and the attempt to get rid of them later may cause additional trouble.[119] The obvious policy is to hold public expenditures within reasonable bounds.[120]

---

[118] Malthus, *Principles of Political Economy* (1836), pp. 361 ff., 409, 411, 434. This work was first published in 1820.

[119] *Ibid.*, pp. 15–16, 435.

[120] The writings of three lesser-known economists—James Mill, J. R. McCulloch, and Nassau Senior—were examined in the course of our investigation. James Mill's opening sentence is of interest: "Political economy is to the State, what domestic economy is to the family." *Elements of Political Economy* (1821), p. 1. By "the State" James Mill meant the total economy. McCulloch's statement on the utility or necessity of taxation is extremely lucid. He believed that taxation "should always be kept within the narrowest limits." Taxation which encroaches on the means of future production "is one of the severest scourges to which a people can be subjected." *A Treatise on the Principles and Practical Influence of Taxation and the Funding System* (1845), pp. 1 ff.

John Stuart Mill, whose *Principles of Political Economy* was published in 1848, was a social philosopher and political theorist, as well as an economist.[121] He believed that public borrowing, which involves a draft on funds engaged in production, or about to be so employed, is equivalent to taking the amounts borrowed from the wages of the laboring classes. The only exceptions are: (1) if the loan represents a draft on foreign capital; and (2) if the funds borrowed would not otherwise have been saved. In general, Mill thought that reduction and elimination of public debts are desirable.[122] The relation between this reasoning and the wages-fund theory of wages is apparent.[123]

Mill's views concerning the role of government differed in some respects from those of his leading predecessors. The distinction he drew between the necessary and optional functions of government suggests a willingness to accept a level of expenditures somewhat above the absolute minimum. Necessary functions are those which "are either inseparable from the idea of a government, or are exercised habitually and without objection by all governments." On the other hand, optional functions may be both expedient and desirable, but their exercise "does not amount to necessity." Mill believed the necessary functions were more numerous than most people were aware. In his view, the idea that governments should confine themselves to affording protection against force and fraud was much too narrow, and he re-

[121] The *Principles* was reprinted in the United States immediately after its appearance in England. It received enthusiastic praise and became the standard authority. Dorfman, *The Economic Mind in American Civilization*, Vol. 2, p. 710.

[122] Mill, *Principles of Political Economy* (1864), Vol. 2, pp. 479–80, 483.

[123] The enormous popularity of the view that wages are limited by the "wages-fund" and its corollary that public borrowing is at the expense of the laboring classes is difficult to appreciate in the present era. The importance attached to free or circulating capital is illustrated by three unidentified quotations cited by one of Mill's contemporaries: (1) "Capital is the fund, out of which wages of labour are paid, and labourers are supported." (2) "Increase the capital, and you increase its power to employ and to remunerate labour." (3) "The power of a country to maintain a population, is in proportion to its capital." Thomas Chalmers, *On Political Economy* (1832), p. 78.

garded as essential a number of activities that did not fall in either category.[124]

Mill's other writings considered in conjunction with the *Principles* suggest that he visualized a changing and more important role for government as the economy became more industrialized and increasingly complex. Though he was reluctant to see the adoption of social controls at the expense of individual responsibility, Mill "was ready to admit the need for legislative and other social measures as a basis for individual freedom." He was "more willing than his predecessors to recognize the importance of political and social factors in the development of the individual."[125] He believed complete or extreme reliance on the laissez-faire philosophy as a guide to action would prove unworkable. However, there is no reason to believe Mill favored a sharp expansion of governmental activities. In common with other classical economists, he looked askance at heavy or onerous taxes. The excess of taxation is a serious "economical evil." It may discourage industry "by insufficiency of reward."[126]

The inability or unwillingness of Mill to accept the laissez-faire philosophy as the sole guide to policy was a noteworthy development in the history of economic thought. The emphasis on political economy as the science of wealth by Mill's leading predecessors, and the relative or total disregard of welfare implications, had led Blanqui to conclude that England had given the subject "a physiognomy and a tendency exclusively industrial. . . . English writers have studied wealth in an abstract manner and independently of the evils which too often accompany its production."[127] Beginning

[124] Mill, *Principles of Political Economy*, Vol. 2, pp. 386 ff. Attempts to classify public expenditures under necessary and optional functions have enjoyed a fairly wide popular vogue since the time of Mill. Such attempts at classification necessarily are strongly subjective.

[125] Frederick Watkins, *The Political Tradition of the West* (1948), pp. 250, 288.

[126] Mill, *Principles of Political Economy*, Vol. 2, p. 492.

[127] Blanqui, *History of Political Economy in Europe*, p. 529. This work considers the development of economic thought to 1842. Mill's *Principles*, as noted above, was first published in 1848.

with Mill, extreme or ultra-rigid adherence to the laissez-faire philosophy by economists was the exception rather than the rule. "In regard to state action, as in so many other respects, Mill occupied a transitional position."[128]

AMERICAN ECONOMISTS,
JOHN MCVICKAR TO HENRY VETHAKE

In the United States there was no single event comparable to the publication of the *Wealth of Nations* to mark the beginning of political economy as a separate and more or less independent discipline. Our reason for beginning this part of the analysis with the *Outlines of Political Economy*[129] by the Reverend John McVickar,[130] which was published in 1825, is that this work has been aptly called "a genuine native literature following the great tradition of Smith and Ricardo."[131] It is not implied that American political economy dates from this work.

McVickar favored meeting all ordinary public expenditures from current revenues. Public loans for emergency purposes may be justified on grounds of "the facility, rapidity, and certainty with which large sums can be raised in a moment of exigency." But the permanent effect of loans "is to cripple the energies of the nation." The repayment of loans is a matter of indifference as far as the progress of the na-

---

[128] C. F. Bastable, *Public Finance* (1892), p. 47.

[129] This work consisted of a reprint of an article by J. R. McCulloch in the 1823 Supplement to the *Encyclopaedia Britannica*, with an introduction and extensive notes by McVickar.

[130] John McVickar was Professor of Moral Philosophy and Political Economy, Columbia College, New York City. He was an Episcopal clergyman before he began to teach at Columbia, and he continued in this role and took an active part in church affairs all his life. The McVickar professorship, long held by E. R. A. Seligman and Robert M. Haig, was created in his honor in 1904.

[131] Dorfman, *The Economic Mind in American Civilization*, Vol. 2, p. 516. "In America, formal political economy maintained its respectability in the halls of learning by keeping close to the traditions of its European ancestry." A. D. H. Kaplan, *Henry Charles Carey: A Study in American Economic Thought* (1931), p. 17.

tional wealth is concerned. The "original capital that government expended has been altogether consumed."[132]

McVickar was especially critical of Adam Smith's attempt to distinguish between productive and unproductive occupations, with public employment arbitrarily placed in the latter category. "The invidious distinction . . . between the various classes of the community by arranging them as productive and unproductive laborers, is one of the narrow and imperfect views which is justly discarded in the liberal system of Political Economy."[133] McCulloch's view that public functionaries are productive he found more acceptable. Referring to the higher class of public officials, McCulloch stated that "when they discharge properly the duties of their high station," they are "the most productive labourers in a state." McVickar believed that in the expenditure of government—as in that of individuals—there may be a false economy as well as a direct extravagance. Salaries may be too low as well as too high for the public good. "Goodness" or quality of service rather than "cheapness" is the test.[134]

In principle Daniel Raymond opposed deficits in the public accounts.[135] He believed the system of supplying a deficiency in the ordinary revenue by loans is "inherently and radically bad." It "will produce national bankruptcy if persevered in, as soon as the interest on the public debt comes to equal the whole revenue of the nation, or the annual product of labour." Nevertheless, emergency borrowing was justi-

---

[132] McVickar, *Outlines of Political Economy* (1825), pp. 173–74.

[133] *Ibid.*, p. 161. Despite his dislike of productive and unproductive as categorical absolutes, McVickar believed that public expenditures are often unproductive. The "expenditure of government is unproductive, except in so far as the security and happiness of society is the result." In a brief discussion of taxes, it was stated that the lowest in amount is to be preferred—"this arises from its very nature, which is unproductive expenditure." *Ibid.*, pp. 172–73.

[134] *Ibid.*, pp. 165, 167.

[135] Daniel Raymond spent his mature years in Baltimore where he began practicing law during the War of 1812. He first attained public recognition with his pamphlet *The Missouri Question* (1819) which had a wide influence. He was an ardent protectionist and helped popularize the case for protection in *The American System*, an anonymous pamphlet published in 1828.

fied and was preferable to hoarding up money or treasure in anticipation of extraordinary needs. A national debt of moderate size was not considered objectionable. Surplus revenues did not present a difficult problem, according to Raymond. There were always a number of public works projects that could be carried forward to advantage, and surpluses could be applied in this direction.[136]

Raymond's views on public debts and budgets are fairly representative of the protectionist school of his period.[137] He sharply questioned the identity of individual interests and the general or public interest under competitive conditions, as expounded by Adam Smith and others. "Public and private interests are often entirely at variance." Intervention by the government, in his view, is justified whenever the welfare of the many makes this the expedient course. For the period in which he wrote, Raymond's views had a strong welfare flavor.[138]

Although Willard Phillips[139] had nothing to say about public debts and deficits, his observations concerning the role of government deserve mention. At the time he wrote, internal improvements by the federal government had become a major issue. Public works, Phillips pointed out, are undertaken with different motives. Some are mainly a reflection of

[136] Raymond, *Elements of Constitutional Law and Political Economy* (1840), pp. 244–46; this was the fourth edition of the volume originally published in 1820 under the title *Thoughts on Political Economy*.

[137] Raymond classified receipts from loans as extraordinary or irregular revenue and all other current income as ordinary revenue. Payments for interest were designated extraordinary expenditure, and all other expenditures were classified as ordinary. An interesting angle of Raymond's thinking is the observation that government loans "transfer the beneficial interest in property to the borrower." *Ibid.*, pp. 241–43.

[138] "A government should be like a good shepherd, who supports and nourishes the weak and feeble ones in his flock, until they gain sufficient strength to take their chance with the strong, and does not suffer them to be trampled on, and crushed to the earth, by the powerful." Raymond, *Elements of Political Economy*, second edition (1823), Vol. 2, p. 13.

[139] Willard Phillips is described by Dorfman as a "converted protectionist." He was a tutor at Harvard University, and was later a member of the state legislature and a judge. He became an expert on marine insurance, patent, and admiralty law.

national glory and vanity; others are of great economic importance since they facilitate the exchange of products. "The work ought to be proportioned to the resources, and correspond to the character and condition of the community."[140]

Phillips was critical of Adam Smith's views on public education. Smith seemed to say that education at public expense was justified only for the children of the poor. In Phillips' opinion this was not a very liberal view, and was "especially uncongenial to the habits of thinking and practice in the United States." He was convinced that after the most wealthy community has done all that it can for public instruction, "room enough will be left for individual effort and the effect of competition."[141]

The work of William Beach Lawrence[142] is of interest for our purpose, because of the analogy he drew between household or individual economy and the economy of governments. "Proceeding upon the simple and undeniable proposition that nations are only collections of individuals," political economy "naturally concludes that the same rules which regulate the economy of families, may be extended to the management of states."[143] This theme was later combined with Lawrence's views concerning the role of government. Taxes for the support of government are a valid charge on every man's income, since the security of persons and property is essential to accumulation as well as to the enjoyment of our acquisitions. The same rule applies to governmental expenditures as to all others. "They should be as small as possible consistent with the objects in view, and most particularly should the public avoid imposing contributions for

[140] Phillips, *A Manual of Political Economy* (1828), p. 268.

[141] *Ibid.*, pp. 270–71.

[142] Lawrence was a student of McVickar at Columbia. His varied experience is described in Dorfman, *The Economic Mind in American Civilization*, Vol. 2, pp. 720 ff.

[143] Lawrence, *Two Lectures on Political Economy* (1832), p. 4. Lawrence defined political economy as the science which relates to the nature and causes of the wealth of nations.

undertakings, which can be carried on by the resources and sagacities of individuals." The government "can seldom step out of its legitimate sphere of action, without ultimately injuring instead of benefitting the common weal."[144]

Lawrence's predilection in favor of private activity is well illustrated by his discussion of internal improvements, which present "some important economical considerations." When roads or canals are commenced at private risk, "it is pretty certain that there is a reasonable prospect of deriving, either from the tolls or the enhancement of property values, advantages more than commensurate with the cost of the undertakings." On the other hand, the disbursement of public funds for internal improvements in a majority of cases is likely to lead to "visionary and absurd expenditures." State financing is preferable to federal; the danger of extravagance and carelessness is the greatest where the responsibility of the agent to the employers is the furthest removed.[145]

The Reverend Francis Wayland's[146] views on public finance and government are of interest mainly because of his observations concerning surplus revenues. Though there is no evidence that Wayland favored unbalanced budgets, he was firmly opposed to surplus revenues—especially surpluses substantial in amount. "A surplus revenue is a public nuisance." Surpluses give government "control of the monetary affairs of the country." They take productive capital from the hands of the owners and vest it "in hands where there is every temptation to spend it uselessly, if not viciously." Moreover, surplus revenues are an invitation to extravagance and waste. In his view, the greater part of the federal surpluses of the 1830's distributed among the states

---

[144] *Ibid.*, p. 64.

[145] *Ibid.*, pp. 64–65.

[146] Francis Wayland, a New Yorker by birth and education, attained prominence as President of Brown University, where he also held the chair of moral philosophy. His major work on political economy first appeared in 1837 and was slightly revised in 1841. It consisted mainly of lectures delivered at Brown University to students of public finance.

had been spent on internal improvements of very doubtful utility.[147] Just before Wayland's book was first published, federal surpluses had been a troublesome problem. They could not be applied to debt reduction for no debt was outstanding. In the circumstances there was no satisfactory way of getting the funds back into circulation.

The Principles of Political Economy by Henry Vethake[148] was characterized by its moderate tone and broad outlook. His principal objection to public loans was that they tend to lead to the extravagant expenditure of public money. A national debt is an evil only if the borrowed funds are used to finance unproductive expenditures. To the extent that the funds are used for productive purposes, the debt represents a national good rather than a loss. He regarded as untenable the argument that if the borrowed funds had been left in the hands of the people, they would have been productively expended, and population and wealth advanced more rapidly.[149]

Since Vethake's argument rests on the distinction between productive and unproductive expenditures, his interpretation of these concepts is a matter of interest. He did not arrogate to himself the right of decision between productive and unproductive expenditures.[150] His sole test was a return commensurate with the amount expended. Expenditures by governments for personal services are productive, when the wages and salaries are no more than necessary to obtain the services desired. Though he did not elaborate, it is clear that

---

[147] Wayland, *Elements of Political Economy* (1840), p. 422. This work was first published in 1837.

[148] Henry Vethake taught a variety of subjects at Columbia, Queen's College (now Rutgers), the College of New Jersey, Dickinson College, New York University, and the University of Pennsylvania. He was President of Washington College (now Washington and Lee) for one year, and Provost of the University of Pennsylvania for five years (1854–1859).

[149] Vethake, *Principles of Political Economy* (1838), pp. 397–400.

[150] Vethake vigorously opposed the efforts of economists to distinguish between productive and unproductive labor; a "practical and *moral* advantage cannot fail to result from getting rid of the distinction between the productive and unproductive labourers." *Ibid.*, pp. 38–39.

in Vethake's thinking the same principle applied to government purchases of all kinds—goods as well as services.[151]

Vethake's views on internal improvements—that important question of the day—were presented in Book 5. The partial title of this book is "On the Interference by Individuals and Governments with the Natural Order of Things." His position on this subject suggests a compromise between conflicting ideas. He proposed that roads and canals should be constructed with private capital, with the profits accruing to the owners for a term of years only. The tolls that could be levied could not exceed the legally prescribed maximum. At the end of the specified period, title to the property would revert to the government on reimbursement of the original cost or other stipulated price.[152]

The ideas of the economists concerning budget policy, public debts, and governmental activities were strongly influenced by accepted theory as to how the economy operates. The analysis of the classical economists led to the conclusion that if equilibrium at full employment is disturbed, forces are set in motion that tend to restore it. Classical economics does not assume the existence of full employment; rather, the full employment norm is the conclusion to which the argument leads.[153]

From the beginning of the nation to the Civil War, economic thought was focused primarily on production and world commerce. A given volume of production having been achieved, a reasonably satisfactory distribution of the annual product and adequate consumption were believed to follow more or less automatically. Under the system posited by

[151] *Ibid.*, pp. 389–91.

[152] *Ibid.*, pp. 313–16.

[153] Wassily Leontief, "Postulates: Keynes' *General Theory* and the Classicists," in *The New Economics*, Seymour E. Harris, ed. (1947), p. 234. In their policy recommendations economists steeped in the classical tradition commonly assumed that full employment was normal. But this is not the same thing as saying that this is an assumption of classical economics.

the economists, neither serious unemployment nor less than maximum use of available resources could be caused by a dearth of consumption. For supply creates its own demand (Say's law). This does not mean that consumption equals production. Rather, consumption plus investment equal annual production. Saving—the excess of the annual output over consumption—is invested and reflected in additions to the capital stock. The necessary balance between saving and investment is maintained through the equilibrating effect of the interest rate.

The principal economic argument in favor of balanced public budgets follows logically from this theory. Deficits mean drafts on savings that otherwise would be available for economic expansion. Governmental competition with private capital needs tends to slow economic progress. This line of reasoning became all the more persuasive as the economy ceased to be predominantly agricultural. With the evolution of business and industry, concomitant with the extension of the frontier, capital became a vital factor in economic growth. Capital needs commonly exceeded domestic saving and were met in part from foreign sources. In the circumstances it was not illogical that public borrowing should be regarded with disfavor except in time of war.

The idea that governmental expenditures should be held to a low level and strictly controlled also follows from the accepted theory. Though a minimum of public activities was deemed essential, government was viewed mainly as a consumer rather than as a producer of needed services. Such public activities as were rated indispensable should be financed to the fullest possible extent by taxes that do not interfere with production and economic growth. A high level of public expenditures resulting from activities well in excess of those sanctioned by laissez-faire conceptions withdraws labor and resources from private employment. Perhaps more important, it impinges on the productive process through the operation of "onerous taxes." As public activities expand, it becomes increasingly difficult to obtain the required resources without serious interference. A nation that thus handicaps itself, while other countries hold public expenditures at or near the permissible minimum, tends to be at a competitive disadvantage.

The Public View[154]

Three key ideas, as we have seen, were generally accepted by both federal officials and economists: (1) a low level of public expenditures was desirable; (2) the federal budget should be balanced in time of peace; and (3) the federal debt should be reduced and eventually extinguished. These ideas were a reflection of views that were deeply rooted in the social fabric. It is not meant to imply that a large majority of the people were seriously concerned about the size of the public debt or that they were capable of appraising budget policies. Rather, the point to be emphasized is that the informed and more influential citizens generally took a rather narrow view of public finance; whatever opinions the general public held usually paralleled closely those of their better informed neighbors.[155]

[154] In using "the public view" in this section and comparable sections of later chapters, it is not meant to imply that the ideas expressed are necessarily a representative cross-section of public opinion concerning budget and debt policies. For the period before the Civil War it would perhaps be impossible to obtain a coverage of public opinion on these subjects comparable to that for the views of public officials and economists.

[155] There were occasional exceptions to the dominant public view on federal finance. For example, early in the nineteenth century Robert Hare pointed out that the fear of bequeathing debt to posterity is absurd and that the analogy between public debt and private debt is false. He defended federal borrowing; in his view the poorer classes gained—they may be called on to pay interest but no more. "The influence of a vigorous system of external defence, and of internal improvement of roads and navigation, furnish an ample and secure field for the employment of our national credit." *A Brief View of the Policy and Resources of the United States* (1810), pp. 48–49, 74, 83, 91. Robert Hare was a prominent chemist who later became Professor of Chemistry at the University of Pennsylvania.

A financial way of thinking about the federal budget predominated among the electorate. The idea that the only sound way of thinking about government is a fiscal one was an important plank in conservative thought.[156] The approach to federal expenditures was in terms of money costs. The economic aspects of federal expenditures were largely ignored. Nor was there any discernible recognition of the contribution of the federal government to the social weal. Governmental expenditures were in the nature of financial costs, and the normal policy goal was to hold their burden within reasonable bounds.

The almost exclusively financial approach to the federal budget was not without a certain internal logic. Aside from national defense and debt service, federal activities were decidedly limited.[157] Neither pensions nor expenditures on account of the Indians, which were separately classified, involved payment for services currently rendered. The remaining federal expenditures were primarily for administration of the three branches of government, including the so-called household activities. The "civil and miscellaneous" and national defense categories had the strongest direct economic impact, in the sense of allocating scarce resources to governmental use.

The narrow compass of federal functions was reflected in the size of the peacetime budget. For example, at mid-century federal expenditures amounted to less than $40 million a year, distributed as shown in the table on page 57; the comparable figures for 1800, 1825, and 1860 are also of interest. On the eve of the Civil War federal expenditures, exclusive of the postal deficit, were only $53 million. The limited nature of federal activities throughout our early history as a

---

[156] Thurman W. Arnold, *The Folklore of Capitalism* (1937), pp. 35–36.

[157] European visitors occasionally commented on the restricted nature of federal activities. For example, following his famous visit in 1831, de Tocqueville expressed the opinion that the Americans "seem to me to have outstepped the limits of sound policy in isolating the administration of the Government." He seemed especially impressed by the absence of common or uniform police regulations. Alexis de Tocqueville, *Democracy in America*, Colonial Press edition (1900), Vol. 1, p. 87.

nation is clearly shown by reference to "civil and miscellaneous" expenditures, a broad classification including expenditures for all purposes other than national defense, pensions, Indians, interest, and the postal deficit. Expenditures in this classification did not amount to as much as $10 million in any year before 1849.

Federal Expenditures, Fiscal Years 1800, 1825, 1850 and 1860[a]

(In millions of dollars)

	1800	1825	1850	1860
Civil and miscellaneous....	1.3	2.7	14.9	28.0[b]
War Department.........	2.6	3.7	9.4	16.4
Navy Department........	3.4	3.1	7.9	11.5
Indians.................	—	0.7	1.6	2.9
Pensions...............	0.1	1.3	1.9	1.1
Interest...............	3.4	4.4	3.8	3.2
	$10.8	$15.9	$39.5	$63.1[b]

[a] *Annual Report of the Secretary of the Treasury on the State of the Finances for the Fiscal Year Ended June 30, 1934*, pp. 302–03.
[b] Includes postal deficit of $9.9 million.

In the circumstances there was some justification for the belief that federal expenditures made little or no contribution to the level of living. Only a minor portion of civil and miscellaneous expenditures were for developmental purposes or contributed more or less directly to living levels. Moreover, expenditures broadly classified as "developmental" frequently were regarded with suspicion or even hostility. While they were accepted as necessary, both defense expenditures and the bulk of civil expenditures were widely regarded as species of overhead costs.

Public attitudes toward the federal budget were influenced by the assumed similarity between governmental finance and private or household finance. The criterion of family or household financial management was the ability to live within one's income. If for any reason a substantial debt was incurred, its early retirement was thought desirable. The disadvantages of going into debt were emphasized, and little attention was paid to the role of debt in the economic process. The traditional English view with respect to non-payment of debts appears to have survived in some degree throughout most of the nineteenth century.[158] Imprisonment for debt was fairly common during the early decades, but this practice gradually disappeared. At the time of the Civil War it was virtually nonexistent.[159] Thus it is not surprising that public debts in any form were distasteful and were widely construed as a sign of weakness.

Thrift ranked among the greatest of individual virtues. Of the influences that established and strengthened the American tradition with respect to individual thrift, none was more important than the homely teachings of Benjamin Franklin. His influence carried over far beyond the period in which he lived—especially in rural America.[160] Later Charles Dickens, who enjoyed enormous popularity in this country, played a part in maintaining the tradition concerning thrift and self-reliance.[161] Thrift had more than an economic conno-

[158] The underlying assumption on which the English debt laws were based was that a debt involves the transfer of property from the lender to the borrower. Failure to return the property or an equivalent value was regarded as little short of outright theft.

[159] Harry Elmer Barnes, *The Repression of Crime* (1926), pp. 203–05. Barnes' discussion of imprisonment for debt relates specifically to Pennsylvania. He regarded the development of criminal law in that state as typical. There were some instances of imprisonment for debt after the Civil War. See p. 138. Thurman W. Arnold has observed that imprisonment for debt continued as a moral lesson long after it had become an economic absurdity. *The Folklore of Capitalism*, p. 231.

[160] "Benjamin Franklin is more than a personage in American history. He wrote so much, traveled so widely, and had so many friends all over the Western world; he was involved in so many matters of the eighteenth century; and he lived so long that he has become an American institution." William D. Grampp, "The Political Economy of Poor Richard," *Journal of Political Economy*, Vol. 55 (1947), p. 132. Franklin "was always very favorably disposed towards the industrious and frugal farmer." W. A. Wetzel, *Benjamin Franklin as an Economist* (1895), p. 44.

[161] For more than a century Mr. Micawber's advice to David Copperfield has been the most frequently cited literary allusion to thrift. Mr. Micawber "solemnly conjured me to take warning by his fate; and to observe that if a man had twenty pounds a year for his income, and spent nineteen pounds nineteen shillings and six pence, he would be happy, but that if he spent twenty pounds one he would be

tation; it was endowed with strong moral overtones. Thrift
and success were assumed to be synonymous.

Thrift and self-reliance were complementary virtues.
Thrift bolstered by a sound instinct for accumulation was an
important part of the process by which one became self-
reliant. The doctrine of the free and unfettered individual
attained its classic expression in nineteenth century America
in the writings of Emerson and Thoreau. In the famous essay
Self-Reliance Emerson extolled the merits of the self-reliant
individual.[162] He "foresaw the day when the advance of the
individual would render the state unnecessary."[163] Thoreau's
contempt for the state was virtually boundless. His essay
Civil Disobedience, which was written at the time of the war
with Mexico, begins with the mild observation: "I heartily
accept the motto,—'That government is best which governs
least'; and I should like to see it acted up to more rapidly and
systematically." He asks the question, "How does it become
a man to behave toward this American government today?" The answer is that "he cannot without disgrace be
associated with it." And later, "I simply wish to refuse alle-
giance to the State, to withdraw and stand aloof from it
effectually."[164] These excerpts suggest that Thoreau regarded state activity, even at the level of the 1840's, as
thoroughly incompatible with individual freedom.

The idealization and practice of thrift by Americans of
virtually all classes were in harmony with the needs of the
economy. Saving and capital accumulation were an integral part of the process by which the economy grew and
progressed. Yet the people generally were reluctant to ac-

---

miserable." David received this advice while visiting Mr. Micawber in King's
Bench prison, where he was imprisoned for debt. *David Copperfield* (1917), Vol. 1,
p. 181. This work was first published in 1850.

[162] *The Complete Essays and Other Writings of Ralph Waldo Emerson*, Modern
Library Edition (1940), pp. 145–69. This essay was first published in 1841 in
Essays, First Series.

[163] Sidney Fine, *Laissez Faire and the General-Welfare State* (1956), p. 5.

[164] *The Writings of Henry David Thoreau* (1894), Vol. 10, pp. 131, 136, 161.

cept the view that debt is merely the obverse side or legal aspect of credit. Going into debt might be permissible for a railroad or other large business. But an individual or family should proceed with extreme care.

Economical government was a parallel social virtue. Practically without exception, economy in government was equated with low-cost government. The idea of administrative economy played only a minor role. Whatever significance was attached to it by the electorate derived mainly from the fact that economies attributable to improved operational efficiency were helpful in holding expenditures within income. Economical government did not flow automatically from the mere fact of democratic government. As stated by de Tocqueville, the American people enjoyed economical government "not only because they live under democratic institutions, but because they are a commercial nation. The habits of private life are continued in public; and we ought carefully to distinguish that economy which depends upon their institutions from that which is a natural result of their manners and customs."[165]

[165] de Tocqueville, *Democracy in America*, Vol. 1, p. 222. "The political values and the ideas of government that had been formed in the rural Yankee world were profoundly influenced by entrepreneurship and the ideal of individual success." Richard Hofstadter, *The Age of Reform from Bryan to F.D.R.* (1955), p. 9.

CHAPTER II

Budget Policy
From the Civil War to 1929

M AJOR WARS OF MODERN times leave a lasting im-
print on the finances of the nations engaged. National
debts are catapulted to new levels and peacetime budgets
are enlarged by sharp rises in pensions and interest, among
other costs. The Civil War, the first major war in which the
United States was engaged, was no exception. In American
public finance, as well as in the broader context of political
and social events, it was a dividing point.[1] Chronologically,
the beginning of Lincoln's administration on the eve of hostilities marked the half-way point in the long period from
the establishment of the federal government under the Constitution to the inauguration of Franklin D. Roosevelt.[2]

Lincoln to McKinley

At the beginning of the administration of Abraham Lincoln (1861–1865), the federal Treasury was in an unsatis-

[1] "There are events in the story of nations which cut their history in two. Nothing
is ever the same again. . . . Such events were the French Revolution, the War
between the North and South in the United States, the Indian Mutiny." Review
by Cecil Woodham-Smith of *The Red Fort: The Story of the Indian Mutiny*, by
James Leasor, *New York Times* (April 21, 1957), sec. 7, p. 1.

[2] On the eve of the Civil War the federal government was serving a nation of
approximately 32 million people, a seven-fold increase over 1790. They were living

factory condition.[3] After the outbreak of hostilities the financial position of the government showed considerable improvement. In December 1861 the President reported that the operations of the Treasury in the preceding months had been conducted with signal success. "The patriotism of the people has placed at the disposal of the Government the large means demanded by the public exigencies."[4]

From the outset the approach to war finance was not a strong one. "The weakest element in the financiering of the Civil War was the delay in applying effective taxation."[5] Thus, in July 1861 Secretary Salmon P. Chase proposed that not less than $80 million of the estimated requirements of about $320 million for the fiscal year 1862 be covered by taxation and that the balance of $240 million be raised by loans.[6] The amount of $80 million was the sum of: (1) $66 million for regular expenditures on a peacetime basis; (2) $9 million for interest; and (3) $5 million for the sinking fund. Covering all extraordinary expenditures from borrowings was rationalized on the ground that suppression of the rebellion would require only a few months—perhaps a half

---

in 34 states and a number of territories. Of the 34 states, the federal government itself had created no less than 21.

[3] The deficits incurred during the preceding administration had brought the debt to about $75 million, most of which was bearing high rates of interest. In January 1861 the Secretary of the Treasury had been forced to admit his inability to pay the warrants submitted by holders. A good summary of federal finances prior to and immediately after Lincoln's inauguration in March 1861 is in Wesley C. Mitchell, *A History of the Greenbacks* (1903), pp. 3 ff.

[4] James D. Richardson, ed., *Messages and Papers of the Presidents* (1897), Vol. 8, p. 3248.

[5] Davis R. Dewey, *Financial History of the United States* (1931), p. 299.

[6] *Exec. Doc. 2*, 37 Cong. 1 sess., p. 6. The "large means" referred to by Lincoln consisted mainly of about $150 million in loans negotiated under a $250 million authorization approved by Congress. The high rate of interest—7.3 per cent for three year notes—and the spirit of loyalty to the government aroused by the rebellion were among the factors that ensured the success of this loan. By no means least important was the fact that the banks were in a liquid condition as a result of the liquidation that occurred immediately after Lincoln's election. The borrowing operations of the Treasury during the Civil War are fully considered in Robert A. Love, *Federal Financing* (1931), Chapters 4 and 5.

year at the outside. The war might be over before a comprehensive program of taxation could be considered and become
effective.

Chase repeated his proposal in December 1861. Recogniz-
ing the effect of the war on customs revenues, he now proposed $50 million in taxes, including (1) a direct tax of $20
million to be apportioned among the states, (2) an income
tax to yield $10 million, and (3) a variety of excises to yield
$20 million. Chase regarded $50 million as a large amount.
"But if the sum is large the means of the people are also large;
and the object to be attained by a consecration of a portion
of them to the public service is priceless."[7] The following
month Congress adopted a more determined policy and announced its intention to enact a revenue measure to yield
$150 million annually. The revenue act approved July 1,
1862 imposed moderate taxes on a large number of objects,
and a measure designed to equalize import duties was enacted the same month.[8]

The following year (December 1862) Chase did not propose any additional revenues, but in 1863 he suggested that
more taxes were needed. "To check the increase of debt must
be, in our circumstances, a prominent object of patriotic
solicitude." A survey of the financing of the war to date led
to the observation: "Hitherto the expenses of the war have
been defrayed by loans to an extent which nothing but the
expectation of its speedy termination could fully warrant."
In a rather strained comparison, the Secretary pointed out
that revenues for 1863 were equal to regular civil expendi-

[7] *Report of the Secretary of the Treasury on the State of the Finances for the Year
Ending June 30, 1861*, p. 15. From the onset of the war Chase took the position
that ordinary or peacetime expenditures should be held "within the narrowest
practicable limits." In his report for 1861 he stated: "Retrenchment and reform are
among the indispensable duties of the hour. . . . All unnecessary offices should be
abolished, and salaries and pay should be materially reduced. In these ways the
burdens of the people, imposed by the war, may be sensibly lightened. . . ." *Ibid.*,
p. 12.

[8] Dewey, *Financial History of the United States*, pp. 300–02; 12 Stat. 432, 543.

tures, interest, and "double" the annual expenses of the Army and Navy on a peacetime basis—with a surplus of $16 million.[9]

The Civil War revolutionized the financial methods of the United States. Nothing was ever the same again. The national banking system was established under the provisions of an act approved in February 1863.[10] A major reason for the creation of the national banks was to afford an outlet for government bonds. National bank notes secured by government obligations became an important component of the currency.[11] The effectiveness of the new monetary system thus created was enhanced by a tax of 10 per cent per annum on the face value of state bank notes. The purpose of this prohibitive rate was to eliminate a thoroughly unsatisfactory component of the circulating medium.

Tax resources before undreamed of were resorted to. The tariff was supplemented by a series of internal taxes. These included an income tax that remained in effect until 1872.[12] The tariff itself was called on to yield more revenue. "The

[9] *Report of the Secretary of the Treasury on the State of the Finances for the Year Ending June 30, 1863,* pp. 9–11. An interesting sidelight in Chase's report for 1862 is that a figure of over $1 billion appeared in the federal accounts for the first time. Expenditures for the fiscal year 1864 were estimated at $1,095 million. The outstanding debt was estimated at $1,122 million on July 1, 1863 and $1,745 million on July 1, 1864. *Report of the Secretary of the Treasury on the State of the Finances for the Year Ending June 30, 1862,* pp. 2, 35.

[10] 12 Stat. 665.

[11] In Chase's report for 1862 he pointed out that "debt, by no means desirable in itself, may, when circumstances compel nations to incur its obligations, be made by discreet use less burdensome, and even instrumental in the promotion of public and private security and welfare." The Secretary considered the "security by national bonds of . . . notes furnished to banking associations" such a use. *Report of the Secretary of the Treasury on the State of the Finances for the Year Ending June 30, 1862,* p. 20. A year later the Secretary reported: "The loan act and the national banking act were followed by an immediate revival of public credit." *Report of the Secretary of the Treasury on the State of the Finances for the Year Ending June 30, 1863,* p. 2.

[12] The aggregate yield of this tax was $347 million, a large amount for the time. The Civil War income tax was the first tax of its kind enacted during our history as a nation. In the Colonial period a faculty or income tax was imposed in New England and the Middle Atlantic areas. Dewey, *Financial History of the United States,* pp. 11, 277, 305–06.

high duties which the war . . . caused to be imposed, at first regarded as temporary, were retained, increased, and systematized, so developing gradually into a system of extreme protection." A large national debt was accumulated, approaching $3 billion as the war ended. "Every resource was strained for carrying on the great struggle."[13]

Lincoln was not greatly concerned by the rise in the federal debt. Toward the end of the war he stated that the federal debt was a species of property. "Held, as it is, for the most part by our own people, it has become a substantial branch of national, though private, property. For obvious reasons the more nearly this property can be distributed among all the people the better. . . . The great advantage of citizens being creditors as well as debtors with relation to the public debt is obvious. Men readily perceive that they can not be much oppressed by a debt which they owe to themselves."[14]

With the federal debt at an unprecedented level, domestic ownership and a wide distribution of outstanding obligations were of no little importance. The difference between foreign holdings and a domestically held public debt, it will be recalled, had figured prominently in Alexander Hamilton's analysis of the public credit. In later decades it was alluded to by Andrew Jackson and Martin Van Buren, among others. The view that this distinction was stressed only by Hamilton and certain modern fiscal theorists, as at times seems to be assumed, is not well founded.

The Civil War was followed by a prolonged period of adjustments. The financial and other problems of the postwar era were complicated by the fact that the war was an internal struggle.[15] An inevitable consequence was that the post-

---

[13] Frank W. Taussig, *The Tariff History of the United States* (1931), pp. 155, 160.

[14] *Messages and Papers of the Presidents*, Vol. 8, pp. 3448–49.

[15] The borrowing operations and debt problems of the period from the close of the Civil War to the 1920's are considered in Love, *Federal Financing*, Chapters 6–13. A more detailed discussion of debt management during the immediate post-Civil War period will be found in Robert T. Patterson, *Federal Debt-Management Policies, 1865–1879* (1954).

war problems of the vanquished merged with those of the victor.

Andrew Johnson (1865–1869) believed that the large post-war debt was an evil and a burden on the economy. The nation, he said, "must aim at nothing less than the complete effacement of the financial evils that necessarily followed a state of civil war." Prominent among these "evils" was the large federal debt—then about $2.5 billion. A debt policy should be devised that "without being oppressive to the people, shall immediately begin to effect a reduction of the debt, and, if persisted in, discharge it fully within a definitely fixed number of years." In Johnson's opinion the debt was "doubly secure—first in the actual wealth and still greater undeveloped resources of the country, and next in the character of our institutions." But he was not willing to have the debt merely fade into insignificance as the wealth and income of the nation expanded. "We should look at the national debt just as it is—not as a national blessing, but as a heavy burden on the industry of the country, to be discharged without unnecessary delay."[16] Johnson suggested a plan that would liquidate the entire federal debt in about 17 years. Foreign holdings, amounting to about one third of total federal debt, were regarded as especially burdensome. Payment of the debt was deemed essential, in order that the nation might "rapidly recover its wonted prosperity."[17]

The President's belief that the debt represented an economic burden was shared by Hugh McCulloch, Secretary of the Treasury. To McCulloch the federal debt was a mortgage—an "incumbrance" on the national estate. "As all

[16] *Messages and Papers of the Presidents*, Vol. 8, pp. 3562–64. The following obeisance to economy was added: "I hold it the duty of the Executive to insist upon frugality in the expenditures, and a sparing economy is itself a great national resource."

[17] *Ibid.*, Vol. 9, pp. 3975 ff. Johnson's desire to reduce the debt promptly was doubtless influenced by his view that it might lead to a financial aristocracy centered in the North. Claude G. Bowers, *The Tragic Era* (1929), p. 116.

men desire to leave to their heirs unincumbered estates, so should it be the ambition of the people of the United States to relieve their descendants of this national mortgage."[18] Neither the advantages of the debt nor its burdens are or can be shared or borne equally by the people. "Its influences are anti-republican. It adds to the power of the Executive by increasing federal patronage. It must be distasteful to the people because it fills the country with informers and tax-gatherers. It is dangerous to the public virtue, because it involves the collection and disbursement of vast sums of money, and renders rigid national economy almost impracticable."[19]

Johnson was unable to reconcile himself to the fact that the war had brought the federal budget to an entirely new level. He pointed out that expenditures for the four postwar years would amount to about $1.6 billion; the total for the entire period 1789 to 1861 was only $1.7 billion. Federal expenditures for 1791 were a little over $1 per capita, by 1860 they were $2 per capita, "while in 1869 they will reach the extravagant sum of $9.78 per capita." The "startling facts" disclosed by the President's financial summary were construed as illustrating "the necessity of retrenchment in the public service."[20]

[18] The idea that federal obligations were in the nature of a mortgage had been used by Jay Cooke in promoting the sale of wartime bond issues. In his most popular circular on the seven-thirty United States loan Cooke stated: "It is as safe as a mortgage on a good farm and pays a better interest. It is, in fact, a *First Mortgage* on all lands, all incomes, all railroad and canal bonds, and bank or other stocks, mortgages, etc." E. P. Oberholtzer, *Jay Cooke: Financier of the Civil War* (1907), Vol. 1, p. 482.

[19] *Report of the Secretary of the Treasury on the State of the Finances for the Year 1865*, p. 16. McCulloch's policies were sharply criticized by the economist Henry C. Carey, among others. See pp. 103–05.

[20] *Messages and Papers of the Presidents*, Vol. 9, pp. 3872 ff. Johnson's attitude toward rising expenditures was in harmony with his views concerning the role of the federal government. He favored a "policy of popularizing all our free institutions" and bringing government "nearer to the people." *Speeches of Andrew Johnson: With a Biographical Introduction by Frank Moore* (1866). p. 55; Bowers, *The Tragic Era*, p. 30.

The idea that the debt incurred during the war represented a serious economic burden was unacceptable to U. S.
Grant (1869–1877). He emphasized that the burden would
decline with the growth of the country. In his first annual
message Grant suggested that the entire public debt could
be paid in ten years, even with lower taxes than imposed during the preceding six years. "But it is not desirable that the
people should be taxed to pay it in that time. Year by year
the ability to pay increases in a rapid ratio."[21] When the debt
was reduced by $86 million in the fiscal year 1871, the Presi-
dent observed that this development strengthened the federal
credit and convinced the citizens of their ability to meet
every dollar of liability. However, so rapid a reduction of the
debt was neither necessary nor desirable. In view of the
growth of the resources of the country and its increasing
ability to meet large demands, tax reduction should take
precedence over extremely rapid debt retirement.[22]

Grant's views concerning the federal debt were broader
than those of most of his predecessors. Without in any way
denying the value of a high federal credit, he was able to
visualize the debt dwindling in importance as an influence
in economic and financial affairs. To him the extreme position that the debt had to be retired—or even repudiated—
before the country could progress was devoid of merit. Well
after his term of office Grant stated that the "war has made

[21] *Messages and Papers of the Presidents*, Vol. 9, pp. 3982–84. It was Grant's
position that every dollar of government debt should be paid in gold, unless otherwise stipulated in the contract. *Ibid.*, p. 3961. He looked with favor upon the act
approved in March 1869 (16 Stat. 1) which declared that the faith of the United
States is solemnly pledged to payment in coin of the United States notes and interest-bearing obligations, except those which could be discharged in lawful money
or other than gold and silver. *Ibid.*, Vol. 10, p. 4224.

[22] *Ibid.*, pp. 4101–02. The views of Secretary George S. Boutwell were narrower
than those of the President. "Whatever arguments may be adduced, or whatever
theories advanced, the fact must ever remain that a public debt is a public evil.
It is especially burdensome to the laboring classes, and it is, therefore, in their
interest to provide for the constant reduction of the existing national debt." *Annual
Report of the Secretary of the Treasury on the State of the Finances for the Year 1870*,
p. XVI.

us a nation of great power and intelligence."[23] The war debt was an incident of the rebellion he had helped to suppress. It was not in his judgment a serious bar to continued economic progress.

The Presidents who served from 1877 to the end of the century, in common with Johnson and Grant, favored a balanced federal budget and the orderly servicing of the public debt. Few, if any, new reasons were advanced in support of the reduction of the debt and its eventual extinguishment. During a large part of this period surpluses were more troublesome than deficits.

Rutherford B. Hayes (1877–1881) advocated a wider distribution of the federal debt among domestic holders.[24] He recommended that

. . . suitable provision be made to enable the people to easily convert their savings into Government securities, as the best mode in which small savings may be well secured and yield a moderate interest. It is an object of public policy to retain among our own people the securities of the United States. In this way our country is guarded against their sudden return from foreign countries, caused by war or other disturbances beyond our limits.[25]

Though Hayes did not press the point, these policies would tend to minimize both the "economic burden" and the redistributive effect of the debt.[26]

Chester A. Arthur (1881–1885) opposed extremely rapid

---

[23] *Personal Memoirs of U. S. Grant* (1886), Vol. 2, p. 553.

[24] When Hayes took office, the country was at the threshold of a new and dynamic era. "Fresh forces, long obscured and hindered by the problems left by the war, were beginning to make their appearance." James A. Barnes, *John G. Carlisle: Financial Statesman* (1931), p. 30. Hayes' administration represented the first step in the transition to orderly and responsible government, following questionable practices disclosed during the "tragic era" of the reconstruction. H. J. Eckenrode, *Rutherford B. Hayes: Statesman of Reunion* (1930), p. 344.

[25] *Messages and Papers of the Presidents*, Vol. 10, p. 4423. During his last year in office Hayes expressed great satisfaction over the progress being made in reducing the public debt. *Ibid.*, pp. 4566–67.

[26] The impact of the silver controversy on the debt was a matter of concern to Hayes. He believed the relation of the government to the holders of the public debt might easily be disrupted by silver coinage proposals. *Ibid.*, pp. 4414–15.

reduction of the federal debt.[27] When the accounts for 1881 showed a surplus of $100 million, relief from the "present onerous burden" of taxation was recommended.[28] Arthur— in common with Grant—emphasized that the growth of the country tended to lighten the burden of the debt.[29] The following year the disadvantages of large surpluses were made more explicit. Such "rapid extinguishment of the national indebtedness as is now taking place is by no means a cause for congratulation; it is a cause rather for serious apprehension." If it continues, either the surplus must lie idle in the Treasury or the government will be forced to buy bonds not yet redeemable at exorbitant premiums. The only other possibility is that the swollen revenues might be devoted to extravagant expenditure.[30]

THE PROBLEM OF SURPLUSES

At this juncture an unusual sort of crisis developed in the national finances. The situation—in the opinion of both Arthur and his successor, Grover Cleveland—called for a reduc-

[27] In his inaugural address James A. Garfield (March 1881–September 1881) emphasized the importance of a high public credit for the economy. In rather ornate language he said: "The prosperity which now prevails is without parallel in our history. Fruitful seasons have done much to secure it, but they have not done all. The preservation of the public credit and the resumption of specie payments, so successfully attained by the Administration of my predecessors, have enabled our people to secure the blessings which the seasons brought." *Ibid.*, p. 4600.

[28] The problem of obtaining tax reductions was complicated by the large proportion of revenues derived from customs duties. For the four fiscal years 1882–1885, customs revenues amounted to $812 million, or slightly over 55 per cent of federal receipts of $1,474 million. *Annual Report of the Secretary of the Treasury on the State of the Finances for the Fiscal Year Ended June 30, 1956*, p. 320.

[29] *Messages and Papers of the Presidents*, Vol. 10, p. 4635. In 1884 Secretary Hugh McCulloch reported that nearly half of the Civil War debt had been paid off and that reduction in the rate of interest had kept pace with the reduction of the principal. Within "a period of nineteen years the debt, which it was feared would be a heavy and never-ending burden upon the people, has been so managed as to be no longer burdensome." *Annual Report of the Secretary of the Treasury on the State of the Finances for the Year 1884*, pp. xxviii–ix.

[30] *Messages and Papers of the Presidents*, Vol. 11, pp. 4721–22. The President also renewed his proposal for tax reduction, and some reductions were made the

tion in revenues. However, strong resistance to tariff reductions developed in the Congress, and this approach to the surplus problem proved unworkable. Members of Congress might agree with Arthur that "swollen revenues" contribute to extravagant expenditure, which "is ever the bane of an overflowing Treasury." But tariff reductions not favored by constituents or other influential interests were not easy to obtain, and requests for action went unheeded.

Large surpluses were deemed undesirable because they contributed to a rise in expenditures. "The temptation to squander money was overwhelming; the Rivers and Harbors Act passed over Arthur's veto in 1882 demonstrated how strongly it lay upon Congress. Pensions, another politically ingratiating form of spending, absorbed increasing amounts, although no new general act was passed."[31] But Arthur did not believe that a liberal spending policy was justified. The "extravagant expenditure of public money is an evil not to be measured by the value of that money to the people who are taxed for it."[32]

Grover Cleveland (1885–1889) took an even firmer stand against continued surpluses and in favor of lower revenues. In his inaugural address the President stated that public ex-

---

following March. In December 1884 the President proposed that further reductions be made in line with his original proposal. *Ibid.*, p. 4831.

The decade of the 1880's marked important changes in the economy. Until this decade agriculture was the principal source of wealth; the census of 1890 showed that manufacturing had forged to the front. Harold U. Faulkner, *American Economic History* (1931), p. 478. The population in 1880 was slightly over 50 millions—by 1890 it had increased to 63 millions. There were 38 states in the Union in 1880 and 44 in 1890. The latter figure includes Idaho and Wyoming which attained statehood in July 1890.

[31] George F. Howe, *Chester A. Arthur: A Quarter Century of Machine Politics* (1934), p. 228. During the decade 1881–1891 federal expenditures for purposes other than national defense and interest more than doubled. *Annual Report of the Secretary of the Treasury on the State of the Finances for the Fiscal Year Ended June 30, 1956*, p. 321.

[32] *Messages and Papers of the Presidents*, Vol. 11, p. 4708. This statement is from the veto message of August 1, 1882. This message was an unusually felicitous statement of the objections an observing executive might raise against the congressional approach to appropriations for rivers and harbors.

penditures should be limited to the actual needs of the government economically administered. It should be the goal of government to relieve the people of unnecessary taxation, thereby preventing the accumulation of a surplus in the Treasury, which would "tempt extravagance and waste." Public extravagance should be avoided; it "begets extravagance among the people." The immediate problem facing the President was the same as the one that confronted Arthur —how to obtain a reduction in revenues in the face of insistent pressures for the continuance of customs rates at existing levels.[33] In December 1886 the President reported that the situation was becoming acute. Application of the surplus to the payment of the debt subject to extinguishment, if continued at the recent rate, would retire that class of indebtedness in less than one year.

The use of the surplus to buy noncallable bonds in the open market was a costly policy. "Higher and higher premiums had to be paid. This meant that large sums which by means of the tariff and internal revenue taxes had been collected from the consuming population, and above all from the masses of poor wage-earners and farmers, were used to pour into the pockets of the investing classes, especially in the East, a heavy unearned increment. The injustice was too obvious to escape notice."[34] In brief, debt retirement through market purchases at exorbitant premiums was objectionable because it was a form of redistribution at the expense of the poorer classes.

Yet the only alternatives were hoarding by the Treasury of "a vast quantity of money, the circulating medium of the people," or "wasteful public extravagance, with all the corrupting national demoralization which follows in its train."

[33] *Ibid.*, pp. 4886–87, 4926. A marked change in tariff policy was not contemplated. It was the President's view that the investments and interests of business and labor should be protected. Within these limitations, a reduction in the revenue derived from a tax on the imported necessaries of life was deemed both possible and proper.

[34] Allan Nevins, *Grover Cleveland: A Study in Courage* (1932), p. 279.

The worst consequence of a surplus, the President observed, is that it involves "a perversion of the relations between the people and their Government and a dangerous departure from the rules which limit the right of Federal taxation." Exactions in excess of legitimate needs become "ruthless extortion" and are "a violation of the fundamental principles of a free government."[35]

In December 1887 the President stated that if revenues in excess of needs continued to accumulate there was "no clear and undoubted executive power of relief." The problem was to provide some legitimate means by which the government could "restore in an emergency, without waste or extravagance, such money to its place among the people." The "present tariff laws, the vicious, inequitable, and illogical source of unnecessary taxation, ought to be at once revised and amended."[36] The problems and dangers incident to continuing large surpluses were summarized in the following language:

When we consider that the theory of our institutions guarantees to every citizen the full enjoyment of all the fruits of his industry and enterprise, with only such deduction as may be his share toward the careful and economical maintenance of the Government which protects him, it is plain that the exaction of more than this is indefensible extortion and a culpable betrayal of American fairness and justice. This wrong inflicted upon those who bear the burden of national taxation, like other wrongs, multiplies a brood of evil consequences. The public Treasury, which should only exist as a conduit conveying the people's tribute to its legitimate objects of expenditure, becomes a hoarding place for money needlessly withdrawn from trade and the people's use, thus crippling our national energies, suspending our country's development, preventing in-

[35] *Messages and Papers of the Presidents*, Vol. 11, pp. 5093–96. To prevent the accumulation of large cash balances, the allocation to the sinking fund for the fiscal year 1888 was expended at the beginning of the year and the funds used to buy bonds not yet redeemable at substantial premiums. In addition, interest payments falling due during the year were anticipated to some extent.

[36] *Ibid.*, Vol. 12, pp. 5166–69. Allan Nevins discusses this message in a chapter entitled "The Great Tariff Message of 1887." *Grover Cleveland: A Study in Courage*, pp. 367 ff.

vestment in productive enterprise, threatening financial distur-
bance, and inviting schemes of public plunder.[37]

The views of high Treasury officials mirrored those of the
President. Daniel Manning, Secretary of the Treasury, believed that surplus financing was redistributive in its effects,
regardless of the disposition of the excess revenues. The employment of surpluses for extravagant appropriations and
their accumulation as "Treasury hoards" were equally indefensible. "Surplus taxation has meant that Treasury operations have promoted the pecuniary advantage of some citizens and involved the pecuniary disadvantage of others."[38]
In 1887 Charles S. Fairchild, Manning's successor, observed
that "taxation beyond the absolute needs of government is
an injury to the people of the country, no matter for what
purposes the proceeds of taxation are expended."[39] A year
later Treasury bonds carrying a rate of 4.5 per cent were sell-
ing on a yield basis of about 1.5 per cent. "To continue
taxation with no other use for its proceeds than such an
investment is a cruel waste of the people's money."[40]

Surpluses continued to be a troublesome problem during
the administration of Benjamin Harrison (1889–1893), but

---

[37] *Messages and Papers of the Presidents*, Vol. 12, p. 5166. The following year
(December 1888) Cleveland broadened the basis of his argument in support of
lower revenues through appropriate reductions in the tariff. A portion of this
message is correctly described as an attack on economic privilege. The President
pointed out that if excessive and unnecessary taxation is continued and the government is forced to purchase its own bonds at substantial premiums, the "loss to the
people will be hundreds of millions of dollars." *Ibid.*, pp. 5359–63, 5372–73.

[38] *Annual Report of the Secretary of the Treasury on the State of the Finances for the
Year 1886*, Vol. 1, pp. XLI–VII.

[39] *Annual Report of the Secretary of the Treasury on the State of the Finances for the
Year 1887*, p. XXIX.

[40] *Annual Report of the Secretary of the Treasury on the State of the Finances for the
Year 1888*, p. XXVI. Though surpluses were not a problem during Grover Cleveland's
second term (1893–1897), he continued to oppose them as a matter of principle. The
accumulation of a fund not needed for immediate expenditure, the President stated,
is not one of the functions of the federal government. "It is immeasurably better to
appropriate our surplus to the payment of justifiable expenses than to allow it to
become an invitation to reckless appropriations and extravagant expenditures."
Messages and Papers of the Presidents, Vol. 14, p. 6174.

as they declined in size they were less annoying. Harrison believed that retirement of outstanding bonds was the only proper and lawful way of getting excess revenues back into circulation. The deposit of government funds in a large number of banks was not the answer. The lending of public funds to the banks without interest on the security of government bonds is "an unauthorized and dangerous expedient. It results in a temporary and unnatural increase of the banking capital of favored localities and compels a cautious and gradual recall of the deposits to avoid injury to the commercial interests."[41]

As Harrison's administration drew to a close, he pointed out that the public debt had been reduced by $259 million. Retirements were running far ahead of requirements under the sinking-fund law. The President concurred in the recommendation of the Secretary of the Treasury that this law should be repealed. "The retirement of bonds in the future before maturity should be a matter of convenience, not of compulsion. We should not collect revenue for that purpose, but only use any casual surplus."[42]

THE EMPHASIS ON ECONOMY

Despite the large surpluses, in the executive branch economy remained a leading goal of public policy. For example, Benjamin Harrison stated: "Expenditure should always be made with economy and only upon public necessity. Wastefulness, profligacy, or favoritism in public expenditures is criminal." Yet Harrison's position was by no means extreme.

---

[41] *Ibid.*, Vol. 12, pp. 5446–47. The problem of getting surplus revenues back into circulation is difficult to appreciate in the present era of central banking and open-market operations. To the extent that surpluses were not returned to the economy, the people were deprived of a portion of the circulating medium. Debt retirements through market purchases frequently meant premiums so large that this course seemed uneconomical. A rise in government deposits in the banks might in some instances have undesirable consequences, which in the absence of central banking could not be offset by appropriate countermeasures.

[42] *Ibid.*, Vol. 13, pp. 5753–54.

On another occasion he observed that it was a misuse of
terms to use economy to describe a "policy that withholds
an expenditure for the purpose of extending our foreign
commerce." In the case of rivers and harbors, he believed
that the wise and economical course was to schedule fewer
projects at a time and push them to completion more
rapidly.[43]

Economy in expenditures, together with limitation of federal functions, was stressed more strongly during Cleveland's second term (1893–1897) than in any other period
during the half century following the Civil War. In his second inaugural address Cleveland stated that frugality and
economy should not be regarded as virtues that we may
safely outgrow. The "waste of public money is a crime"
against the citizen. "It is a plain dictate of honesty and good
government that public expenditures should be limited by
public necessity, and that this should be measured by the
rules of strict economy; and it is equally clear that frugality
among the people is the best guaranty of a contented and
strong support of free institutions."[44]

Cleveland demanded that federal appropriations be limited
to public purposes. In vetoing a rivers and harbors bill, he
pointed out that many of the projects were for the benefit
of limited localities or in aid of individual interests. "Economy and the exaction of clear justification for the appropriation of public moneys by the servants of the people are not
only virtues, but solemn obligations."[45]

When an economic recession or financial panic occurred,
official policy without exception called for a doubling of economy efforts. U. S. Grant, as we have seen, had a decidedly
optimistic outlook on federal finances. But when the recession or financial panic of 1873 set in, his optimism was tem-
pered by the sharp decline in revenues. The situation, in the

[43] *Ibid.*, Vol. 12, pp. 5447, 5477, 5492.

[44] *Ibid.*, Vol. 13, pp. 5822–23.

[45] *Ibid.*, Vol. 14, pp. 6110–11. Secretary John G. Carlisle lamented the upward
trend in federal expenditures during the preceding decade. *Annual Report of the
Secretary of the Treasury on the State of the Finances for the Year 1896*, pp. LXXXV–VI.

thinking of the times, required economy. Three approaches
were suggested: (1) reduced appropriations for public
buildings; (2) lower expenditures for rivers and harbors; and
(3) more rigorous control of claims for losses incurred during
the Civil War.[46]

The economy theme was strongly emphasized during the
recession of 1893 and the economic and financial difficulties
that followed. The obvious requirement, in Cleveland's
opinion, was that "legislation be so limited by strict economy
as to exhibit an appreciation of the condition of the Treasury
and a sympathy with the straitened circumstances of our
fellow-citizens."[47] The President was ably seconded by Secretary John G. Carlisle. The "present and prospective condition of the Treasury and the general state of the country,
demand a policy of the strictest economy in public expenditures consistent with an efficient administration of the
laws. . . . Genuine economy and frugality can be secured
only by the repeal of statutes authorizing or requiring unnecessary expenditures."[48] The same thought was stressed
again two years later. "At a time when the people . . . are
compelled to practice the closest economy in their business
and domestic affairs in order to meet their obligations and
re-establish their trade and industries, it is more than ever
the duty of the public authorities to avoid waste and extravagance in the appropriation and disbursement of the
revenues."[49]

[46] *Messages and Papers of the Presidents*, Vol. 10, p. 4197.
[47] *Ibid.*, Vol. 13, p. 5890.
[48] *Annual Report of the Secretary of the Treasury on the State of the Finances for the
Year 1893*, p. LXXXIV.
[49] *Annual Report of the Secretary of the Treasury on the State of the Finances for the
Year 1895*, p. LXVIII. Considering the adverse economic situation, the combined deficit of $125 million for the four years of Cleveland's second administration appears
rather moderate. It was not the deficits that were at the heart of the financial difficulties. The central problem was a direct outgrowth of the vagaries of the monetary
system, especially the silver legislation. A major reason for the increase in debt was
to obtain gold with which to redeem United States notes. These notes were issued to
pay for silver tendered to the government under provisions of the Sherman Act of
1890, among other legislation. They not only were redeemable in gold, but they could
be reissued. The details concerning the several bond issues and Treasury finance are
fully presented in Barnes, *John G. Carlisle: Financial Statesman*, Chapters 13–16.

William McKinley (1897–1901) took the position that when economic conditions became unsatisfactory the "Government should not be permitted to run behind or increase its debt." Economy "is demanded in every branch of the Government at all times, but especially in periods, like the present, of depression in business and distress among the people." In a message to Congress called in special session to consider the government's financial needs, the President observed: "With unlimited means at our command, we are presenting the remarkable spectacle of increasing our public debt by borrowing money to meet the ordinary outlays incident upon even an economical and prudent administration of the Government." Ample revenues should be supplied not only for current expenses including pensions, but also for "the liquidation of the principal and interest of the public debt."[50]

The emphasis on economy does not mean that federal activities remained stationary from the Civil War to the close of the nineteenth century. Forces at work were destined to increase the scope of federal functions, notably in the regulatory field; for example, the Interstate Commerce Act was approved in 1887 and the Sherman Anti-Trust Act in 1890. Land and other grants in aid of higher education were influential in helping to break down the provincial outlook on federal activities that characterized the period before 1860.[51]

[50] *Messages and Papers of the Presidents*, Vol. 14, pp. 6237–38, 6244–46. The continuing drain on the gold reserve caused by the reissue of redeemed United States notes remained a troublesome problem. To obviate this difficulty, McKinley recommended that the redeemed notes be set aside and be used only to pay for gold. *Ibid.*, pp. 6252–53, 6340.

[51] In the last three and one half decades of the nineteenth century "the federal government was no slave to the doctrine of the negative state. The exigencies of the time and the pressure of politics compelled it to do considerably more than most proponents of laissez faire thought necessary. It promoted the interests of businessmen and farmers and also undertook the regulation of certain business activities. It initiated a national conservation policy and sought to promote the education, health, and morality of its citizens." Sidney Fine, *Laissez Faire and the General-Welfare State* (1956), pp. 362–63.

With the development of a network of railways, the internal improvement question became less important. This great issue was solved without the benefit of a constitutional amendment, as the strict constructionist philosophy faded into the background after the Civil War.

Though it is not possible to consider here the forces operating to shape federal fiscal trends, the discussion would be deficient without mention of the arguments for federal aid for the public schools advanced by three Presidents. Rutherford B. Hayes was the first President to urge strongly that the federal budget include grants for public school education. The basis of all prosperity, he observed in his inaugural address, "lies in the improvement of the intellectual and moral condition of the people. Universal suffrage should rest upon universal education. To this end, liberal and permanent provision should be made for the support of free schools by the State governments, and, if need be, supplemented by legitimate aid from national authority."[52]

A federal education policy that would embrace grants for public school purposes was recommended in all four of Hayes' annual messages. The President was especially concerned by the fact that one seventh of the voting population were unable to read and write. "It is vain to hope for the success of a free government without the means of insuring the intelligence of those who are the source of power."[53] Illiteracy and responsible self-government were said to be irreconcilable. "Whatever Government can fairly do to promote free popular education ought to be done. Wherever general edu-

[52] *Messages and Papers of the Presidents*, Vol. 10, p. 4396. Commenting on this proposal, a recent biographer states: "Sixty years later this kind of recommendation would bring the charge of socialism against anyone who made it. But in 1877 Hayes made it as the spokesman of Republican conservatism. Harry Barnard, *Rutherford B. Hayes and His America* (1954), p. 409.

[53] *Messages and Papers of the Presidents*, Vol. 10, p. 4431. In 1879 the President observed: "No more fundamental responsibility rests upon Congress than that of devising appropriate measures of financial aid to education, supplemental to local action." *Ibid.*, p. 4531.

cation is found, peace, virtue, and social order prevail and civil and religious liberty are secure."[54]

In Hayes' thinking the question of federal aid for education was closely tied in with the reconstruction problems of the South. He was convinced that "the enormous mass of ignorance in the South was too much for the old slaveholding States in their impoverished condition to cope with alone." In perhaps his strongest plea for federal grants for the schools he said: "To perpetuate the Union and to abolish slavery were the work of the war. To educate the uneducated is the appropriate work of peace."[55]

The position of Chester A. Arthur on this question was comparable to that of Hayes. His initial proposal was that the federal government should assist in the financing of public school education by setting aside the proceeds of the sales of public lands, or by some other course. The amounts thus becoming available would be distributed among the states according to the ratio of illiteracy. Educational aids based on illiteracy were proposed again in the next two annual messages,[56] but no action was taken by Congress.

Federal grants for education were also advocated by Benjamin Harrison. In accepting the Republican nomination in 1888, he stated:

The nation, not less than the States, is dependent for prosperity

[54] *Ibid.*, pp. 4554–55.

[55] Charles R. Williams, *The Life of Rutherford Birchard Hayes* (1914), Vol. 2, pp. 288–90; Barnard, *Rutherford B. Hayes and His America*, p. 494. Hayes suggested that the problem should be dealt with on the public works principle. "That principle is, that wherever a public improvement is of national importance, and local and private enterprise is inadequate . . . to its prosecution, the general Government should undertake it. . . . Wherever in the United States the local systems of popular education are inadequate, they should be supplemented by the general Government, by devoting to the purpose, by suitable legislation and with proper safeguards, the public lands, or, if necessary appropriations from the Treasury of the United States." The excerpts here cited are from an address delivered at Columbus, Ohio, August 11, 1880.

[56] *Messages and Papers of the Presidents*, Vol. 10, p. 4645; Vol. 11, pp. 4730–31, 4771.

and security upon the intelligence and morality of the people. This common interest very early suggested national aid in the establishment and endowment of schools and colleges in the new States. There is, I believe, a present exigency that calls for still more liberal and direct appropriations in aid of common-school education in the States.[57]

A change from land grants to money grants in aid of education was not an important consideration. The emancipation of the slaves and the impairment of the ability of the southern states to finance education and other services were among the reasons cited in defense of money grants. But Harrison's argument was couched in broader terms. "No one will deny that it is of the gravest national concern that those who hold the ultimate control of all public affairs should have the necessary intelligence wisely to direct and determine them."[58]

As the nineteenth century drew to a close, the Spanish-American War engaged the attention of the American people. Because of the war, deficits were incurred during the fiscal years 1898 and 1899—the first two years of McKinley's administration. The financing of this war did not present a serious problem. A $200 million loan floated for war purposes was over-subscribed.[59] For the first time in our history "the credit of the country was so used that it grew stronger rather than weaker from its use."[60] The necessary funds were obtained promptly and without serious disturbance of the money market. The economic and financial impact of the

[57] *Public Papers and Addresses of Benjamin Harrison* (1893), p. 5.
[58] *Messages and Papers of the Presidents*, Vol. 12, pp. 5489–90. This statement is from the annual message submitted in December 1889, in which Harrison proposed that federal grants be made to the states. By 1892 he apparently believed that federal grants were not urgently needed. *Public Papers and Addresses of Benjamin Harrison*, p. 21.
[59] *Messages and Papers of the Presidents*, Vol. 14, pp. 6314–15.
[60] C. C. Plehn, *Finances of the United States in the Spanish War* (1898), p. 419. This pamphlet is a reprint from University of California, *The University Chronicle*, Vol. 1, No. 5.

war was extremely light, and no significant inflationary pressures developed.[61]

Toward the end of the calendar year 1899 the federal government was again running a modest surplus. The accounts for the fiscal year 1900 showed a surplus of about $80 million and debt retirements were resumed.[62] The administration looked with satisfaction on the return to surplus financing after six deficits in succession, which it was hoped were merely "a temporary interruption to a history of twenty-eight years when each year showed annual expenditures less than annual revenues." The official view was expressed by Secretary Lyman J. Gage: "An annual excess in receipts over expenditures is the best indorsement of the national credit, while a deficit is a depressing factor in public finance."[63]

Theodore Roosevelt to Coolidge

At the turn of the century federal activities were expanding.[64] There was a growing awareness that the federal government could not remain the simple mechanism with limited

[61] The cost of the war with Spain has been placed by James Ford Rhodes at $300 million. The same authority estimates the cost of suppressing the Philippine insurrection at $170 million. *History of the United States: The McKinley and Roosevelt Years 1897–1909* (1923), p. 112.

[62] *Messages and Papers of the Presidents*, Vol. 14, pp. 6358, 6437. In recent Treasury reports the surplus for 1900 is shown as a little over $46 million.

[63] *Annual Report of the Secretary of the Treasury on the State of the Finances for the Fiscal Year Ended June 30, 1900*, pp. LXXXI–XII. At the end of the nineteenth century, the United States was experiencing rapid growth in resources and in population. For example, the value of the output of the iron and steel industry for 1899 was almost 70 per cent larger than for 1889; the increase during the succeeding decade was slightly larger. In both periods there was a moderate decline in the number of establishments. Faulkner, *American Economic History*, p. 509. The population in 1900 was 76 millions, an increase of over 50 per cent in two decades. There were 45 states; Oklahoma, New Mexico, and Arizona attained statehood after 1900.

[64] The expansion of activities and expenditures during the first half of the present century is fully considered in Solomon Fabricant, *The Trend of Government Activity in the United States Since 1900* (1952).

duties that it was during most of the nineteenth century. To an increasing extent, the role of the government was construed to be a facilitating one. Acceptance of this interpretation was an important step in the transition from the laissez-faire conception of the role of government to the idea of a clearly defined public sector of the economy.

ROOSEVELT, TAFT, AND WILSON

The thought that government should play a facilitating role was well expressed by Theodore Roosevelt (1901-1909) in his first annual message.

Fundamentally the welfare of each citizen, and therefore the welfare of the aggregate of citizens which makes the nation, must rest upon individual thrift and energy, resolution, and intelligence. Nothing can take the place of this individual capacity; but wise legislation and honest and intelligent administration can give it the fullest scope, the largest opportunity to work to good effect.

The "sharp division of authority between the Nation and the several States" had been advantageous to development, in Roosevelt's opinion. But the change in industrial conditions required a reassessment of their respective roles, especially with respect to the use of the police power.[65] In 1907 the President lamented that the federal laws relating to commerce and industry were "of a negative or prohibitive rather than an affirmative kind." Comments such as this did not mean that a revolutionary change was in the offing. Rather, certain nineteenth century conceptions were being questioned with increasing effectiveness. In particular, individual initiative and self-reliance should not be carried to unwarranted extremes.[66]

---

[65] *Messages and Papers of the Presidents,* Vol. 15, p. 6643; Vol. 16, pp. 7024-25.

[66] *Ibid.,* p. 7453. "With genius, audacity and courage," Theodore Roosevelt aroused the long slumbering civic conscience and awakened the people to a realization of their patrimony in the Nation's natural resources." Claude G. Bowers, "The Great Presidents Had Certain Traits in Common," *Washington Post* (Jan. 21, 1957), p. C-5.

In his inaugural address William Howard Taft (1909–1913) pointed out that the "scope of a modern government in what it can and ought to accomplish for its people has widened far beyond the principles laid down by the old 'laissez faire' school of political writers, and this widening has met popular approval."[67] The normal growth in expenditures—about 4 per cent annually for a number of years—was not viewed with alarm. Though economy was a favorite theme, the idea that low-cost government was synonymous with economical government was given little credence. "Real economy is the result of efficient organization. By perfecting the organization the same benefits may be obtained at less expense. A reduction in the total of the annual appropriations is not in itself a proof of economy, since it is often accompanied by a decrease in efficiency."[68]

Both Theodore Roosevelt and Taft favored a balanced federal budget. In 1901 Roosevelt stated: "The utmost care should be taken not to reduce the revenues so that there will be any possibility of a deficit; but, after providing against any such contingency, means should be adopted which will bring the revenues more nearly within the limit of our actual needs." In the President's opinion a large surplus was undesirable. A close correspondence between revenues and expenditures was conducive to economy.[69] Mainly because of the recession of 1903 and the financial panic of 1907, the progress toward a closer balance in the federal accounts was

[67] *Messages and Papers of the Presidents*, Vol. 17, pp. 7750–51. Conservation of natural resources, improvement of agricultural methods, supervision of railways and industrial combinations, and prosecution of unlawful business practices were mentioned as activities that widened the role of government. Incurrence of debt for permanent improvements such as the Panama Canal was favored by Taft.

[68] *Ibid.*, Vol. 18, pp. 8061–62, 8078–79. Similar views were expressed by Franklin MacVeagh, Secretary of the Treasury. "It would be a great mistake . . . to let this epoch of economy discredit itself and come to an untimely end by reason of losing the sense of difference between reductions of appropriations that we are better without and reductions of the appropriations that we are better with." *Annual Report of the Secretary of the Treasury on the State of the Finances for the Fiscal Year Ended June 30, 1909*, p. 3.

[69] *Messages and Papers of the Presidents*, Vol. 15, pp. 6652, 6861.

not especially noteworthy.[70] When Taft took office, the government was operating at a substantial deficit, largely as an aftermath of the 1907 panic. In the President's words, it "is imperative that such a deficit shall not continue." Adjustments in tariff rates were recommended, and a few months later the income tax amendment was proposed, together with an excise on corporations.[71]

In principle Woodrow Wilson (1913–1921) favored balanced peacetime budgets. Early in his career he observed that "money is being spent without new taxation, and appropriation without accompanying taxation is as bad as taxation without representation." In order to ensure "the preservation of political health under a popular constitution, taxation and appropriation must go hand in hand."[72] When in December 1915 Wilson deemed it necessary to request additional federal revenues, he observed that borrowing money "is short-sighted finance." But public borrowing was not ruled out in all circumstances. Borrowing can be justified "only when permanent things are to be accomplished which many generations will certainly benefit by and which it seems hardly fair that a single generation should pay for."[73]

Wilson's attitude toward debt reduction was less rigorous than that of most earlier Presidents. The orderly management of the debt was merely one of a number of considerations in the formulation of an appropriate policy. Writing in 1888, he observed that "an ideal financial policy" would not at the present time "hasten the payment of the national

[70] Secretary George B. Cortelyou questioned the adequacy of budgetary methods and the classification of accounts. In his report for 1908, it was stated that a system of accounts that did not distinguish clearly between operating expenditures and capital outlays was no longer adequate. *Annual Report of the Secretary of the Treasury on the State of the Finances for the Fiscal Year Ended June 30, 1908*, pp. 86–87.

[71] *Messages and Papers of the Presidents*, Vol. 17, pp. 7750, 7759, 7769–72. A corporation excise of one per cent on net income over $5,000 was approved and became the forerunner of the modern federal income tax. 36 Stat. 112.

[72] Woodrow Wilson, "Taxation and Appropriation," in *The National Revenues*, Albert Shaw, ed. (1888), p. 108.

[73] *Messages and Papers of the Presidents*, Vol. 18, p. 8492.

debt."[74] After World War I Wilson favored a planned reduction of the federal debt; he approved the sinking-fund provision in the Victory Liberty Loan Act of 1919.[75] In his last annual message the desirability of debt reduction was stressed, together with the importance of obtaining a better distribution of outstanding federal debt.[76]

Wilson's views concerning the role of government were more sophisticated than those of his immediate predecessors.[77] His conception of government was an evolutionary one. "The one idea that dominated Wilson's thought on society and government was the idea of evolution, with all its organismic corollaries." He did not accept the view that a nation is the numerical sum of its members. Rather, it is an

[74] Wilson, "Taxation and Appropriation," p. 110.

[75] See footnote 8, p. 317. An interesting development during World War I relates to the federal debt limit. The first wartime bond issue was floated under an authorization of $5 billion, in addition to unused portions of prior authorizations; authority to issue certificates of indebtedness in an amount not to exceed $2 billion outstanding at any one time was also granted. 40 Stat. 35. The Second Liberty Loan Act consolidated unused bond authority under previous legislation and authorized an additional $4 billion, bringing the total to $7,539 million; the figure for certificates was increased to $4 billion. 40 Stat. 288. For later changes, see *Debt Limit of the United States*, Hearing Before the Committee on Ways and Means, 85 Cong. 2 sess (1958), pp. 7–8. It was not until 1938 that a single limitation became applicable to all forms of indebtedness—bonds, notes, certificates, and bills. The limit then established was $45 billion. 52 Stat. 447.

[76] *Messages and Papers of Woodrow Wilson* (1924), Vol. 2, pp. 15–16. The outstanding federal debt was then approximately $24 billion. A detailed discussion of budget and financial policy during World War I is not included in the present study. Though taxes reached unprecedented levels in the fiscal years 1918 and 1919, receipts covered less than 30 per cent of expenditures. See the table and summary in the Appendix, p. 317. The borrowing operations of the Treasury during World War I and significant developments of the postwar decade are considered in Love, *Federal Financing*, Chapters 8–13.

[77] The point is sometimes made that basically Woodrow Wilson was an academician—"a product of academic groves"—and that he had learned statecraft from books, except for his two-year term as Governor of New Jersey. See, for example, Louis M. Hacker and Benjamin B. Kendrick, *The United States Since 1865* (1932), p. 456. Wilson possessed a knowledge of economics and was well schooled in the classical tradition. William Diamond, *The Economic Thought of Woodrow Wilson* (1943), pp. 18, 29. At an early stage of his career, he collaborated with two prominent American economists—Richard T. Ely and Davis R. Dewey—in the preparation of an unpublished history of American economic thought.

organic unit which has an existence aside from its individual members. "Society, the state, government, all three go through a process of development, changing under the pressure of competition and adaptation to new circumstances." Wilson's views have been aptly described as a "middle path between what he called socialism and extreme laissez faire." He considered a purely police state as absurd as a society leaning "fondly upon government for guidance and assistance in every affair of life."[78] A cardinal plank in his philosophy was that government has a positive role to play. The implications are obvious. If it is to function effectively, modern government cannot restrict its activities to the merely essential, or even remotely consider limiting its functions to those acceptable to extreme advocates of laissez faire such as Sumner and Spencer.[79]

Wilson looked with favor on all constructive economies in federal expenditures. "The duty of economy is not debatable. It is manifest and imperative. . . . The only thing debatable and upon which we should be careful to make our thought and purpose clear is the kind of economy demanded of us." The people of the United States "are not jealous of the amount their Government costs if they are sure that they get what they need and desire for the outlay, that the money

[78] *Ibid.*, pp. 39, 46; Wilson, *The State* (1911), pp. 629 ff. This work was first published in 1889. As governor of New Jersey, a dominant element in Wilson's thought was "the conception of government as a third party, an umpire to smooth away the friction between groups and interests and to serve the whole of society." Diamond, *The Economic Thought of Woodrow Wilson*, p. 80.

[79] In his earlier writings Wilson had distinguished between the essential and optional powers of government; the latter included the regulation of economic life, internal improvements, and social welfare legislation. The only test of the functions and activities under these headings that government should undertake is wisdom. The sphere of government "is limited only by its own wisdom . . . ."Government "does now whatever experience permits or the times demand. . . ." It is "by gaining practical experience, . . . by long processes of historical experience, that states modify their practices." *The State*, pp. 621, 625, 628. Diamond, *The Economic Thought of Woodrow Wilson*, p. 45. On Sumner and Spencer, see the later discussion at pp. 109–12.

is being spent for objects of which they approve, and that it is being applied with good business sense and management."[80] After World War I Wilson pointed out that vigorous economy was needed. In his last annual message he observed that it was impossible to overemphasize the necessity of economy in governmental appropriations and expenditures.[81]

Others high in the councils of the administration feared that the war would be followed by a careless attitude toward federal expenditures. For example, Secretary Carter Glass said that "it becomes the clear duty of this department to point out that there appears to be grave danger that the extraordinary success of the Treasury in financing the stupendous war expenditures may lead to a riot of public expenditures after the war, the consequences of which could only be disastrous."[82] Secretary David F. Houston was equally emphatic a year later. "The need of the exercise of plain common sense, of patience, of the effective realization that burdens of war do not end with the fighting, of hard work, of thrift and of economy, private and public, Federal, State, county, and municipal, is so obvious as to render emphasis and discussion of it unnecessary." Individuals and communities should return to a normal degree of self-help and self-reliance. "We have demobilized many groups, but we have not demobilized those whose gaze is concentrated on the Treasury."[83]

[80] *Messages and Papers of the Presidents,* Vol. 18, pp. 8399–8400. On the same occasion—December 1914—the President stated that "it is generally agreed that there should be a systematic reorganization and reassembling" of the several parts of the federal establishment "so as to secure greater efficiency. . . . But the amount of money saved in that way would . . . be relatively small . . . in proportion to the total necessary outlays of the Government." *Ibid.,* p. 8400.

[81] *Messages and Papers of Woodrow Wilson,* Vol. 2, pp. 1215–17.

[82] *Annual Report of the Secretary of the Treasury on the State of the Finances for the Fiscal Year Ended June 30, 1919,* pp. 22–23. Glass stressed the relation between a high level of public expenditure and the cost of living, together with the desirability of an early return to a balanced budget.

[83] *Annual Report of the Secretary of the Treasury on the State of the Finances for the Fiscal Year Ended June 30, 1920,* pp. 1, 4, 49.

THE HARDING-COOLIDGE ERA

Return to normalcy was a major theme of Warren G. Harding (1921–1923). To say that "normalcy" included a balanced federal budget and debt reduction is superfluous. Finance received major emphasis in the inaugural address. "We can reduce the abnormal expenditures, and we will. We can strike at war taxation, and we must. We must face the grim necessity, with full knowledge that the task is to be solved. . . . Our most dangerous tendency is to expect too much of government, and at the same time do for it too little." The immediate task is to put "our public household in order." A "rigid and yet sane economy" is needed.[84] A few months later the President said: "Government, to a greater extent now than ever before, is under obligation to give the greatest service for the lowest possible cost. But it is for certain obvious reasons difficult to do this, because government is not under the necessity to earn profits, nor to obey laws which regulate competition."[85] War "is not wholly responsible for staggering costs; it has merely accentuated the menace which lies in mounting cost of government and excesses in expenditure which a successful private business would not tolerate."[86]

The problem of controlling and reducing expenditures and indebtedness was not regarded as solely a federal one. In the budget message submitted in December 1922, the President expressed his concern over increasing state, county, and municipal indebtedness. "I am fearful lest this condition

[84] Inaugural address of President Warren G. Harding, March 4, 1921, *Congressional Record*, Vol. 61, Pt. 1, p. 5. At that time postwar adjustments were not complete, and the peacetime level of federal expenditures remained uncertain. That it would be well above the prewar level was obvious; interest requirements alone were substantially larger than total federal expenditures before the war.

[85] Address of President Harding at the luncheon of the Academy of Political Science, New York City, May 23, 1921, *ibid.*, Pt. 9, p. 8246.

[86] Address of President Harding to the Senate on the Soldiers' Bonus, July 12, 1921, *ibid.*, Pt. 4, p. 3597.

may be in part attributable to the expenditures made by Government pursuant to its Federal-aid laws."[87] The President was even more emphatic the following summer. Speaking at Salt Lake City in the presence of Senator Reed Smoot, Harding said: "I find myself involuntarily thinking when I come to your State, of the menace of mounting taxes and growing public indebtedness. The removal of this menace is not alone a Federal problem, for we are recording gratifying progress so far as the nation is concerned, but the larger menace today is to be faced by municipality, county and State." The President deplored the fact that state and local governments had not been following the example of the federal government and spending less than their income. A single rule applies to citizens and governments alike. "Learn to spend somewhat less than your income all the time."[88]

Harding's philosophy was given strong backing by Secretary Andrew Mellon, among others. Referring to federal expenditures of over $5 billion for 1921, Mellon stated that the "Nation can not continue to spend at this shocking rate. . . . The country is staggering under the existing burden of taxation and debt and clamoring for gradual relief from the war taxation."[89] The "increasing burden of local taxation" was a matter for grave concern. "These taxes are affecting land values unfavorably" and "causing a state of discontent which does not always place the blame where it belongs."[90]

[87] *Message of the President of the United States Transmitting the Budget for the Service of the Fiscal Year Ending June 30, 1924*, p. IX.

[88] Address of the President of the United States on Taxation and Expenditures at Salt Lake City, Utah, *New York Times* (June 27, 1923), p. 12. "Harding was convinced that one of the greatest services he could perform would be to get government spending back to a peacetime basis, with the national balance sheet showing healthy annual surpluses. Repeatedly during his 28 months in office he preached to the public on economy, lectured Congress on economy, admonished the personnel of the government on economy." Mark Sullivan, *Our Times: The Twenties*, Vol. 6 (1935), p. 207.

[89] Letter of April 30, 1921 to the Chairman of the Committee on Ways and Means, in *Annual Report of the Secretary of the Treasury on the State of the Finances for the Fiscal Year Ended June 30, 1921*, p. 31.

[90] *Annual Report of the Secretary of the Treasury on the State of the Finances for the*

When Calvin Coolidge (1923–1929) became President in August 1923, budget policy was focused even more strongly on lower taxes and debt reduction. It was not the official policy to strive for the largest possible surpluses. Rather, the goal was to keep revenues at a level "not too greatly in excess of expenditures."[91] In line with this policy, the Treasury recommended tax reduction on several occasions, and reductions were effected by the Revenue Acts of 1924, 1926, and 1928.[92] Nevertheless, the surpluses shown by the federal accounts were substantial. The average annual reduction in debt for the six fiscal years 1924–1929 was over $900 million.

Economy was more than the keystone of budget policy during the Coolidge years. It was the central element of all public policy in the domestic sphere. A few months after taking office the President observed that for "seven years the people have borne with uncomplaining courage the tremendous burden of national and local taxation. These must both be reduced. . . . High taxes reach everywhere and burden everybody. . . . Of all services which the Congress can render to the country, I have no hesitation in declaring this one to be paramount."[93] The following summer this philosophy was stated even more succinctly: "I am for economy. After that I am for more economy. At this time and under present conditions that is my conception of serving all the people."[94]

Fiscal Year Ended June 30, 1923, p. 3. As a consequence of the decline in war-influenced expenditures and the economy drive, federal expenditures exclusive of debt retirements amounted to $3.1 billion for 1923, compared with $5.1 billion for 1921. (See appendix table, p. 318.) During the two Harding years outstanding debt was reduced by over $1.6 billion. In addition, the first step toward tax reduction had been taken, with the approval of the Revenue Act of 1921 in November of that year. 42 Stat. 227.

[91] Andrew Mellon, *Taxation: The People's Business* (1924), p. 51.

[92] 43 Stat. 253; 44 Stat. 9; 45 Stat. 791.

[93] Annual Message of the President of the United States, Dec. 6, 1923, *Congressional Record*, Vol. 65, Pt. 1, p. 97.

[94] "Address of the President," *Addresses of the President of the United States and the Director of the Bureau of the Budget at the Seventh Regular Meeting of the Business Organization of the Government*, June 30, 1924, p. 6. The emphasis on economy was a lifelong practice of Mr. Coolidge. When he was Mayor of Northampton, Mass., "it was said of him that he was greedy to save time, greedy to save words, and greedy

In his inaugural address (March 1925), Coolidge stated
that the policy that stands out with greatest clearness is that
of economy in public expenditures with reduction and reform
of taxation. "The principle involved in this effort is that of
conservation. The resources of this country are almost beyond computation. No mind can comprehend them. But the
cost of our combined governments is likewise almost beyond
definition."[95] Some five weeks earlier the President had attributed the prevailing prosperity mainly to the economy
movement. "Our Nation is prosperous. Its prosperity is due
largely to the economy which had been effected in the cost
of Government. It is this economy that has encouraged business, abolished unemployment, made wages high and work
plentiful."[96]

Underlying the drive for economy was the assumption that
an abnormal situation prevailed in governmental finance.
The depression of 1920–1921, it was asserted, had "resulted
in no small measure from the prohibitive taxes which were
then levied on all productive effort."[97] The beneficiaries of
the economy program were the American people. The task
"is in essence restoring our country to the people of our
country."[98] After the end of hostilities, the President observed, "relief from the gigantic burden the World War imposed upon the people had been no less urgent than the call
to arms." The people "had made their sacrifices to enable

to save taxes." William Allen White, *Calvin Coolidge: The Man Who is President*
(1925), p. 52.

[95] "Inaugural Address of President Calvin Coolidge," March 4, 1925, *Congressional Record*, Vol. 67, Pt. 1, p. 6. At the time of the 1925 inauguration Coolidge had
been President for 19 months.

[96] "Address of the President," *Addresses of the President of the United States and the
Director of the Bureau of the Budget at the Eighth Regular Meeting of the Business
Organization of the Government*, Jan. 26, 1925, p. 2.

[97] Annual Message of the President of the United States, Dec. 3,1924, *Congressional Record*, Vol. 66, Pt. 1, p. 52.

[98] "Address of the President," *Addresses of the President of the United States and
the Director of the Bureau of the Budget at the Ninth Regular Meeting of the Business
Organization of the Government*, June 22, 1925, p. 1.

the Federal Government to meet the great emergency. It was for that Government to take the lead in the effort to restore their financial and economic structure."[99]

A balanced budget, rigid expenditure control, and reduction of the federal debt constituted the three major planks in the program that the President and other high officials regarded as essential for the restoration of the nation's finances. In 1927 Coolidge reported that the "work of restoring the national finances has met with large success." But the federal debt—then about $18 billion—was viewed with grave concern. "It is a menace to our credit. It is the greatest weakness in our line of national defense. It is the largest obstacle in the path of our economic development. It should be retired as fast as possible under a system of reasonable taxation. This can be done only by continuing the policy of rigid Government economy."[100] A few weeks later the President stated: "The Nation must make financial sacrifices, accompanied by a stern self-denial in public expenditures, until we have conquered the disabilities of our public finance." To achieve this objective, we "must keep our budget balanced for each year."[101]

The President and other officials were not content to confine their economy efforts to the federal government. A virtue of the economy movement, in their view, was that it afforded an example to state and local governments. These governments, Coolidge pointed out, accounted for about 60 per cent of all taxes in the early 1920's.

It is therefore highly desirable that an example of determined and insistent economy be set by the Federal Government for the

[99] "Address of the President," *Addresses of the President of the United States and the Director of the Bureau of the Budget at the Thirteenth Regular Meeting of the Business Organization of the Government,* June 10, 1927, p. 1.

[100] Address of President Coolidge Before the Union League Club of Philadelphia, *New York Times* (Nov. 18, 1927), p. 4.

[101] Annual Message of the President of the United States, Dec. 6, 1927, *Congressional Record,* Vol. 69, Pt. 1, pp. 103–04.

sake of its influence upon every body which possesses the authority to levy taxes. I am firmly persuaded that if the National Government will reduce its expenditures and its levies . . . , it will have a highly salutary effect in inducing greater economies in all other departments of public taxation.

A reduction in federal taxes "would certainly tend to align the whole people in support of economical administration of Government."[102]

Federal grants to the states were criticized on the ground that they resulted in increased expenditures from state funds. "While Federal taxes have been reduced, State and other governmental taxes have been steadily increasing. Federal aid to States has influenced this latter condition." The entire cost of highways and other federal-aided activities falls on the people. Though the need for good roads is constantly increasing, "they should not be constructed faster than the taxpayers can afford to pay for them. The amount that taxpayers can afford to pay can best be determined by the citizens of each State."[103]

Under the impetus of insistent demands, especially for education and highways, state and local expenditures and debts increased each year during the 1920's. That some increases were justified seems not to have been recognized by high federal officials. In 1926 the President stated: "How great a need exists to emphasize the homely fundamental virtue of government economy is seen when we contemplate the mounting tide of expenditure and indebtedness of municipal and State governments. This tendency is one of great

---

[102] *Message of the President of the United States Transmitting the Budget for the Service of the Fiscal Year Ending June 30, 1925*, pp. v, VIII. This message is dated December 3, 1923. A few months later the President observed that the "National and local Governments ought to be unremitting in their efforts to reduce expenditures and pay their debts." Address of the President of the United States before the National Republican Club at the Waldorf-Astoria Hotel, Feb. 12, 1924, *New York Times* (Feb. 13, 1924), p. 2.

[103] *Message of the President of the United States Transmitting the Budget for the Service of the Fiscal Year Ending June 30, 1927*, p. VII.

concern." It was asserted that from 1921 to 1925 state and local expenditures had increased by more than $4 billion, which meant a corresponding increase in tax levies on the people or in indebtedness.

There is cause for concern in this situation. It is fraught with grave consequences to the public welfare. The Federal Government has decreased its costs by practicing the homely virtue of thrift. This has not been an easy task. It has required co-operative effort and sacrifice in every direction. If the interests of the people demanded this action on the part of the Federal Government, surely they would seem to demand similar action with regard to the increase in these other local governmental costs.[104]

The persistent upward trend in state and local expenditures was regarded with even more serious misgivings in the last year of Coolidge's administration.

This steady increase in governmental cost on the part of the States and municipalities is a menace to prosperity. It can not be ignored. It can not longer continue without disaster. It will not correct itself. I can conceive no more dependable guarantee of genuine prosperity than a nation-wide effort in behalf of less and wiser spending by State and local governments.[105]

The economy drive was endowed with strong moral and spiritual overtones. In his second annual message, Coolidge observed: "Economy reaches everywhere. It carries a blessing to everybody." And in his inaugural address: "Economy is idealism in its most practical form," and the "result of economic dissipation to a nation is always moral decay."[106] The economy challenge, a prominent federal official pointed out, was accepted "in the interest of the States, cities, and

---

[104] "Address of the President," *Addresses of the President of the United States and the Director of the Bureau of the Budget at the Tenth Regular Meeting of the Business Organization of the Government*, Jan. 30, 1926, p. 4; *Eleventh Regular Meeting*, June 21, 1926, p. 7.

[105] "Address of the President," *Addresses of the President of the United States and the Director of the Bureau of the Budget at the Fifteenth Regular Meeting of the Business Organization of the Government*, June 11, 1928, p. 4.

[106] *Congressional Record*, Vol. 66, Pt. 1, p. 52; Vol. 67, Pt. 1, p. 6.

towns, the lesser governing agencies in this country, which must look to the Federal Government to point the way to financial redemption."[107]

Economical government and low taxes were said to be conducive to peace with other nations.

If we can make the circumstances of the people easy, if we can relieve them of the burden of heavy taxation, we shall have contributed to that contentment and peace of mind which will go far to render them immune from any envious inclination toward other countries. If the people prosper in their business, they will be less likely to resort to the irritating methods of competition in foreign trade out of which arise mutual misunderstandings and animosities.[108]

At times the economy movement seemed to take on the attributes of a moral crusade. The moral or spiritual content was supplied in large part by the Director of the Bureau of the Budget. Speaking at the tenth regular meeting of the Business Organization of the Government, Director Lord expressed his appreciation of "the gallant fight" the President was making "for the tax-ridden people of this country." President Coolidge, he observed, had "kept intimately and continuously in mind the welfare of those who suffer under the burden of heavy taxes." Addressing the President, Director Lord said:

Under your leadership the Federal service has won many battles. We still follow you, Mr. President, singing the old and tried battle song, 'Economy with efficiency,' one and inseparable. May we continue to sing it until in a noble paean of praise it heralds the day when taxes cease to be burdensome and serve but as the grateful expression of our appreciation of the numberless privileges and boundless blessings we enjoy in this most favored Nation of the earth.[109]

[107] "Address of General H. M. Lord," *Addresses of the President of the United States and the Director of the Bureau of the Budget at the Eighth Regular Meeting of the Business Organization of the Government*, Jan. 26, 1925, p. 17.

[108] Address by President Coolidge at the Memorial Exercises at Arlington, May 31, 1926, *Congressional Record*, Vol. 67, Pt. 9, p. 10415.

[109] "Address of General H. M. Lord, Director of the Bureau of the Budget,"

With a view to holding the line, various clubs were proposed by Director Lord. The goal during the mid-1920's, it may be recalled, was to keep federal expenditures other than debt retirements at a figure of not more than $3 billion a year. The first of the clubs was a two per cent personnel club, which had as its object cutting personnel by two per cent a year. A second club was a correspondence club, which was designed to save money in the handling of correspondence. In June 1927 another club was proposed. The underlying thought was that the economy movement had about reached its limits, but that minor economies were still possible on the initiative of individual federal employees.

It may be conservation of Government time, it may be more economical use of Federal supplies, it may be actual saving in money. It may be big, it may be little, but, big or little, it will be voluntary and will constitute a free-will offering to our economy and efficiency campaign. In the interest of those who may have no opportunity to do big things but who . . . are desirous of making some sort of showing, of making some sort of contribution to the cause, the Loyal Order of Woodpeckers is herewith inaugurated. It will embrace in its membership all those who definitely determine to do something more than perfunctorily to perform their usual and routine duties.[110]

One who peruses our fiscal and financial history cannot avoid concluding that governmental economy was a favorite theme of statesmen and public officials from the beginning of the nation. In some instances the impression is unavoidable that references to economy were little more than obeisances

---

Addresses of the President of the United States and the Director of the Bureau of the Budget at the Tenth Regular Meeting of the Business Organization of the Government, Jan. 30, 1926, p. 16.

[110] "Address of General H. M. Lord, Director of the Bureau of the Budget," *Addresses of the President of the United States and the Director of the Bureau of the Budget at the Thirteenth Regular Meeting of the Business Organization of the Government,* June 10, 1927, pp. 12–13. General Lord saluted the new club, as follows: "All hail to the Loyal Order of Woodpeckers, whose persistent tapping away at waste will make cheerful music in Government offices and workshops during the coming year. . . . I am confident if these things be done, the humble woodpecker will be given place in history as symbol of a great national thrift crusade."

expected by influential sectors of the electorate. No one even slightly familiar with the record of the Coolidge years could possibly misread it in this regard. The drive for economy was absolutely sincere. To the President and others economical and low-cost government was more than a laudable fiscal objective. It was an end in itself—a virtue of unexcelled purity.[111]

[111] The social outlook of Coolidge and principal members of his administration "was not only prewar; it antedated the whole era of Theodore Roosevelt and Woodrow Wilson, and was the most frankly conservative which had been expressed in America since the days of Mark Hanna." Walter Lippmann, *The Method of Freedom* (1934), p. 8. "Mr. Coolidge gave the country a dignified and business-like administration of its affairs. His words were few and his actions sensible. He went about the day's work with the genius of common sense; and as for economy, he got more 'mileage out of a dollar' than the oldest inhabitant of Aberdeen." Thomas F. Moran, *American Presidents: Their Individualities and Their Contributions to American Progress* (1933), p. 242.

CHAPTER III

Views of Economists and the Public
From the Civil War to 1929

FROM THE CIVIL WAR to the beginning of the great depression, official attitudes toward the federal budget, the public debt, and the role of government found support in economic thought. At times there seemed to be considerable divergence between official views and those of the economists, especially with respect to the scope of governmental activity. To some extent this was a result of changing trends in economic thought. It was also in part a consequence of the tendency of official pronouncements and public policy to lag behind the views of the economists. The basic ideas about public finance and the role of the federal government held by the public changed slowly. The view most widely held was that governmental expenditures and debts were burdens on the people and the economy.

British Economists

At the time of the Civil War John Stuart Mill was widely regarded as the foremost economist—British or American. Beginning with Mill, as stated in Chapter I, strict adherence to the laissez-faire philosophy was the exception rather than the rule. Mill's influence in the United States extended beyond his role in loosening the rigidities of laissez faire. After the war he publicly supported the Republican position that in accord with the "spirit of the laws" the principal of the war debt should be paid in specie. The bonds paying interest in specie implied payment of the principal in specie, and this implication had enabled the government to obtain its loans at a low rate.[1]

Of the British economists who followed Mill, John E. Cairnes deserves mention—for two reasons. First, his work in effect rounded out a century of writings on political economy in the classical tradition. Second, his essay on "Political Economy and Laissez-Faire" is of interest because of the underlying philosophy. Compared with the paternal state, he believed "laissez-faire to be incomparably the safer guide." But "it is a *practical rule*, and not a doctrine of science." This rule is "in the main sound, but like most other sound practical rules, liable to numerous exceptions."[2]

If this reference to Cairnes' essay should seem in the nature of a digression, it is well to remember that laissez faire was not merely an economic doctrine or philosophy. "It involved a theory of government and the state, a social and individual philosophy, and a theory of evolutionary development."[3] As stated by Myrdal, the "principle of laissez faire is . . . not confined to economic policy. The ideal state is held to be the state of justice and the art of government is the art of refraining as much as possible from governing."[4] Modification of the laissez-faire philosophy and the introduction of

[1] *The Nation*, Vol. 7 (Oct. 15, 1868), p. 308; Joseph Dorfman, *The Economic Mind in American Civilization*, Vol. 3, 1865–1918 (1949), p. 11.

[2] Cairnes, *Essays in Political Economy* (1873), p. 251. Neither of Cairnes' two principal works contains any significant observations concerning governmental budgets and public debts. The reference here is to *The Character and Logical Method of Political Economy* (1857), and *Some Leading Principles of Political Economy Newly Expounded* (1874).

[3] Scott Gordon, "The London Economist and the High Tide of Laissez Faire," *Journal of Political Economy*, Vol. 43 (1955), p. 480.

[4] Gunnar Myrdal, *The Political Element in the Development of Economic Theory* (English edition, 1953), p. 30.

alternative conceptions inevitably implied an expanding role for government and higher levels of public expenditures.

The views of Alfred Marshall concerning government and the necessity of public expenditure were much broader than those of most earlier economists.[5] In a memorandum prepared near the end of the century, he said that "the constructive work of government, and especially of local government, is life itself in one of its highest forms." In a country such as England, which has rid herself "of all taxes which are in themselves mischievous, the reform of taxation should be subordinated to the development of the constructive work of government."[6] Marshall believed that the constructive activities which the modern age required from government were "probably growing much faster than its power of getting through its work."[7] In one of his later books he observed that the State is the most precious of human possessions, and no care can be too great to be spent on enabling it to do its special work in the best way.[8]

There is reason to believe that Marshall was not greatly concerned about about either the size or possible economic effects of the British public debt. In *Money, Credit and Commerce* published in 1923, there are brief references to the public debt. The discussion is wholly dispassionate, and there is nothing to indicate that he regarded Britain's rather large postwar debt as a hindrance to economic progress.[9]

[5] Marshall's *Principles of Economics* was the most influential work in economics to appear during the last half of the nineteenth century. In this work he does not discuss either governmental budgets or public debts. Taxes are discussed only incidentally, and mainly for the purpose of illustrating certain economic principles. The only detailed examination of taxes pertains to local rates (property taxes), which are considered in an appendix. *Principles of Economics* (1920), pp. 794–804. There is also a brief criticism of Ricardo's doctrine with respect to taxes and improvements in agriculture. *Ibid.*, pp. 833–37.

[6] "Memorandum on the Classification and Incidence of Imperial and Local Taxes" submitted in 1897 to the Royal Commission on Local Taxation, *Official Papers by Alfred Marshall* (1926), pp. 358–59.

[7] "Memorandum on Fiscal Policy of International Trade (1903), *ibid.*, p. 396.

[8] Marshall, *Industry and Trade* (1920), p. 647.

[9] Marshall favored a degree of supervision by the central government over local debts. "The central government should remain the guardian of the ratepayer of the

Toward the end of the nineteenth century public finance began to develop into a separate discipline or field of specialization. In Great Britain *Public Finance* by C. F. Bastable published in 1892 epitomized this trend. Bastable was especially critical of British and other writers on governmental finance who confined their discussion to taxation and ignored public expenditures.

In principle Bastable favored a balanced budget. "The practical rule is to aim at a slight excess of receipts over outlay in order to prevent the chance of a deficit." But there is a place for public borrowing, which he viewed as a creation of the constitutional period and a consequence of the credit system. The refined financial mechanism by which public borrowing is carried out enables extraordinary expenditure for a short period to be transformed into ordinary expenditure for a long one. Bastable regarded as fallacious the idea that public debt is relatively unimportant because it is in effect owed by the right hand to the left hand. The action of indebtedness on the economy cannot be altogether without influence or effect.[10]

Bastable recommended the exercise of caution and restraint in the use of the public credit. "We should remember that so-called extraordinary expenditure is itself recurring. Purchase of productive property or creation of revenue-yielding works may fairly be defrayed by loans." This concession to the policy of borrowing, however, "should not be stretched to include the cost of works or other state action that yield no revenue."[11]

Bastable's views concerning public expenditures and the role of government were fairly advanced for his period. The "several items of expenditure" should be treated on a positive basis. The doctrine of the less expenditure the better ac-

---

future against debts incurred for extravagant expenditure in the present." *Official Papers by Alfred Marshall*, p. 359.
[10] Bastable, *Public Finance* (1892), pp. 42, 125, 550, 579.
[11] *Ibid.*, pp. 586–87.

cepted by Say and Ricardo "is palpably incorrect." When applied to various categories of expenditure, terms such as "necessary," "useful," and "superfluous" have little meaning; they carry with them "an already-formed judgment."[12]

American Economists

Before the Civil War the efforts of American economists were largely overshadowed by the work of foreign economists of international renown—Adam Smith, David Ricardo, and John Stuart Mill, among others. Beginning with Henry C. Carey this gap was gradually narrowed. In the latter decades of the nineteenth century a number of economists in this country attained wider recognition than the earlier American economists considered in Chapter I.

HENRY C. CAREY TO FRANCIS A. WALKER

Henry C. Carey was perhaps the most widely known American economist of the mid-nineteenth century.[13] An ardent protectionist, he was a prolific writer of books, pamphlets, and letters. Though his *Principles of Political Economy* was published several decades before the Civil War, Carey's views are considered at this point because of his prominent role in the controversy over postwar debt policy.

In Carey's opinion immediate and rapid reduction of the Civil War debt was not required. Because of the heavy taxa-

---

[12] *Ibid.*, pp. 7, 43, 138.

[13] Carey was the first American economist to win a following abroad. Paul T. Homan states that his influence abroad was probably greater than at home. *Encyclopedia of the Social Sciences*, Vol. 3 (1930), pp. 226–27. A. D. H. Kaplan has observed that as a stimulant to controversy, perhaps only Ricardo excelled Carey. *Henry Charles Carey: A Study in American Economic Thought* (1931), p. 89.

tion entailed, this might prove to be a disastrous course.[14]
On the question whether it was essential to pay the debt—
both principal and interest—in gold, Carey disagreed strongly with Secretary Hugh McCulloch who took the affirmative.
During the war large bond issues had been floated under laws
that made no mention of the currency in which the principal
should be paid. To Carey it seemed irrational to pay in gold
in the absence of a clause requiring payment in gold or coin.
Yet this is precisely what the Secretary proposed.

In language both blunt and vitriolic Carey berated Mc-
Culloch who "in his recent voluminous and most feeble report, devoted much space to a lecture on the absolute necessity for paying the debt in gold, both principal and interest."
The course proposed would plainly add to the burdensome-
ness of the debt. Carey strongly implied this was McCulloch's intention "on the day on which the Secretary entered
on his most destructive career." In other countries the public
credit improves with diminution of the need for loans, but
"under our admirable system of finance" it seems to deteri-
orate as the debt is more and more diminished.

Were it not for the Secretary's profession of desire to maintain the
public faith we should be much disposed to believe that, determined upon bringing about repudiation, he had arrived at the
conclusion that the shortest road thereto lay in the direction of
making the debt from day to day more burthensome. Certain it is
that had such been his wish, he could have chosen no better course
of operation than that he has so consistently pursued almost from
the hour that he was so unfortunately placed in the direction of the
national finances.[15]

The contrast in debt attitudes was never sharper than at
the time of Carey's unrestrained castigation of Secretary
McCulloch. Official policy called for payment in gold or coin.

[14] Carey, *The Public Debt, Local and National: How to Provide Its Discharge While Lessening the Burthen of Taxation* (1866). This pamphlet consists of a letter to David A. Wells, Esq., Chairman of the Board of Revenue Commissioners.
[15] Carey, *The Finance Minister, the Currency, and the Public Debt* (1868), pp. 21–24.

To many this seemed an essential part of the process by which the return to financial stability would be achieved. But Carey and other opponents believed this policy was both inopportune and excessively costly. As stated by Carey in 1868, the late holders of the 7.30's—as they were called—were receiving in gold the equivalent of 8.50 per cent in lawful money.[16] Carey's pronouncements formed a rallying ground for those who feared that the postwar debt would be intolerably burdensome. Though his views were not accepted, they played a role in the evolution of policy.

Carey's concept of government was an evolutionary one. He believed that the citizen desires from government security of person and property, together with the power of retaining and having the enjoyment of the whole fruits of his labor.[17] But property cannot be deemed secure when it is in the power of any person, or collection of persons, to compel the remainder of the community to contribute for the support of government a larger proportion of their incomes than is necessary for the effectual maintenance of that security. When more is demanded than is necessary, the surplus is wasted. Both extremes—excessive and niggardly payment of public employees—should be avoided. Wasteful and unproductive expenditure should not be tolerated; with every increase of unproductive expenditures, there has been a diminished power of accumulating capital.[18] In this respect Carey's views coincided with those of the classical economists.

Amasa Walker gained considerable prominence as an economist before the Civil War.[19] Though his specialty was money and banking, he held rather firm views on public finance and the role of government. Walker's principal work, the *Science*

---

[16] *Ibid.*, p. 24.

[17] Carey, *Principles of Political Economy* (1838), Vol. 2, pp. 11–12.

[18] *Ibid.*, pp. 107, 125.

[19] Amasa Walker lectured on economics at Oberlin and Amherst colleges, and from 1853 to 1860 he was an examiner in political economy at Harvard. He was a successful shoe manufacturer in Boston and also a railroad promoter.

of Wealth, was published in 1866. The statements concerning public debt in this volume are of special interest, for the reason that it was the first widely read work in political economy to appear after the war.

In an article published in January 1865 Walker had taken the position that the war debt could be "easily borne" and, if wisely managed, "paid off in thirty years without difficulty."[20] But after the war the size of the federal debt—almost $2.8 billion in 1866—seemed to trouble him greatly.[21] He stated categorically that the "economy of a national debt, under the modern financial system, must always impoverish the productive classes." The entire influence of such a debt on the productive classes is oppressive. "It deprives them of their honest reward," not only by a false currency which "robs them of a large share of their nominal wages," but it also imposes on them through indirect taxation an undue proportion of the public burdens.[22]

Walker's debt philosophy becomes understandable only when one considers that he was an ardent disciple of the wages-fund doctrine. Though perhaps not so intended, a national debt is "a stupendous enginery" for depressing the working classes. Alluding to the large postwar debt and heavy annual interest payments, Walker emphasized the importance of understanding the whole subject of modern finance by the people themselves. For "without such an understanding of it, however much they may suffer, they cannot hope for relief. They must know the causes of their sufferings, or they cannot apply the remedy."[23]

[20] Amasa Walker, *The National Finances*, a reprint from *Hunt's Merchants' Magazine and Commercial Review*, p. 15.

[21] Federal interest requirements after the war were in the range of $125 to $145 million a year, or approximately double federal expenditures for all purposes before the war.

[22] Amasa Walker, *Science of Wealth* (1866), p. 370.

[23] *Ibid.*, pp. 370–71. In Walker's opinion the impoverishing effect of a national debt was especially apparent in England. He introduced his discussion of the effect of the newly created debt in this country with a dramatic reference to English experience. "What has become of that YEOMANRY, once the pride of the country? Their little estates have disappeared, have been swallowed up by the terrible system

Nowhere in the *Science of Wealth* does Walker say that he favors a balanced budget in time of peace. But it was scarcely necessary, for the moral of his admonitions is obvious. A further increase in federal debt was something to be avoided. The budget should not merely be balanced. If at all possible, additional revenues should be raised and applied to debt reduction. These inferences are so apparent from his analysis that it is almost unnecessary to state them. Walker has little to say concerning the role of government. The entire volume is written in the laissez-faire tradition. A cardinal principle of this philosophy was that government should undertake nothing that can be left to individual enterprise. To this basic tenet Walker added a second: government should do nothing for display.[24]

Arthur Latham Perry was, to quote Joseph Dorfman, a "distinguished and extremely popular elaborator of Walker's views."[25] His conception of economics was consciously limited to the market place.[26] Perry's principal work does not include a discussion of public debts and their economic effects. His chapter on taxation is of interest to the student of public budgets.

Perry's approach to taxation and public expenditures was consistent with his market approach. "Value resides in services exchanged; and since government is an essential prerequisite to any general and satisfactory exchanges, since it contributes by direct effort to the security of person and property, it justly claims from every citizen in return a compensation for the service thus rendered to him." Perry recog-

---

of taxation to which they have been subjected." He pointed out that in 1858 the middle and working classes paid £51 million in taxes out of a total of £73 million. *Ibid.*, pp. 369–70. The authority for these figures was Leone Levi, *On Taxation: How It Is Raised and How It Is Expended*, London ed. (1860), p. 32.

[24] Walker, *Science of Wealth*, pp. 403–04.

[25] Arthur Latham Perry was a graduate of Williams College. He was professor of history and political economy for many years at the same institution.

[26] Dorfman, *The Economic Mind in American Civilization*, Vol. 3, pp. 56–57. Both Perry and Amasa Walker "found their intellectual fatherhood" in Frederic Bastiat, whose *Economic Harmonies* had received wide acclaim. *Ibid.*, pp. 49–50.

nized that government does not exist solely for the protection of persons and property and that not all the operations of government can be brought down within the sphere of exchange. Government also exists for the improvement of society, and "many of its high functions are moral, to be performed under a lofty sense of responsibility to God and to future ages."[27]

To Francis A. Walker there was little or no place in the study of political economy or economics for a consideration of governmental budgets and public debts.[28] "Political economy, or Economics is the name of that body of knowledge which relates to wealth." It "has to do with no other subject, whatever, than wealth."[29] Since taxes impinge on or affect the production of wealth and other phases of the economic process, Walker devoted a chapter to the principles of taxation. But there is nothing on either the agenda of government or the significance of public debts.

Walker was critical of the failure of American economics to adjust to changing conditions. Long after the English economists admitted many qualifications of the doctrine of laissez faire, he said in 1890, the professors of political economy in the leading American colleges continued to write about the economic man of Ricardo and James Mill as if he were worth all the real men who ever lived. The editors of the journals and reviews "greeted with contumely every suggestion of an exception to the rule of individualism. . . . Even the complete establishment of such an exception in the policy of half a dozen nations, and its triumphant vindication in

[27] Perry, *Elements of Political Economy* (1869), p. 472. This is the fifth edition of Perry's work. The first edition was published in 1866. The last edition was the twenty-second, published in 1895.

[28] Francis A. Walker was the son of Amasa Walker. He attended Amherst College and was an officer in the federal army during the Civil War. His academic career was spent at the Sheffield Scientific School where he was professor of political economy and history, and the Yale Graduate School. From 1881 to his death in 1897 Walker was President of the Massachusetts Institute of Technology.

[29] Walker, *Political Economy* (1883), p. 1.

practical working . . . constituted no reason why these high priests of economic orthodoxy should accept it." In the circumstances, there "is small occasion for wonder that . . . our economists, as a body, should be able to do little in stemming the tide of socialism which has set in so strongly of late."[30]

Our main reason for referring to the work of Francis A. Walker is his effective refutation of the wages-fund doctrine. This theory, as we have seen, was a major plank in the arguments of opponents of public debts. Its refutation was an essential step in the process by which a more realistic approach to public borrowing was achieved. In an analysis of great simplicity, Walker pointed out that wages may be advanced out of capital, but are paid out of the product.[31] By clearly stating this elemental principle, Walker did more than help lay low a fallacy that strongly influenced public-debt attitudes. He and others who took a similar position cleared the way for a scientific approach to the determinants of wages, including factors such as productivity and effective management.

SUMNER AND "PURE" LAISSEZ FAIRE

In any consideration of the cross currents in political economy that developed toward the close of the nineteenth century, the work of William Graham Sumner deserves a prominent place.[32] Sumner was the arch-exponent of laissez faire in its most rigid form. He extolled laissez faire both as a philosophy and as a principle of action. In his thinking there was no

[30] Walker, "The Tide of Economic Thought," *Publications of the American Economic Association*, Vol. 6 (1891), pp. 20-21.

[31] Walker, *The Wages Question* (1876), Chapters 8-9; *Political Economy*, pp. 377 ff.

[32] William Graham Sumner gained wide renown as Professor of Political and Social Science at Yale University. In his later years his interest was mainly in sociology, but he continued to give courses in advanced economics. His most famous work is *Folkways* published in 1907.

place for the regulatory and ameliorative efforts of government. The concept of the "survival of the fittest" was at the heart of his creed.

Laissez faire, as Sumner used the term, "includes avoidance of all anticipatory legislation, of all interference by the state in the industrial organization except such as is necessary to maintain that equilibrium of rights and duties which liberty and justice require, and of all state projects in the interest of 'the poor,' 'the needy,' or any class whatsoever." Anticipatory legislation, according to Sumner, is both irrational and harmful; "attempts to create future conditions thereby have proved futile."[33] The modern industrial system is "a great social co-operation. It is automatic and instinctive in its operation. The adjustments of the organs take place naturally. The parties are held together by impersonal force—supply and demand." Society does not need any care or supervision.[34]

To say that under the Sumnerian system the role of government was a modest one would be an understatement. The maintenance of peace, order, and the guarantee of rights appear to represent the scope of permissible functions. Even the maintenance of order is narrowed to a point scarcely recognizable by modern standards. Sumner frowned on the efforts of society—through police, sheriffs, and various institutions—to protect people against themselves; that is, against their own vices. Such efforts and social reform in general prevent the normal operation of nature's fierce discipline—the law of the survival of the fittest.[35] The only justification for government is that "some kind of formal organi-

---

[33] Harris E. Starr, *William Graham Sumner* (1925), p. 464; Sumner, *The Challenge of Facts and Other Essays* (1914), p. 253.

[34] Sumner, *What Social Classes Owe to Each Other* (1883), pp. 66, 119.

[35] *Ibid.*, pp. 12, 130–32. "When we see a drunkard in the gutter we pity him. If a policeman picks him up, we say that society has interfered to save him from perishing. 'Society' is a fine word, and it saves us the trouble of thinking. The industrious and sober workman, who is mulcted of a percentage of his day's wages to pay the policeman, is the one who bears the penalty."

zation is essential to the attainment of any social good. The state must exist to enforce the rights that conduce to societal welfare."[36]

A man "whose labor and self-denial may be diverted from his maintenance to that of some other man is not a free man, and approaches more or less toward the position of a slave."[37] This is in essence the same thesis that was advanced by Herbert Spencer, the British sociologist, who regarded the proportion of income taken by taxes as measuring the degree of slavery.[38] In Spencer's thinking government "is begotten of aggression and by aggression." Though Sumner did not state the matter in this way, the basic tenets of his philosophy support this view. To him interference with the operation of natural law was a principal characteristic of a large part of the efforts of government, and all such efforts were misguided.

To our knowledge Sumner nowhere stated any views concerning public debts or the desirability of balanced budgets. His philosophy of individual action and self-reliance is here considered not because of any contribution toward our understanding of the evolution of public budgets and the use of public credit. Our sole reason for referring to Sumner is that he summarized in extreme form a creed that was accepted in influential circles in the late nineteenth and early twentieth centuries. His version of laissez faire was more uncompromising than that of any other prominent economist, American or British. It served effectively as a rallying point for those

[36] Robert G. McCloskey, *American Conservatism in the Age of Enterprise* (1951), p. 63.

[37] Sumner, *What Social Classes Owe to Each Other*, p. 15.

[38] Herbert Spencer, *The Man Versus the State* (1884), pp. 34–35. "The essential question is—How much is he (the citizen or taxpayer) compelled to labour for other benefit than his own, and how much can he labour for his own benefit? The degree of his slavery varies according to the ratio between that which he is forced to yield up and that which he is allowed to retain; and it matters not whether his master is a single person or a society. If, without option, he has to labour for the society, and receives from the general stock such portion as the society awards him, he becomes a slave to the society." *Ibid.*, p. 35.

who looked with trepidation on every expansion of the role of government.[39]

LATER ECONOMISTS

Whatever influence Sumner's views had on the evolution of economic thought in this country, especially as it pertained to the role of government, was offset in some degree by an opposing trend. In the latter decades of the nineteenth century a number of young American economists went abroad— mainly to Germany—for the purpose of continuing their studies. The German historical school was then in the ascendency. A conspicuous feature of German thought was that the role of government was conceived to be broader than under either traditional or modified laissez faire. The use of public credit in the construction of appropriate public works was entirely acceptable, according to the German view. Expansion of state activities as society evolved was an observable historical fact; that such expansion would continue in the future was completely in accord with all evolutionary tendencies and the lessons of experience.

It is not one of our purposes to assess precisely the impact of German and other European thinking on American economic thought during the late nineteenth century. Nor shall we consider the merits of the oft-repeated assertion that the German historical school established too strong a presumption in favor of state activity. It suffices to point out that Edmund Janes James, Henry Carter Adams, Richard T. Ely, Simon N. Patten, and E. R. A. Seligman, among others, continued their studies abroad. If there was ever any possibility that men such as these might have accepted even a watered-

---

[39] Sumner's interpretations and philosophy continue to serve this function in limited degree at the present time. There have been several recent printings of *What Social Classes Owe to Each Other*. In the foreword to the 1952 edition, William C. Mullendore states that this work "is even more pertinent today than at the time of its first publication."

down version of Sumnerian orthodoxy, it was dispelled by their breadth of outlook attained in part by study in other countries.

The philosophical origins of what has been termed "The New Political Economy" were largely European. Leading new school economists believed that economic truth "is relative rather than absolute," a principal tenet of the German historical school. The progress of history gives rise to new facts and new conditions, and "economic theory and economic laws must be adjusted to the conditions of a particular age and a particular locale." Other motives than self-interest and the pursuit of gain influence man's activities.[40] Under this interpretation government ceases to be regarded primarily as a necessary evil. As society evolves and becomes more complex, government is compelled to assume a positive and more important role. To the young American economists who were dissatisfied with the rigidities and largely deductive character of traditional economics, ideas such as these were stimulating and conducive to greater realism in the approach to economic problems.

Edmund Janes James was one of the leaders of the "new school" group. He attained prominence during the latter part of the nineteenth century as a writer, teacher, and administrator.[41] James was among the first to champion the view that a more realistic approach to governmental activities was essential. The new school was simply adapting itself to changed conditions.

The state, James said, "is an economic factor of prime importance." Its function "in the sphere of economics is a varying one." The idea that the state was a "purely negative factor" in economic and social life, "a necessary evil which did most good when it did least harm," he found completely un-

[40] Sidney Fine, *Laissez Faire and the General-Welfare State* (1956), p. 198.
[41] Edmund Janes James became director of the Wharton School of the University of Pennsylvania while in his early 30's. He was later President of Northwestern University and the University of Illinois.

acceptable. The investigation of historians throughout the nineteenth century "has proven conclusively that the state, so far from being the source of innumerable evils, has always been not only the absolutely essential condition of human progress, but also one of the most important, if not, indeed, the most important factor, in the economic evolution of society itself."[42]

A corollary of the increasing recognition accorded to the role of government was that public finance came to be regarded as a separate discipline.[43] In this area the contributions of Henry Carter Adams were outstanding.[44] Adams' views on public expenditures were decidedly forward looking. He emphasized that the "social income rather than the governmental necessities" is the starting point for a theory of public expenditures. He agreed with Lorenz von Stein, the German authority, that "public and private needs are integral parts of a common necessity." In appraising the claims and needs of government, the margin of the social income over essentials is of major importance. The "general income of the people from which the income of the State in large measure arises, should as a matter of right and does as a matter of fact exert a decided influence upon the extent and character of the functions which the State may undertake." The state of industrial development plays a major role in determining the character and level of public expenditure. In Adams' view "government is essential to civilized existence." In an evolving society such as the United States, the role of government becomes relatively greater as the economy be-

[42] James, "The State as an Economic Factor," *Science Economic Discussion* (1886), pp. 24–28.
[43] It was not until the 1930's that public finance was fully restored to the mainstream of economic thought. The latter development, curiously enough, also resulted in part from recognition of the increasingly important role of government in the economy.
[44] Henry Carter Adams was "one of the most creative figures in American economics." Joseph Dorfman, "The Seligman Correspondence," *Political Science Quarterly*, Vol. 56 (1941), p. 270.

comes increasingly industrialized and complex.[45] This philosophy contrasted sharply with the role of government under the laissez-faire rationale, which continued to be influential in shaping public policy.

A cardinal element of Adams' thesis was that, within bounds, society is capable of directing its own development. He did not look with favor on indiscriminate or needless state intervention. "The State exists for its citizens, and its chief service is to provide conditions under which the activities of citizens may prosper." But there is no logical basis for a policy of restricting public powers within the narrowest possible limits. Such a policy "tends to render government weak and inefficient, and a weak government placed in the midst of a society controlled by the commercial spirit will quickly become a corrupt government. . . . " An extension of state functions beyond those sanctioned by the laissez-faire philosophy would result in harmony between public and private interests.[46]

The complementary relations of government and the individual were emphasized by Adams. What might be called a complementary theory of public expenditure is implicit in his analysis. There is no overpowering presumption in favor of either the English or German view concerning the role of the state.

The fundamental error of English political philosophy lies in regarding the state as a necessary evil: the fundamental error of German political philosophy lies in its conception of the state as an organism complete within itself. Neither the one nor the other of these views is correct. *Society* is the organic entity about which all our reasoning should center. Both state action and the industrial activity of individuals are functions of the complete social organism. . . . It is not proper to consider individual activity as

[45] Adams, *The Science of Finance* (1898), pp. 25ff., 37–40, 328.

[46] *Ibid.*, pp. 31–32; *Relation of the State to Industrial Action and Economics and Jurisprudence*, Joseph Dorfman, ed. (1954), pp. 89–90; Dorfman, "The Role of the German Historical School in American Economic Thought," *American Economic Review*, Supplement, Vol. 45 (May 1955), pp. 25–26.

supplementary to state powers, or to look upon the functions of the state as supplementary to personal activity.[47]

Adams believed that only three conditions justified public borrowing or deficit finance: (1) temporary deficits resulting from inability to estimate revenues and expenditures precisely; (2) fiscal emergencies such as wars; and (3) public works requiring substantial outlays. Though he looked with favor on public borrowing under proper safeguards, Adams was careful to point out that dangerous tendencies are "bound up in deficit financiering." A national debt may be a national evil, especially if the borrowing entailed leads to relaxation of popular control of the public purse. But it would be rash to close this source of funds, for such a decision might result in greater evils. Governments might be forced to adopt other and more injurious methods of raising money.[48]

That Adams favored a balanced federal budget, and balanced governmental budgets in general, is strongly suggested by the foregoing discussion. He recognized, of course, that a budget could never be balanced precisely. He believed that a small deficit is preferable to a constant surplus—for three reasons. First, the moral effect of a deficit on the electorate and legislators is desirable. Second, expenditures are more likely to be controlled effectively; appropriations for the previous year will be reviewed. Third, the money supply tends to be contracted by a government surplus.[49]

Of the "new economists," Richard T. Ely was most intensely concerned with giving economics a new slant. In his opinion a crust had formed over the old economics, and it had failed to make a satisfactory adjustment to changing conditions.[50] Ely was greatly impressed by the German ap-

---

[47] Adams, *Relation of the State to Industrial Action and Economics and Jurisprudence*, pp. 82–83.

[48] Adams, *Public Debts* (1893), pp. 22, 78–101. This work was first published in 1887.

[49] *Ibid.*, pp. 80–83.

[50] We "found a failure in the conclusions reached by the older economists to har-

proach. In sharp contrast with the emphasis on wealth by most British and American economists, the German tradition elevated man to the central place in economics. According to Karl Knies, Ely's principal teacher in Germany, the "starting-point as well as the object-point of our science is man." The German economists "had given 'a new and living' attitude toward the study that enabled Ely to utilize his religious concepts and his zeal for humanitarian reform." In admitting frankly that he believed there were higher values than the profit motive, Ely was in effect adopting a welfare approach to economics and economic policy. In his view, the "law of society is actually service for one's fellows."[51]

The contrast between Ely's views and those of the laissez-faire economists could scarcely have been sharper. "For him the older school of orthodox laissez-faire advocates was expounding a doctrine that was not only ruinous to public policy, but essentially contrary to the social Christianity he believed."[52] In Ely's opinion, the type of science Sumner was advocating "seemed to endorse an egoistic struggle for the desirable things in life, and to make the winner in the struggle, regardless of the means by which success was achieved, appear to pursue a socially beneficent course of conduct."[53]

Ely's philosophy implied a new and broader approach to the role of government. Implicit in the welfare type of economics, which he favored, is an expansion of governmental activities as well as a more hospitable attitude toward government. Throughout his life he believed that the effort to

---

monize with the life that was unfolding about us. We found also that . . . the conclusions of the other economists, as they existed in the popular mind, and as they existed in the minds of leaders of thought and action, especially, stood in the way of real progress." Ely, *Ground Under Our Feet*, an autobiography (1938), pp. 154–55.

[51] John R. Everett, *Religion in Economics* (1946), pp. 82, 85, 91. This theme was developed by Ely in *The Social Law of Service* (1896), a work characterized by strong religious overtones.

[52] *Ibid.*, p. 85.

[53] Ely, "Social Progress," *The Cosmopolitan*, Vol. 31 (May 1901), p. 61.

fit political institutions to complex economic society was a
continuing and important task.[54] On a number of occasions
he said that there is no greater inequality than the equal
treatment of unequals. This observation, which apparently
was not original with Ely, served his purpose admirably.
Recognition of its essential accuracy is a prerequisite for the
development of welfare economics.

Ely played a major role in breaking through the cloud of
negativism, which was a principal characteristic of most
earlier discussions of governmental activity. The first sentence of the platform of the American Economic Association
which was developed by Ely in 1885 is of interest: "We regard the state as an educational and ethical agency whose
positive aid is an indispensable condition of human progress."[55] The use of "positive" was at once a challenge to
those who regarded all governmental activities beyond the
protection of life and property as questionable, and an expression of faith that the work of government could be
greatly improved if a more realistic attitude were taken
toward its role. A cardinal principle of Ely's philosophy was
that "the way to improve government was to give government essential tasks and make it real and vital to us all."[56]

Though he envisioned a broader role for government as
society evolved, Ely's views on public finance—especially
governmental debts—were conservative by modern standards. In one of his ealier works he had occasion to refer to
Henry Carter Adams' compilation of the debts owed by civilized governments, which were placed at $27 billion. After
pointing out that alarm has often been expressed concerning
the magnitude of public debts, Ely stated categorically that
they "are undoubtedly a misfortune and should be paid as
soon as possible." At the same time, he believed that "serious

[54] Ely, "Progressivism, True and False—An Outline," *Review of Reviews*, Vol. 51
(1915), p. 209.
[55] "Report of the Organization of the American Economic Association," (March
1886), *Publications of the American Economic Association*, Vol. 1, No. 1 (1887), p. 6.
[56] Ely, *Ground Under Our Feet*, p. 253.

apprehension was not called for so far as Germany, England, and the United States are concerned."[57] There is a clear implication that in time of peace balanced budgets coupled with a policy of debt retirement were desirable.

The idea that private and public activities were complementary was an important element in Ely's thought. "There is no such thing as a purely private enterprise, and we may perhaps say, also, that there is no such thing as a purely public enterprise. Certainly in the vast majority of the enterprises with which we are familiar private and public activities are combined in varying proportions." Ely believed that the growth of private activity would mean increased state activities. "We may lay it down as a general principle that, as society becomes dependent upon the individuals in control of an industry, it protects itself by State activity."[58]

Ely believed, with John Stuart Mill, that "the intellectual and moral grounds of socialism deserve the most attentive study, as affording in many cases the guiding principles of the improvements necessary to give the present economic system of society its best chance." In an article published in 1894 he stated that socialism is "a force which has stimulated the consciences of many and transformed beneficially the lives of not a few."[59] Ely's approach to the study of socialism was objective. His study of the subject seems to have been motivated by a desire to develop ideas that would be helpful in formulating the economic and social principles applicable to an evolving society of ever-increasing complexity.

Simon N. Patten stressed the dynamic nature of society to a greater extent than any of his contemporaries. He was constantly endeavoring to correlate economic conditions

[57] Ely, *An Introduction to Political Economy* (1892), p. 295. The first edition of this work appeared in 1889.

[58] Ely, *Outlines of Political Economy* (1893), pp. 249–50.

[59] Ely, "Fundamental Beliefs in My Social Philosophy," *The Forum*, Vol. 18 (October 1894), p. 180. The full title of the book which led to the articles in *The Forum* was "*Socialism: An Examination of Its Nature, Its Strength and Its Weakness, With Suggestions for Social Reform* (1894).

with the thought of the times; his interest was in developing economic theories applicable to a changing society. In Patten's work "the dynamic concept intrudes so incessantly upon the stage" that one is "continuously aware that the society under discussion is a dynamic society."[60] The idea of natural and universal laws in the field of economics he believed entirely unwarranted. There is nothing absolutely fixed about any formulation.

Several features of Patten's work are essential by way of background for an understanding of his ideas concerning public finance and the role of government. Patten placed greater emphasis on consumption than any other economist of his era. He believed that it is "the consumer who makes the economic system function." The progress of society had witnessed a more or less continuous change in consumption habits. Through a process of selection a better adaptation of consumption habits to the environment is obtained. This emphasis on consumption was more than a refreshing note in the evolution of economics. It suggested strongly that the formal treatises that approached the subject from the side of production, and in which consumption was either sketchily treated or ignored, were not acceptable explanations of how the economy functions.

Until the time of Patten, economics had placed great stress on "the niggardliness of nature." Man was pictured as engaged in wrestling the economic necessities plus perhaps a minimum of comforts from a reluctant and resistant environment. Whatever merits this approach may have had under primitive conditions, it did not ring true to Patten in the United States of the late nineteenth and early twentieth centuries. In the economy in which he lived the law of increasing returns (decreasing cost) was of greater import than diminishing returns. It was a surplus economy, not a deficit econ-

[60] James L. Boswell, *The Economics of Simon Nelson Patten* (1933), p. 133.

omy. This surplus was a consequence of economic growth—of the general progress of society. It was a surplus in which all the agents of production might share.[61]

Basically Patten was a philosopher working in the field of economics, among other disciplines. The role of government in the changing environment of a surplus economy was of greater interest to him than budgeting and debt policy. He envisioned a broader and more important role for government as society evolved. Taxes should "not be limited to the lowest minimum that the *laissez-faire* conception of government would allow. A high rate of taxation, when used economically to further public ends, raises the standard of life by furnishing the conditions needed for a wholesome regular social progress." Public education, parks, roads, and drainage and sanitation systems for cities were mentioned as objects for which surplus revenue could be expended to advantage. "We have passed beyond those primitive conditions in which an increase of taxation necessitates a decrease of that portion of the produce of industry which the average individual enjoys, if the sources of national revenue are taxed, and not the income of individuals."[62]

The context in which the latter observation appears suggests that Patten was visualizing a rise in taxation that absorbed a portion of—but in no case more than—the increase in national income attributable to productivity gains. This statement may not be strictly accurate, since he foresaw other sources of the "fund" on which government might draw to meet its expanding needs. Prominent among these were elimination of waste throughout the economic system and improved consumption habits. "Every invention, every change in production, every increase in human energy, every economy in consumption creates a surplus which abides. This

[61] *Ibid.*, pp. 134–36.
[62] Patten, *The Stability of Prices*, Publications of the American Economic Association, Vol. 3, No. 6 (1889), p. 62.

may be reserved for public benefit or be permitted to pass
into private hands to be used in personal consumption. An
increase of taxation means a larger use of this fund for public purposes."[63]

In Patten's thinking the welfare function of government
enjoyed a high ranking. His views on this subject were discussed under "the right to relief." Every one, said Patten, is
liable to misfortunes; "health breaks down, accidents happen, employment is uncertain, and sickness reduces families
to a condition where aid is necessary. Against these and similar hardships no individual can adequately provide, and if he
could, it would be more economical to have them guarded
against by public measures."[64] To say that this proposal was
motivated solely by Patten's desire for the economical handling of relief, together with his humanitarianism, would be
far from the whole story. That his approach was much broader is suggested by the fact that his ideas were developed in a
book dealing with the theory of prosperity.

"The orderly development of higher wants, tastes, and
standards is delayed or prevented by any disturbing fear that
the forethought and energy providing for them will not attain
the desired end. . . . The energy and the skill of each person
should be left free so that the reward for work can come to
the worker; but misfortune is not an individual affair due to
conditions that individuals make." The evil may lie in the
environment—crop failures, accidents for which others are to
blame, diseases, and bad local conditions. "In such cases
social evils should be met by social action. Make the individual responsible for the results of his own acts, but do not
let him suffer from what he could not avoid." The heart of
Patten's reasoning follows: "A system of relief is an essential
to industrial freedom; economic activity will not reach its
maximum until it is so effective that the energy of individuals

[63] Patten, "Liquidation Taxes," *Annals of the American Academy of Political and Social Science*, Vol. 75 (January 1918), p. 169.

[64] Patten, *The Theory of Prosperity* (1902), p. 227.

can be applied to the satisfaction of their own wants. The social surplus is more than sufficient to provide for all the exigencies that persons cannot control."[65] In brief, an adequate relief or welfare program is essential for orderly economic and social progress.

Perhaps the sharpest contrast between Patten's thought and orthodox laissez-faire economics relates to the planning function. Patten believed that the central political unit can act as the agency for intelligent social planning. "There is no reason to fear the tyranny of planning since everyone would be motivated by a desire to cooperate. This does not mean government ownership of the factors of production. It merely means that all who own or produce work toward the same end." In Patten's thinking there was no such thing as coerced co-operation.[66]

Patten's writings on finance during World War I were at once provocative and optimistic. Instead of straining the economy, the government could draw on a surplus that was much larger than its requirements. The "real surplus," said Patten, "is the difference between the amount produced and that needed to maintain the personal welfare of the population." This surplus he placed at about $40 billion, of which it appeared the government would require $15 billion.[67] To those whose thinking was restricted within the narrow compass of the federal budget, Patten's reasoning was difficult to follow. He was thinking in terms of real national income. He was less interested in the balance or lack of balance in the economy than in balancing increased costs against possible improvements—productivity gains, elimination of waste, improved consumption, and the like.[68]

Patten was the first economist of prominence to minimize

[65] *Ibid.*, pp. 227–28.

[66] Everett, *Religion in Economics*, p. 140.

[67] Patten, "The Tomorrow of Finance," *Annals of the American Academy of Political and Social Science*, Vol. 76 (March 1918), pp. 259–62.

[68] Patten, "Making National Debts National Blessings," *ibid.*, Vol. 82 (March 1919), pp. 40–45.

the financial and economic burden of the World War I debt.
A "national budget" of increased costs and a second "national budget" of possible improvements suggested to him
that the answer was in enlarged production. By way of historical background, he pointed out that it "was the debt of
the Revolutionary War that forced the adoption of the national constitution, which constitution, through its benefits,
paid for the war without taking a dollar from the pockets of
anyone." The Civil War debt, he continued, "was paid not
by the sweat of labor but by the great inventions of the
epoch."[69] To those who regarded the higher debt and budget
levels as barriers to a return to "normalcy," statements such
as these were baffling as well as provocative.

The influence of Adams, Ely, and Patten, along with other
economists of similar outlook, was substantial. Their forward-looking views with respect to state action and the role
of government represented a sharp break with prevailing
conceptions. Their influence on public policy was a gradual
one. Even their staunchest critics were forced to recognize
that their ideas concerning public activities had a broad appeal and represented an effective antidote to the pronouncements of Sumner and other exponents of extreme laissez
faire. It was largely because of these ideas that the traditionalists found the new economics unacceptable.

Arthur T. Hadley challenged the approach of the new
school economists. Writing in 1894, he came to the defense
of traditional economics. "It is because of success in serving
the community that individualistic economics holds the position which it does at the present day." The old-school economists did not deny others the right to think differently. "But
they strongly disapprove the attempt to 'popularize' economics by giving too much weight to uninstructed public senti-

[69] *Ibid.*, pp. 39 ff.

ment."[70] Hadley did not hold that the individualistic theory was perfect in practice.

Even those who emphasize most clearly what self-interest has done for political and industrial progress are compelled to recognize that it will not do everything. Its successes have been great, but they have not been unmixed with failures. It is a powerful stimulant, but it is by no means that panacea for social ills which so many economists and moralists have considered it. The exalted hopes of the individualistic philosphers during the first half of the nineteenth century have been followed during the second half by a correspondingly depressing reaction.[71]

Hadley regarded what he called the "movement toward state socialism" during the Theodore Roosevelt-Taft era with serious misgivings. This movement was "very different in character" from anything that occurred in the nineteenth century. The Interstate Commerce Act of 1887, he pointed out, was supplemented by the Elkins Act of 1903, the Hepburn Act of 1906, and the Mann-Elkins Act of 1910. Twenty years earlier these laws would have been regarded as "distinctly socialistic in tenor." Of even greater consequence was the increased activity shown in enforcing old laws. "By the mere action of public sentiment the Department of Commerce and Labor . . . was given an importance which its sponsors hardly anticipated. By the same force of public opinion, statutes which at first had been little more than dead letters were brought into active use as agencies of industrial control."[72]

In his later years Hadley continued to deplore the increasing reliance on government. He disliked the "increasing demand for ill-considered legislation" during the 1920's, together with "increasing readiness of would-be reformers to rely on authority rather than on public sentiment" for secur-

[70] Hadley, "Ely's Socialism and Social Reform," *The Forum*, Vol. 18 (1894), pp. 190–91.
[71] Hadley, *The Education of the American Citizen* (1901), pp. 17–18.
[72] Hadley, *Undercurrents in American Politics* (1915), pp. 76, 86–87.

ing their objectives. "Today, it is from the law maker rather than from the law breaker that our American traditions of self-government have most to fear." A key question, in Hadley's opinion, was: "What can we do to protect ourselves from the spirit of over-regulation?"[73] A lack of confidence in the trend of developments is suggested. Though he apparently did not say so directly, in his view a great deal of regulatory legislation was properly regarded as state interference. In his thinking legislation in itself was not necessarily the vital consideration. The important matter is the spirit in which government is administered.[74]

Hadley believed that all ordinary public expenditures should be covered from current revenues. There are apparently but two cases where recourse to loans is desirable. First, borrowing is permissible in "an extraordinary emergency like war." Second, borrowing is justified in the case of "permanent productive investments, like state railroads or telegraphs, which are made once for all, and offer the prospect of national and fiscal advantages for a long series of years." Debts for industrial enterprises which do not promise a commercial return should follow the same rule as war debts—hold them to a minimum. "Sewers, harbor improvements, highways and other things which cannot pay for themselves commercially" should in general be "paid for by assessment or not built at all." Hadley believed that capital expansion within the public sector should proceed slowly. "Unless fiscal checks are rigidly applied and fiscal deficits made up by present taxation rather than by promises for the

---

[73] Hadley, *Education and Government* (1934), pp. 5, 8. This work consists of addresses before Yale students during Hadley's last years.

[74] Hadley, *The Relations Between Freedom and Responsibility in the Evolution of Democratic Government* (1903), p. 1. Hadley's knowledge of men and of human institutions "convinced him that permanent progress is best assured by the slow organic growth of institutions and not by sudden and violent changes in the existing order." Irving Fisher, "Obituary: Arthur Twining Hadley," *Economic Journal*, Vol. 40 (1930), p. 531.

future, the danger of waste far outweighs the probability of good."[75]

To Frank W. Taussig the pronouncements of economists concerning the role of government were out of bounds. Replying to Edmund Janes James in 1886, he stated that James and others who expressed similar views were not speaking as economists. It was Taussig's position that "economic science does not answer and should not pretend to answer" the questions raised by James. "It merely helps to answer them, by investigating one aspect of man's activity." In expressing themselves on the sphere of government, economists "have spoken, not as economists, but as speculators on the theory of the state and of society at large." Political economy "investigates and explains the phenomena of wealth." Economic science may be helpful in solving the general problem of what the state should do, but "it does not pretend to solve it by laying down a rule of *laissez faire* or one of state interference."[76]

Taussig's views concerning the disparateness between economics and speculations as to the role of government never changed appreciably during his long career. Interference with the distribution of income through steeply progressive tax rates he regarded with misgivings; "the principle of ability leads to no clear conclusion on the question of progression." He was never impressed by the ability theory, as expounded by Seligman and others, which sanctioned progressive rates and viewed the resulting redistribution as a consequence of the application of a fiscal principle. "They are influenced, tho not always consciously, by an underlying belief that the rich in general are in an unduly favored position and that it is therefore equitable to apply

[75] Hadley, *Economics: An Account of the Relations Between Private Property and Public Welfare* (1896), pp. 479–84.
[76] Taussig, "The State As An Economic Factor," *Science Economic Discussion*, pp. 34–35.

to public charges a different rule from that which holds in other affairs."[77]

Though his attitude was one of tolerance, not even the great depression converted Taussig to the merits of governmental intervention in economic affairs. Perhaps all informed persons would agree with him that there was small likelihood the hortatory approach would accomplish anything during extreme economic adversity. Taussig thought that large expenditures for public works "may have a sort of catalytic effect"; but "they may fall flat." The same holds for free extensions of credit, easy and plentiful money, and loans to concerns temporarily embarrassed. "Any of these if used too widely or too freely may easily lead to false starts, then relapse, eventual prolongation of the depression. No one can tell how the psychological factor will work."[78]

The same skepticism was evidenced early in 1934. Taussig did not condemn the program of the Roosevelt administration out of hand. Expressing the hope that it would enjoy a measure of success, he nevertheless seemed to doubt that it represented a major contribution toward hastening recovery. He continued to hold that the main cause of the nation's economic difficulties was to be found in "the maladaptation of production to consumption, and the failure of increased output to take the form of well-balanced output." We had had "a particularly bad wrench," and the inevitable process of readjustment "is going on, or has begun to set in." For an ultimate attainment of a good balance "we must look . . . to the operations of private industry."[79]

In common with Taussig, only a minor part of the writings of Irving Fisher are of interest for this study. Fisher saw clearly that the role of government would necessarily expand

---

[77] Taussig, *Principles of Economics* (1924), Vol. 2, p. 511.

[78] Taussig, "Doctors, Economists, and the Depression," *Harper's Magazine*, Vol. 165 (1932), p. 364.

[79] Taussig, "Wanted Consumers," *Yale Review*, New Series, Vol. 23 (1934), pp. 438 ff.

as the economy became more complex. Writing in 1907, he pointed out that the gradual abandonment of the laissez-faire conception had resulted from the effect of accumulated experience rather than the development of any rival abstract doctrine. In "hundreds of individual cases" men have been brought face to face "with the practical limitations of the let-alone policy." The revival of governmental activity in economic affairs was due to causes which are partly political and partly economic. In some instances the government acted in self-defense. "It has been felt . . . that if the government did not control the railroads, the railroads would control the government."[80]

The premises underlying the negative state of laissez-faire theorists were challenged vigorously by Fisher. The idea that governmental interference in economic matters is unnecessary and harmful is no longer entitled to credence. A generation ago, he pointed out, the Manchester school (a British school of economic thought) "would have regarded numerous social welfare activities as not only impracticable, but as unnecessary and possibly harmful." The work of the Child Labor Committee and the effort to prevent and control tuberculosis were mentioned as examples. We can not, said Fisher, "let any dogma of laissez faire prevent us from checking suicidal ignorance." The belief that in following or serving his own interest, the individual is serving the public interest was questioned with equal vigor. Individual actions are by no means uniform in their social effects. They fall into three classes: (1) They may benefit the individual himself and have no effect on others. (2) They may benefit the individual and at the same time benefit society. (3) They may benefit the individual and at the same time injure society. The mistake of the laissez-faire doctrinaires is that they "overlook the third, especially that part where the injury to society out-

[80] Fisher, "Why Has the Doctrine of Laissez Faire Been Abandoned?" *Science*, Vol. 25 (1907), p. 18.

weighs the benefits to individuals." In numerous cases legal restraints are necessary in the social or public interest.[81]

One of Fisher's lesser-known contributions was his effective questioning of the narrow approach of federal officials to the financing of government during the 1920's. Those who contrasted the decline in federal debt and the rise in state and local debt, and at the same time reflected on the thrift of the states and localities, were not justified in their interpretation of the facts, according to Fisher. The national and local debts were not comparable; the federal debt was a war debt. He agreed with C. E. Rightor's observation that it "seems illogical to compare the trend of local debt with the downward trend of federal debt, and infer that the former should also be gradually reduced." The schools, highways, hospitals, and other capital facilities financed by state and local borrowings were urgently needed and were not indicative of extravagance. In general, the economic gains outweigh the costs.[82]

Probably no economist of his era saw more clearly than Fisher the role of debts, both public and private, in our society. At the same time, he was keenly aware of the dangers inherent in an unbalanced or top-heavy debt structure. "Excessive debts sooner or later precipitate excessive liquidation. Thus are booms the cause of depressions." Total debt as of 1929 was placed by Fisher at $234 billion, of which the $9.5 billion of brokers' loans was the most unstable of all.[83] In an article dealing with the debt-deflation theory of depressions, Fisher favored the efforts of the Roosevelt administration to arrest the deflation and institute a recovery. In his opinion, "debt and deflation, which had wrought havoc

---

[81] *Ibid.*, pp. 19–22.

[82] Fisher, "City and State Debts Justified." This reprint by the Portland Cement Association (1928) is item No. 37 in *Collected Papers in Economics of Irving Fisher,* an unbound collection in the Library of Congress. C. E. Rightor was then a statistician for the Detroit Bureau of Governmental Research; he was later Chief of the Governments Division, U. S. Bureau of the Census.

[83] Fisher, *Mastering the Crisis* (1934), pp. 39–40.

up to March 4, 1933, were then stronger than ever and, if let
alone, would have wreaked greater wreckage than ever after
March 4. Had no 'artificial respiration' been applied, we
would soon have seen general bankruptcies of the mortgage
guarantee companies, savings banks, life insurance companies, railways, municipalities, and states." What Fisher
was saying was that under the conditions prevailing in the
spring of 1933 there was no definable limit to the deflationary
spiral.[84]

Edwin R. A. Seligman may appropriately be classified
as a "new school" economist. He was not impressed by the
immutability at times claimed for classical doctrine. He
believed that economic thought was relative and that it must
adjust to changing conditions and changing times. The
modern school "holds that the economic theories of any generation must be regarded primarily as the outgrowth of the
peculiar conditions of time, place, and nationality, under
which the doctrines were evolved, and that no particular set
of tenets can arrogate to itself the claim of immutable truth,
or the assumption of universal applicability to all countries
or epochs."[85]

Seligman specialized in public finance to a greater extent
than any other prominent economist of his era. He believed
that increased use of public credit was a logical development
in an evolving society. "Public credit has been utilized in
increasing measure not only because modern business life
lays continually more stress on credit, but also because under
the dynamic conditions of a rapidly augmenting national
wealth the weight of a given public debt tends gradually to
diminish. Public credit is not only a natural, but within
bounds a salutary, phenomenon."[86] There is here a sugges-

[84] Fisher, "The Debt-Deflation Theory of Great Depressions," *Econometrica*, Vol. 1
(October 1933), pp. 346–47.

[85] Seligman, "Continuity of Economic Thought," *Science Economic Discussion*,
pp. 1–2.

[86] Seligman, *Currency Inflation and Public Debts* (1921), p. 7.

tion that in certain circumstances—especially emergencies—
the burden of financing is better handled if there is appropriate recourse to the public credit.

European and American theories with respect to public
debts were contrasted by Seligman near the end of World
War I. The European theory of a perpetual debt, he observed,
rests on two chief arguments. First, with a "progressive increase in the wealth and productive capacity of modern
nations a fixed debt constitutes a continually diminishing
burden upon the community." Second, in so far as a nation
has "to deal with a domestic debt, there is virtually no burden upon the community as a whole." The American theory
has been the reverse, largely for reasons dependent on "the
disparate economic conditions of the United States." The
"growth of our wealth and social income has been so prodi-
gious that the country has experienced no appreciable dis-
comfort in getting rid of a continually diminishing burden.
So productive and so easily tapped have been the ordinary
sources of revenue that from the war of 1812 to the period
after the Civil War the extinction of the debt took place
almost automatically." Our troubles almost always involved
a surplus.[87]

In Seligman's judgment rapid repayment of a public debt
was favorable to enterprise. "One of the first problems of
reconstruction will be the rapid repayment of the war
debt."[88] That is to say, a balanced budget was deemed desirable after World War I and, in addition, ample revenues
should be provided to ensure rapid and systematic reduction
of the war debt. However, a few years later he questioned
the rather inflexible sinking-fund requirement which had
been enacted in 1919. "Where, as at present, the burdens
of an excessive war taxation are still so serious as to impair

[87] Seligman, "Fiscal Reconstruction," in *American Problems of Reconstruction*,
E. M. Friedman, ed. (1918), pp. 429–30.
[88] *Ibid.*, pp. 430–33.

the replenishment and the increase of the social capital, the question arises whether it would not be desirable to introduce more elasticity into the process of debt payment." A "sound debt-payment policy will compare the advantages of a rapid diminution of the debt burden with the corresponding advantages of a rapid decrease of the tax burden, and with the possibility of adjusting the tax system to fundamental principles."[89]

In principle Seligman continued to favor a balanced budget during the early years of the great depression. In an address delivered in January 1932 he pointed out that the "fiscal leaders at Washington are perfectly right in emphasizing the necessity of the country's balancing the budget in order to maintain the federal credit. Unless the Government upholds the public credit, there can be no firm foundation for private credit. Any sacrifice, however severe, is justifiable to achieve that end." This succinct summary of his credit philosophy led to a timely question: What magic is there in the term of twelve months? Why a budget balanced over a period of twelve months rather than three months or two years! "Balancing the budget is indeed a necessity, but why should not the fat years be permitted to atone for the lean years?"[90]

The same theme was reiterated the following spring. Though budgetary balance is an absolute necessity, "we must not be too meticulous in defining the period." The danger of a surplus, Seligman said, is almost equal to that of a deficit: "We have had in the United States on the whole more difficulties with surplus than with deficit financing." A budget is annual, but a budgetary balance is not necessarily restricted to a single year. "The requirements of a balanced budget are substantially met if there is an equilibrium after

[89] Seligman, "The State of Our National Finances," *American Economic Review*, Vol. 12 (1922), pp. 25–26.

[90] Seligman, American Institute of Consulting Engineers, Inc., *Proceedings of the Annual Meeting Held January 18, 1932*, p. 14.

not too protracted a period." In the spring of 1932 two annual deficits in succession were a certainty, and a third one—for 1933—was clearly indicated unless there was a sharp turn in the economic tide. At this juncture Seligman's cautious approach to any departure from budgetary balance became evident, and he concluded that "under the actual circumstances it would be hazardous further to prolong the period of balancing."[91]

In common with other economists, Seligman was aware that the debt increases resulting from deficits incurred during the depression were offset in part by additions to government-owned assets. Early in 1934 he observed that "in the broader sense all these peace outlays are not only as legitimate as those of war, but perhaps less disadvantageous because in large measure susceptible of being credited to capital account." The dual budget system then in effect met with his approval.[92] "We need, in addition to the ordinary budget, an extraordinary budget dealing with emergency and capital outlays. In balancing one we must include the interest and amortization of the other."[93]

From the Civil War to the depression of the 1930's adherence to the laissez-faire philosophy by economists was the exception rather than the rule. John Stuart Mill and Alfred Marshall, whose works were widely used in this country, recognized that increasing governmental activity was a virtual certainty as the economy became more complex. The same is true of prominent American economists of the immediate post-Civil War decades such as Arthur L. Perry and Francis A. Walker. To these and most other economists of their era, the dictum that a government which governs least governs best was long since outmoded. In their

[91] Seligman, "Toward a New Tax Program," *The Nation*, Vol. 134 (April 27, 1932), p. 484.
[92] See the discussion at pp. 177-78.
[93] *New York Times* (Jan. 9, 1934), p. 34.

view this and similar slogans were useless as a guide for policy in a rapidly developing industrial society.

In the latter decades of the nineteenth century marked differences of opinion developed among American economists with respect to governmental activities and the role of government in the economy. At one extreme the writings of William Graham Sumner represented as uncompromising an advocacy of individualistic economics as this country has ever seen. His underlying philosophy differed only in degree from that of Henry David Thoreau, who in an earlier period seemed to condemn the very existence of organized government. Yet at the very time that Sumnerian orthodoxy was reaching the peak of its popularity, the new school of political economy was in the ascendency. Henry Carter Adams, Richard T. Ely, and others of this group believed that intervention in economic affairs and the assignment of new activities to government were absolute necessities if society were to progress in an orderly manner.

The mainstream of American economic thought from about 1890 to 1930, in so far as it relates to governmental activity, followed a course somewhere between Sumnerian orthodoxy and the "new economics." At times the main current seemed to be fairly close to one extreme or the other, but at no time could it be said that either of the two philosophies was dominant. No economist or group of economists typified the main course of developments.

In contrast with the pronounced differences concerning the scope of governmental activity, there was a marked unanimity of opinion with respect to federal budget and debt policy. Those economists who expressed an opinion believed that a balanced peacetime budget was desirable and that, when a large federal debt was outstanding, debt reduction was in the public interest. To the extent that there were disagreements, they related mainly to the level at which the budget should be balanced and the rate at which the debt should be reduced.

The Public View

As the Civil War drew to a close, the informed public generally took the position that the huge war debt would not represent an intolerable burden. One of the remarkable aspects of this conflict was the enthusiastic support of the people in shouldering a heavy tax burden. It was scarcely conceivable that on the cessation of hostilities the same people would regard the fiscal requirements imposed by the war debt as unbearable.

How the national debt might be paid was considered in a pamphlet designed to influence public opinion issued by Jay Cooke just before the end of the war. The author, William Elder of the Treasury Department, pointed out the real significance of the debt was not the principal sum, but the ratio of "current interest to the current annual product of wealth" (national income). Placing the debt at the end of the war at $3 billion, he showed that for the three years 1865–1867 the ratio of interest to national income would be approximately 3 per cent. This ratio would decline with the growth of the country. In less than two decades it might not be much over one per cent. Elder visualized retirement of the principal over a twenty-year period beginning in 1870. His study pointed to the conclusion that the debt could be serviced and paid off without too great difficulty.[94]

In the process by which public opinion was influenced and debt policy fashioned, resort to hyperbole was by no means uncommon. In another pamphlet issued by Jay Cooke, Samuel Wilkeson made the point that the interest rather than the principal is the measure of the burden imposed by a domestically held government debt. But his other arguments were unconvincing. Though economic understanding was not at a high level, the people generally were not

[94] Elder, *How Our National Debt Can Be Paid* (1865), pp. 3–7, 13–15.

willing to believe that the national debt was "just so much capital added to our wealth." Nor were they willing to accept the thesis that to pay the debt and "lose this wealth" would be an "inconceivably grave national misfortune." They were not convinced that "our National War Debt should be held forever in place as the political tie of the States and the bond forever of a paternal nationality."[95]

If some of Wilkeson's assertions seemed merely ineffective propaganda, they were no less so than the near-hysterical outbursts of the advocates of repudiation during the late 1860's. The question whether the war debt should be paid in specie or in depreciated currency figured prominently in the campaign of 1868. It was one on which men of good will might reasonably differ. In a nation that had long regarded a public debt as evil—or even immoral—it was not illogical to expect that the war-incurred debt would be regarded by some as calling for drastic action.

The large federal debt was little short of anathema to some people fairly prominent in American life. For example, a few years after the war Isaac Butts, a former editor of the *Rochester Daily Union and Advertiser*, made an impassioned plea for repudiation of the debt incurred to finance the war. His arguments were addressed principally to the industrial classes; their "welfare is more seriously involved than any other." The tenor of Butts' pamphlet is suggested by a section heading entitled " 'The World's Progress' in War Debts and Popular Enslavement." With a shrill crescendo, he paid his respects to public debts: "Of all the schemes ever devised by the perverse ingenuity of man for making the rich richer and the poor poorer, the weak weaker and the strong stronger, the funding system, with its accessories, holds the highest rank, unchallenged and unchallengeable."[96]

[95] Wilkeson, *How Our National Debt May Be a National Blessing* (1865), pp. 3–6. The author was a member of the editorial staff of the *New York Tribune*.

[96] Butts, *Brief Reasons for Repudiation; Applicable to the War Debts of All Countries* (1869), pp. iii, 67, 92.

There is no reason to believe that Butts' emotional reactions to the post-Civil War debt were in any way typical. At the time he wrote, indecision and controversy were important features of federal administration—financial and other. His observations were ineffective because they lacked perspective. A balanced view would have taken into account factors other than "the funding system" and the size of the debt. An appraisal of postwar debt burdens that gave no consideration to the prospects for economic expansion and population growth was obviously unrealistic.

A more rational view was taken by Edward Learned, who believed the growth factor was of major importance. The future promised "a population and a wealth almost too vast for imagination." The debt should not be permitted to interfere unnecessarily with the favorable outlook. Indecision and agitation tended to magnify the debt problem.[97] Though national income and wealth data were not then in vogue, informed observers were able to visualize a reduction of debt burdens through economic growth and territorial expansion.[98]

The Civil War did not bring about a marked change in popular attitudes toward public and private debt. The idea that debt was evil or immoral seems to have received less emphasis after the war, but the change was one of degree. Before the war, as mentioned previously, imprisonment for debt had virtually disappeared. Yet there were instances of this practice during the reconstruction period. Referring to

---

[97] "Bright as are those prospects, they are dimmed by a cloud of overhanging debt, which, gathering intensity from our indecision, distracted counsels, diversities of interests, and political differences both as to the obligations of the debt and our ability to discharge it, causes damaging apprehensions among those who hold our obligations, but who do not appreciate our resources, and our determination to maintain our national faith untarnished." Learned, *How to Pay It: or a Method for Discharging the National Debt, and Lessening the Burden of Taxation* (1869), p. 6.

[98] See, for example, Edward Atkinson, *The National Debt* (1868). In a table (p. 8) showing how the Civil War debt might be eliminated in 15 years, Atkinson assumed a rise in population from 38 millions in 1868 to 61 millions in 1884.

the situation in South Carolina, W. A. Swanberg states: "Destitute widows of soldiers were being evicted from their homes. Even returned soldiers were cast into prison for debt."[99] It is apparent that even by the mid-1860's not everyone was convinced that imprisonment for debt was "an economic absurdity."

There was no decline after the war in the emphasis on thrift. The half century after the war was an era of pronounced economic expansion. Capital accumulation through saving was an integral part of the process by which the economy grew and progressed. Throughout most of this period the demand for capital exceeded domestic saving and was met in part from foreign sources. The legacy of larger fiscal requirements from the war was merely an added reason for the careful husbanding of resources.

Thrift, as in the earlier period, had more than an economic connotation. It continued to be endowed with strong moral overtones. In the popular literature thrift was commonly extolled as the greatest of individual and social virtues. Thrift and industry combined with a fair share of luck or good fortune were regarded as synonymous with success, particularly in the prolific writings of Horatio Alger.[100]

Attitudes toward government were strongly influenced by the widely held popular belief that the people were capable of governing themselves. "The most deep-rooted political instinct which Americans have, an instinct which determines all their thinking, is the feeling that they can and will . . . govern themselves. No other kind of government could possibly be considered proper."[101] To say that faith in self-

[99] Swanberg, *Sickles the Incredible* (1956), p. 287. The author cites as his authority, F. B. Simkins and R. H. Woody, *South Carolina During Reconstruction* (1932), pp. 246–47.

[100] Horatio Alger (1832–1899) produced a large number of novels of the success type which were widely read by American youth. Four titles beginning with "S" are suggestive: *Sink or Swim, Shifting for Himself, Seeking His Fortune,* and *Strive and Succeed.*

[101] Carl Becker, *The United States: An Experiment in Democracy* (1920), p. 67.

government was a logical corollary of individual initiative and self-reliance would not be strictly accurate. Rather, they are interrelated and interdependent. As stated by Henry C. Carey: "Self-reliance, and the power to command the confidence of others, grow with growth in the habit of self-government."[102]

Nineteenth century attitudes carried over well into the present century. In 1912, the year Woodrow Wilson was elected President, David Starr Jordan published a small volume entitled *Unseen Empire*. The author's position with respect to public debts and the public credit corresponded closely with the more extreme views voiced during the previous century. Underlying the entire volume was the assumption that public debts are immoral. On the title page there is a Bulgarian proverb: "God is not sinless; he created borrowers." The federal government was not the only offender. "In any discussion of national debt, we must remember that other branches of government are not sinless."[103] Presumably debts of all kinds—public and private—could not be reconciled with elementary morality.

Jordan lamented the fact that the federal government had not continued its earlier policy of paying off the outstanding debt as rapidly as possible. "Up to 1900, it had always been the policy of the government to pay off its interest-bearing debts as soon as possible in order to avoid unnecessary burden on the taxpayers. But at present this policy has been more or less cast aside in the interest of military expenditures and unwarranted river and harbor improvements."[104]

The American people were living in a spendthrift age, ac-

---

[102] Carey, *Review of the Decade 1857–1867* (1867), p. 11.

[103] Jordan, *Unseen Empire* (1912), p. 26. The author of this volume was a renowned naturalist, educator, and publicist. He was president of Stanford University from 1891 to 1913.

[104] *Ibid.*, p. 44. At the close of the fiscal year 1912 the federal debt was less than $1.2 billion or $12.52 per capita. Federal interest payments for 1912 were $22.6 million, or about 3.3 per cent of budget expenditures. *Annual Report of the Secretary of the Treasury on the State of the Finances for the Fiscal Year Ended June 30, 1956*, pp. 321, 392.

cording to Jordan. The editor of a contemporary magazine
was quoted with approval. "The expanded credit of the
world, according to the editor of Life, may be likened to 'a
vast bubble on the surface of which, like inspired insects,
we swim and dream our financial dreams. . . . ' We have long
since passed the simple or kindergarten stage of living beyond
our incomes. We are now engaged in living beyond the incomes of generations to come."[105] One is reminded of the
Jeffersonian thesis that the present belongs to the living
generation.

After World War I it was widely asserted that the high
level of peacetime public expenditures would interfere with
economic development and would cause a decline in the
level of living. Thus, Irving T. Bush believed that the tri-
pling of federal expenditures, as compared with the immediate
prewar years, would make serious inroads on the capital
formation essential for normal economic growth. "A prosperous nation before the war was one that conserved about
10 per cent of its national income and put it back into productive industry and productive commerce. Without such
accretions of capital, nations do not grow. We have seriously
cut our own savings account. We are beginning to live almost
from hand to mouth." In Bush's opinion the American people
had not been compelled to reduce their living expenses, but
"we shortly must, for we are cutting down our ability to
produce, and therefore, our ability to buy. We are headed for
a lower standard of living." He lamented the fact that the
efforts of President Harding "to cut into the civil expenditure" had aroused only mild interest. "There is nowhere a
realization that only as the Government strips itself can the
people clothe themselves. There is still a lurking desire to
have the Government do more rather than less."[106]

It is difficult to characterize pronouncements such as those

---

[105] Jordan, *Unseen Empire*, p. 51. The publication *Life* here referred to is the
humorous magazine published from 1883 to 1936.
[106] Bush, "Too Much Government," *Collier's*, Vol. 69 (Jan. 28, 1922), pp. 5–6.

of Jordan and Bush, other than to say that they were fairly typical of conservative business and professional opinion at the time they were made. Numerous individuals prominent in business and the professions believed that governmental expenditures were continuously on the verge of getting out of control. With the development of a public highway system, the complementary nature of public and private activities became more apparent than ever before. Yet for the most part, discussions of public activities continued to emphasize the money costs of government. The modern concept of a public sector of the economy that complements the private sector had gained only limited acceptance.

CHAPTER IV

The Hoover Years: Conflicting Views

W HEN THE DEPRESSION BEGAN IN 1929, federal budget policy was firmly anchored to the idea that the budget should be balanced annually. A balanced budget was regarded as the principal test of sound fiscal management. The Treasury had just enjoyed a decade of surpluses, and debt incurred during World War I had been sharply reduced. At the prevailing rate of retirement, the federal debt would be eliminated in less than two decades. If any one had suggested that large peacetime deficits were imminent, he would have received scant hearing.

The historical record shows that the surpluses of the 1920's were followed by an unbroken series of ten peacetime deficits.[1] So large a number of deficits in succession was to become a new phenomenon in our fiscal annals.[2] With deficits in the federal accounts apparently becoming habitual, it was to be expected that prevailing views concerning budget policy would be re-examined. If the origin of the new theories and their role in the evolution of public policy are to be understandable, an appreciation of the environment in which

[1] The deficit for the fiscal year 1941 is not included; expenditures for this year were strongly influenced by the defense program instituted after the invasion of the Low Countries in May 1940. The figures for the years 1931–1940 are shown in appendix table, p. 319.

[2] Prior to the 1930's the largest number of successive deficits was eight, incurred in the period ended in 1865. Four—perhaps five—of these deficits were attributable to the Civil War.

143

they were developed is essential. In particular, fiscal developments and public attitudes during the early years of the great depression are of considerable importance.

The Struggle for a Balanced Budget

The federal budget for 1931 was submitted by President Hoover on December 2, 1929, about six weeks after the collapse of the stock market. There was no indication in this budget of impending fiscal difficulties. Surpluses were estimated for 1930 and 1931, as may be seen in the table on page 145. The President proposed that a reduction of one percentage point be made in the rates on 1929 incomes for both the personal and corporate income taxes, as recommended by the Secretary of the Treasury.[3] This recommendation was enacted into law in December 1929. The revenue loss was placed at $160 million, divided about equally between the 1930 and 1931 budgets.[4]

At no time during the calendar year 1930 was there a direct admission that large deficits might soon be incurred.[5] Income

[3] The rates on personal incomes for 1929 ranged from 0.5 per cent on the first $4,000 of taxable income to 24 per cent on net income above $100,000; an earned income credit of not to exceed 25 per cent of the computed tax was allowed. The corporate rate for 1929 was 11 per cent.

[4] *Message of the President of the United States Transmitting the Budget for the Service of the Fiscal Year Ending June 30, 1931*, pp. ix–x, 46 Stat. 47. The modest size of this reduction was influenced by the fact that the estimated surpluses, as officially announced, were much smaller than the figures shown in the table on p. 145. Official policy called for a balanced budget on a basis that included statutory debt retirements in expenditures.

[5] In April President Hoover stated that "the indicated income of the Government and the expenditures to which the Government is already committed" suggested a deficit of $20 to $30 million for the fiscal year 1931. Any further large amounts of expenditures, he continued, "will jeopardize the primary duty of the Government, that is, to hold expenditures within our income." Letter to Senator Wesley L. Jones, *State Papers and Other Writings of Herbert Hoover* (1934), Vol. 1, p. 240.

tax revenues remained at a high level throughout the year. The fact that they were based mainly on 1929 incomes helped place the budget situation in a favorable light. The surplus for the completed fiscal year 1930 announced early in July was $738 million, with statutory debt retirements excluded from expenditures. The 1932 budget released in December 1930 indicated surpluses for the fiscal years 1931 and 1932.[6]

Estimated and Actual Budget Surpluses and Deficits
Fiscal Years 1930–1933[a]

(In millions of dollars)

Fiscal Year	Initial Budget Estimate[b]	Revised Budget Estimate[b]	Surplus or Deficit for Completed Year[b]
1930..........	+614	+ 856	+ 738
1931..........	+758	+ 262	− 462
1932..........	+499	−1,711	−2,735[c]
1933..........	−923	−1,146	−2,602

[a] Estimated surpluses and deficits computed from data in the federal budget. Figures for completed years from *Annual Report of the Secretary of the Treasury on the State of the Finances for the Fiscal Year Ended June 30, 1956,* p. 323.

[b] A surplus is indicated by (+) and a deficit by (−).

[c] The deficit for 1932 shown in the 1934 budget was $2,467 million; the difference of $268 million between the larger figure in this table and the budget figure is accounted for by expenditures of the Reconstruction Finance Corporation financed from borrowings.

The administration remained committed to a policy of debt reduction. No change was recommended in the practice of including statutory debt retirements in the expenditure totals used in computing the surplus or deficit. In the message transmitting the budget for 1932, the President stated that he did not look with favor on attempts to meet the 1931 "deficit" by reduction of the statutory debt redemptions. The adverse balance, it was pointed out, could be met by

[6] On the basis then used—that is, including statutory debt retirements in expenditures—there was an estimated deficit of $179 million for 1931 and a surplus of $31 million for 1932. *Message of the President of the United States Transmitting the Budget for the Service of the Fiscal Year Ending June 30, 1932,* pp. A8–A10.

drawing down the general fund or cash balance. The small "favorable margin" of receipts over expenditures for the fiscal year 1932 was stressed by the President. This situation, it was believed, merely required that expenditure proposals be examined with extraordinary care. "When we stop to consider that we are progressively amortizing our public debt, and that a balanced Budget is being presented for 1932, even after drastic writing down of expected revenue, I believe it will be agreed that our Government finances are in a sound condition."[7]

In retrospect it would be easy to find fault with this point of view on the ground that in a period of depression balancing a budget that included almost $500 million for debt retirements was an illogical—perhaps impossible—goal. Nor would it be difficult to criticize the estimates for 1932. It should be remembered, however, that only a little more than a year had elapsed since the stock market crash and that the Treasury had just enjoyed eleven successive annual surpluses. Moreover, recovery from earlier depressions had usually occurred soon enough to avoid fiscal difficulties.

As the depression deepened, it became apparent that the budget estimates had been far too optimistic and that the Treasury would soon be faced with larger deficits than any previously incurred in time of peace. The long period of deficit financing began in January 1931, or at the middle of the fiscal year 1931. The accounts for the first half of the fiscal year showed a surplus. In placing the date when deficit financing began so precisely, the pertinent fact is that January-March 1931 was the first quarterly period to show a deficit.[8]

An early return to a balanced budget remained the dominant goal of budget policy. The estimated deficits for 1932

[7] *Ibid.*, pp. XVIII–XIX.

[8] Because of the concentration of income tax receipts in four months—March, June, September, and December—the accounts for individual months are not a significant factor.

and 1933 announced in December 1931 were of unprecedented magnitude, on the basis of peacetime standards. Extensive federal borrowings were regarded as undesirable by
President Hoover because they interfered with "recovery of
employment by detouring capital away from industry and
commerce into the Treasury of the United States."[9] In this
situation the President recommended an increase in taxes
for a period of two years based primarily "upon the general
plan of taxation which existed under the revenue act of
1924."[10] The increased revenues, it was believed, would enable the government to balance the budget for the fiscal
year 1933 except for statutory debt retirements, and would
make possible a fully balanced budget—including debt retirements—for the following year.[11]

The financial integrity of the federal government, in the
President's opinion, required prompt action directed toward
the restoration of a balanced budget. The federal finances
would not permit the assumption of any obligations that
would enlarge expenditures. Interested individuals and
groups were advised that "the most patriotic duty" they
could perform was to refrain and to discourage others from
seeking "any increase in the drain upon public finances."[12]
In retrospect the most unusual feature of the 1933 budget
message, which was submitted more than two years after the

[9] Address on Business Depression and Policies of Government, Indianapolis,
Indiana, June 15, 1931, *State Papers and Other Public Writings of Herbert Hoover*,
Vol. 1, p. 578.
[10] Under the Revenue Act of 1924 the Treasury relied on income taxes, the
estate tax, and a group of excises to meet its requirements. The taxes on cigarettes
and other tobacco products were the most productive excises.
[11] *Message of the President of the United States Transmitting the Budget for the
Service of the Fiscal Year Ending June 30, 1933*, pp. I, VII, A8–A9. When the accounts for 1932 were in, the deficit was placed at almost $2.5 billion. In the Treas-
ury's historical series the 1932 deficit is shown as $2,735 million. See footnote c in
the table on page 145. Expenditures for 1932 were inflated by the inclusion of $500
million on account of the purchase by the Treasury of the capital stock of the
Reconstruction Finance Corporation and $125 million for additional capital stock
of the federal land banks. Investments of this type were regarded as a proper charge
against current revenues, even under conditions of extreme depression.
[12] *Ibid.*, p. XVII.

onset of the depression, was that the policy objective remained unchanged. The goal was a level of receipts that
would cover all expenditures, including statutory debt retirements.

The next month—January 1932—the President made
another appeal for retrenchment and declared: "We cannot
squander ourselves into prosperity." In March he appealed
for further economies, which "must be brought about either
by reorganization of the Federal machinery or changes in
the legal requirements as to expenditures of the various services."[13] A few weeks later Hoover called a balanced budget
"the very keystone of recovery" and predicted that if the
federal accounts were not brought into balance, the depression would be prolonged indefinitely.[14]

The view that the budget should be balanced without delay was accepted by the opposition party, as well as the administration. When the revenue bill of 1932 was under consideration, Jouett Shouse, Chairman of the Democratic
National Executive Committee, urged party members in
Congress to support a nonpartisan plan to balance the
budget. The Democratic membership of the House was asked
to unite on a sales tax bill. A sales tax, Shouse said, is a
Democratic concession to necessity.[15] Henry T. Rainey,
Democratic leader of the House, declared that the federal
government was "bankrupt": the time has come, as prophe-
sied by Thomas Jefferson, when "all the tax resources" would
have to be called into force "to maintain the credit and economic stability of the State." Speaker John N. Garner was
firmly of the opinion that a balanced federal budget was essential for the restoration of confidence and economic
recovery. He issued several statements in March 1932, re-
affirming his conviction that balancing the budget was the
first step in relieving the burden of depression.[16]

---

[13] *Current History*, Vol. 35 (March 1932), p. 835; Vol. 36 (April 1932), p. 85.
[14] *New York Times* (March 26, 1932), p. 2.
[15] *Ibid.* (March 14, 1932), p. 1; (March 18, 1932), p. 2.
[16] *Ibid.* (March 18, 1932), p. 1; (March 19, 1932), p. 1; (March 20, 1932), p. 1.

Whether a general sales tax should be adopted became a major issue in the early months of 1932. Such a tax, it was argued, would aid in balancing the budget and at the same time broaden the tax base. The administration did not look with favor on a broadly based sales tax at this juncture. Appearing before the Committee on Ways and Means in January, Secretary Andrew Mellon and Under Secretary Ogden L. Mills opposed a general sales tax. In the Secretary's opening statement he said: "We laid aside all thought of a general sales or turnover tax, not only because generally speaking it bears no relation to ability to pay and is regressive in character, but because of the great administrative difficulties involved and the almost inevitable pyramiding of the tax in the course of successive sales." A tax on manufacturers' or producers' sales only of the type employed in Canada was not favored; it was extremely doubtful that such a tax "would meet with the success in our country that it has across the border."[17] The following month Secretary Mills informed the Committee on Ways and Means that the Treasury had further considered such a tax, and that it continued to favor a limited group of excises.[18] Nevertheless, pressures for a broadly based sales tax continued to mount. The issue came to a head on March 24, when a proposed manufacterers' sales tax of 2¼ per cent was defeated by the House.[19] The sales tax agitation had the effect of exacerbating the budget

---

[17] *Revenue Revision, 1932*, Hearings Before the Committee on Ways and Means, 72 Cong. 1 sess., p. 4.

[18] In a letter to the committee Secretary Mills stated: "We hold to our original opinion that a limited group of selected excise taxes is a preferable method of raising the required revenue, not only from the standpoint of administration but also from that of basic economic considerations." *New York Times* (Feb. 17, 1932), p. 4. Ogden L. Mills became Secretary of the Treasury on February 13, 1932.

[19] *Ibid.* (March 25, 1932), p. 1. Early in March Secretary Mills stated that if such a tax were enacted, it would be accepted by the administration. *Ibid.* (March 2, 1932), p. 1. An important reason for the opposition to this tax was the rather widespread belief that if a sales tax were enacted, it might eventually replace the income tax. This view was not shared by Thomas S. Adams, Treasury tax adviser. Speaking later in the year at a meeting of the National Industrial Conference Board attended by the author, Adams stated that it was his considered judgment that a sales tax—more than any other factor—would solidify the position of the income tax in the federal tax structure.

controversy. William Randolph Hearst and the Hearst press, among others, seemed unwilling to accept the House vote as conclusive, and continued to regard the sales tax as the key to the budget problem.[20]

The drive for a balanced budget gained momentum during the spring of 1932. In the President's opinion, congressional action on the revenue bill and economy measures was being delayed unnecessarily. Early in May a message demanding a prompt balancing of the budget was dispatched to the Congress. "Nothing is more necessary at this time than balancing the budget. Nothing will put more heart into the country than prompt and courageous and united action in enacting the legislation which this situation imperatively demands." The Congress was reminded that "the necessity for these measures is born of a great national emergency."[21]

When the end of May arrived without final action on the revenue bill, President Hoover took the unusual course of going to the Senate to urge immediate action. The Senate passed this measure the same day, and it was announced in the press that the estimated additional revenues of over $1.1 billion would balance the budget.[22] A few days later, however,

[20] Though the Hoover administration later recommended a general sales tax, the effort to revive the sales tax also proved abortive. See p. 167.

[21] *New York Times* (May 6, 1932), pp. 1, 8. One member of the President's party suggested that the federal fiscal emergency might not be solvable by customary democratic processes. On the day the President's economy message was received, Senator David A. Reed of Pennsylvania said: "I do not often envy other countries their governments, but I say that if this country ever needed a Mussolini it needs one now." Senator Reed explained that he was not proposing that Hoover become a Mussolini; if we are "to get economies made they have to be made by some one who has the power to make the order and stand by it." Reed's statement was challenged by three Senators before the day's debate was terminated. *Congressional Record*, Vol. 75, Pt. 9 (May 5, 1932), pp. 9644–46.

[22] *New York Times* (June 1, 1932), p. 1. The Revenue Act of 1932 (47 Stat. 169) was signed by the President on June 6, 1932. This act increased the rates for the personal and corporate income taxes, the estate tax, and a number of stamp taxes. Exemptions for the personal income tax were reduced from $1,500 to $1,000 for a single person and from $3,500 to $2,500 for a married couple or head of family. The specific exemption for the estate tax was reduced from $100,000 to $50,000. A number of excise taxes that had been repealed during the 1920's were reimposed and additional excise taxes were imposed on various commodities, including radio sets and equipment, mechanical refrigerators, and gasoline.

it was reported that there remained a gap of $350 million, which presumably might be closed by additional economies.[23] Because of the deteriorating economic situation, among other reasons, the budget had not been brought into balance. The fight for a balanced budget had been made, but the battle was never won.

Though the Hoover administration sought an early return to a balanced budget, occasional references to the accelerated debt reduction of the preceding decade suggested that the fiscal situation was not so serious as was assumed. For example, Secretary Mills stated that, because of the large surpluses over and above statutory debt retirements that had been applied to debt reduction, the government "had in effect accumulated a reserve . . . which could be drawn upon in the lean years, and which fortified the position of the Federal finances."[24] This "reserve" amounted to about $3.5 billion; for the eleven-year period ended in 1930, debt retirements had exceeded by this sum those required by the sinking-fund and other statutes. However, no reserve in any meaningful sense had been established. There had never been any announcement that debt obligations equal to retirements over and above those required by statute might be reissued at some future time. In the official reports the rapid reduction of the debt had been treated as though it were a permanent accomplishment.[25]

It would be erroneous to conclude that the views of Secretary Mills differed appreciably from those of the President and others high in the councils of the administration. In 1932

[23] *New York Times* (June 3, 1932), p. 18.

[24] *Annual Report of the Secretary of the Treasury on the State of the Finances for the Fiscal Year Ended June 30, 1932*, pp. 22–23. The same theme had been developed by the Secretary in several addresses.

[25] In the opinion of Robert M. Haig, the reserve argument might have been more convincing if some part of the retirements from surplus had been earmarked. "The State of the Federal Finances," *Yale Review*, New Series, Vol. 22 (1932–1933), pp. 247–48. Mills' usage of "reserve" as equivalent to debt retirements in excess of statutory requirements was an unusual one. The unused borrowing power represented by the difference between the statutory debt limit and the debt existing at a given time is at times referred to as though it constitutes a reserve. See p. 300.

achievement of a balanced budget at an early date seemed well-nigh impossible. Mills was merely trying to present the picture in a less dismal hue than was then customary. Though his statement in regard to a reserve conveys a suggestion of what later came to be known as compensatory fiscal action, it would be stretching the point to claim that his primary interest was in finding a plausible rationalization for continuing deficits.

The Hoover administration never deviated from traditional attitudes toward the budget problem. The trend in expenditures was upward, mainly because of larger outlays for public works and the ameliorative efforts of the Reconstruction Finance Corporation. It was not claimed that expenditures such as these would do more than cushion and perhaps help to arrest the decline. There was no intention to develop a broad program based largely on the federal credit that might bring the nation out of the depression.

In insisting that a balanced federal budget was an essential condition for recovery, the President and other officials were acting in accordance with accepted doctrine. A balanced budget was regarded as a prerequisite for a revival of business confidence. Federal borrowing was viewed as competitive with business and other private borrowing; interest rates were higher because of federal competition for loan funds. Normal capital flows, it was reasoned, could not be restored as long as the government continued to borrow large sums. The exigencies of the times required a balanced budget "not merely for maintaining unimpaired the credit of the Government, but also for reinvigorating the entire credit structure of the country."[26]

An additional reason why a balanced budget was regarded as essential was that an unbalanced federal budget was equated with inflation. Unless the budget were brought into balance, it was believed that a loss of confidence in the federal

[26] Statement by Andrew Mellon, *Congressional Digest*, Vol. 11 (1932), p. 138.

credit and in the monetary unit might ensue and a disastrous inflation occur. A closely related view was that a balanced budget was necessary to show that the federal government was in control of its own actions. A government that tolerated a succession of unbalanced budgets in time of peace did not qualify as a responsible government. Only if taxes and other receipts equaled or exceeded expenditures could prevention of economic waste be assured. To those who held that acceptance of unbalanced budgets would be followed by profligacy and carelessness in public expenditures, a serious moral issue was involved.

The budget policy of the early 1930's was questioned during President Hoover's term of office. Even sharper criticisms have been voiced over the past quarter of a century. In these criticisms one important aspect of the budget policy of the early years of the great depression is frequently not mentioned or is not given the emphasis it deserves. In making a balanced budget the primary policy goal, the President, officials of the executive branch, and the leadership of both parties in Congress were acting in accordance with accepted principles. The idea that sound finance required a balanced budget in time of peace was deeply rooted in tradition. Over the years the primacy of the balanced budget had become an article of faith. President Hoover and others who demanded that the budget be balanced under adverse conditions were acting in conformity with "high principle."

Early Dissents: Why Balance the Budget?

During the last half of President Hoover's term of office the belief that a balanced federal budget was essential for recovery was challenged, at times with great vigor. To some observers it seemed that cutting expenditures and raising taxes would merely add a strong deflationary influence to a situation that required the arrest of persistent deflationary forces. In their opinion the times called for a broader approach to fiscal policy.

The idea that balancing the federal budget should be the primary policy goal during a depression was unacceptable to William Trufant Foster and Waddill Catchings, whose work had attracted wide attention during the 1920's.[27] The philosophy of the negative state, which emphasizes that reliance must be placed solely on the private sector of the economy for the generation of income and the maintenance of the level of national income, was not in accord with reality. On the eve of the great depression they wrote: "The Federal Government is the largest business in the world; the largest consumer; the largest spender. As such it inevitably affects prices, markets, and public confidence." Foster and Catchings were among the most ardent advocates of long-range planning of public works. Carefully planned public works programs would serve as a balancing factor and help to sustain income. They believed the public credit should be used when the need arises. Flexibility in a portion of government budgets was essential if unemployment was to be prevented. Index numbers of unemployment, consumer income, and retail prices should be perfected and used as a guide for policy.[28]

[27] In beginning this section with the views of Foster and Catchings, we do not mean to imply that these authors initiated the trend of thought that with the passing of time flowered into present-day fiscal theory. The roots of the compensatory doctrine antedate the works of Foster and Catchings by at least several decades. In the early 1920's, Herbert Hoover had played a leading role in the efforts to chart a course that would lead to greater economic stability. When he was Secretary of Commerce, Mr. Hoover served as Chairman of the President's Conference on Unemployment, which met in Washington in September 1921. The volume entitled *Business Cycles and Unemployment* (1923) was an outgrowth of this conference. The possibilities of countercyclical public works were explored by Otto T. Mallery, "The Long-Range Planning of Public Works," pp. 231 ff.

[28] Foster and Catchings, "Better Jobs and More of Them," *Century*, Vol. 118 (1929), pp. 277–83. This article was published in the July 1929 issue. During the 1920's Foster and Catchings had written extensively on economic subjects. The great need of the times, in their opinion, was improved balance in the economy. A balanced economy implied something more than well-balanced production. The

To Foster and Catchings, the destruction of purchasing power as the deflationary process continued through 1931 and 1932 was a tragedy of the first magnitude. The depression and the severe deflation of the credit and price structures, in their judgment, were not the consequences of inevitable and uncontrollable forces. Rather they were man-made; in large degree they were attributable to erroneous policies and faulty economics. In the spring of 1932 Foster stated:

> We must conquer the depression by collective action. This necessarily means the leadership of the Federal Government—the only agency which represents all of us; the only agency with power enough to use our resources. We must abandon our policy of defeatism, our worship of the budget, our false economy programs, our complete reliance on individual initiative. Instead, we must collectively put into use enough currency and credit to restore the commodity price level of 1928.

This "degree of counter-deflation," Foster believed, would have a widespread restorative effect on the economy; "in one process, we could increase the national debt and reduce the *burden* of the debt."[29]

Increases in expenditures designed to cope with the depression coupled with heavy taxation were condemned as idle gestures during the hearings and debates that preceded enactment of the Revenue Act of 1932.[30] The validity of heavy taxes under conditions of extreme depression was sharply

---

key to a prosperous economy, they emphasized, was sustained consumption at a level high enough to absorb the output of consumer goods. Underlying much of their argument was the assumption of optimum levels of consumption and saving. The economy could not be counted on to function continuously at or near peak efficiency, however, even though the relation between consumption and total income approximated the ideal. Upward and downward movements could not be prevented entirely, and they tended to become cumulative. Public works programs were needed to maintain balance. Their principal works were *Money* (1923); *Profits* (1925); *Business Without a Buyer* (1927); and *The Road to Plenty* (1928). "Foster and Catchings had in some respects the most striking insights of any American economists of the decade. . . . *The Road to Plenty* was a triumph of seductive explanation." Arthur M. Schlesinger, Jr., *The Crisis of the Old Order: 1919–1933* (1957), p. 134.

[29] Foster, Address at a special meeting of the Taylor Society, *American City*, Vol. 46 (June 1932), p. 51.

[30] See, for example, the statement by Representative John W. Flannagan, *Congressional Digest*, Vol. 11 (1932), p. 141.

questioned. There "is a limit to the burdens that taxpayers can endure without endangering the private industry and the country's economic structure. Government ought not to exceed that limit nor make the burden of taxation actually oppressive."[31] The budget deficits, it was emphasized, were an inadequate point of departure for determining additional tax requirements. Expenditures for 1932 included $500 million for the capital stock of the Reconstruction Finance Corporation and $125 million for additional capital stock of the federal land banks. Moreover, in the early 1930's the expenditure totals used in computing the official deficits included statutory debt retirements; for 1932 these amounted to $413 million.

The need for more spending was stressed in the spring of 1932 by Sumner Slichter, Professor of Business Economics at Harvard University. He stated categorically that

... the way to reduce taxes is to revive business. ... One need not be a student of economics to understand that we shall never again regain prosperity by spending less and less. Prosperity can be restored only by spending more. And in this spending more, must not the government do its share and, indeed, take the lead? Surely it is far better able to risk an increase in expenditures than are most individuals and business enterprises.[32]

The argument for a balanced budget, Slichter pointed out, asserts that a revival of business depends on easy money and a revival of confidence, which in turn depends in large degree on a balanced budget. Living within one's income is the test of balance. He favored giving the public a balanced budget "in the sense that all current expenses are paid out of current receipts." But in his opinion there was no logic whatever in trying to balance a budget that included public works and other capital outlays, large investments in capital stock of the Reconstruction Finance Corporation and the like, and

[31] Statement by H. T. Newcomb, Vice President of the Delaware and Hudson Railroad Co., *ibid.*, p. 143.
[32] Slichter, "Shall the Budget Be Balanced?" *New Republic*, Vol. 70 (1932), p. 262.

statutory public debt retirements. The pronouncements of
public officials who insisted on the necessity of balancing a
budget that included such items were characterized as
alarmist. Our leaders "by their reckless speeches have fostered a dangerous popular psychology both here and abroad
—a psychology which greatly increases the difficulty of shifting to a sensible fiscal policy."[33]

In similar vein Virgil Jordan, economist for the McGraw-
Hill Publishing Co., asserted: "At this time, above all, when
private spending is at its lowest, is the time to expand public
spending. Just as we saved our way into depression, we must
squander our way out of it." In the same address it was
stated:

No highly developed industrial nation can escape increased public spending as a means of diverting excessive savings from production of competitive products into social services, which not only
expands current purchasing power for products of established private business but raises the general standard of living. Such public
expenditure supported by public credit is especially important in
periods of depression.[34]

The expansion of purchasing power was regarded by Jordan as ample justification for expenditures financed from
loans under conditions of depression. More significant, he
took the position that public spending in excess of revenue
would be permanently necessary in order to prevent money
savings from damming up and destroying the income flows
that are essential for continued prosperity. The view that
more or less continuous public investment was needed to
offset savings in excess of private demand did not gain widespread acceptance until five or six years later.

In the autumn of 1932 Simeon E. Leland, Professor of
Economics at the University of Chicago, stressed the perverse effects of the approach to public budgets then current.

[33] *Ibid.*, pp. 262–64.
[34] Jordan, address at the 1932 annual banquet of the Pennsylvania State Chamber
of Commerce, *American City*, Vol. 46 (June 1932), p. 51.

Some demands for expenditure control are legitimate, but an indiscriminate demand for expenditure reduction also exists. It is directed at the amount of expenditure rather than the services rendered.

The real crisis is whether in its efforts to assist business out of the doldrums government may not adopt policies which will have the opposite tendency and whether the attempts of business to deflate government may not impair the social usefulness of that institution, thus injuring the very parties who are trying to help themselves. The crisis represents a conflict between the social and the individualistic philosophy of government.[35]

In Leland's opinion public expenditure policies, so far as possible, should "be synchronized with economic rhythms." Capital outlays for needed public improvements should be undertaken and "no hesitancy should be shown in borrowing to finance them." Interest rates were low and the purchasing power of the public dollar high, and "every advantage should be taken of these favorable circumstances to secure needed improvements." It was recognized that the credit reserve of some governments had been exhausted, but this was by no means generally true.[36]

The continued emphasis on the annual budget was regarded by Leland as responsible for some of the real and imaginary crises facing government. The task of the finance officer is to bring revenues and expenditures into equilibrium.

It is erroneously conceived that this is the only proper policy year in and year out, regardless of economic conditions. . . . A wise fiscal policy requires not only an annual budget but also a long-term financial program. The latter should take account of the fluctuations of the business cycle and should control the policy of the annual budget. The long-term budget should be balanced with reference to economic periods and the equilibrium between surplus

---

[35] Leland, "How Governments Can Best Meet the Financial Crisis," in The International City Managers' Association, *City Manager Yearbook: 1933*, pp. 105–06. This address was delivered at the convention of the Association in Cincinnati on October 24, 1932.

[36] *Ibid.*, pp. 109–10.

and deficits should be struck over a period of years rather than annually.[37]

This proposal was later amplified and offered for the consideration of the federal government. "It is by no means axiomatic that the federal government should annually collect revenues sufficient to cover even its ordinary operating expenses." Deficits are defensible if in accordance with deliberate and well-designed long-range planning.

The balancing of budgets should be regarded as a series of long-term operations in which deficits will be incurred and debts increased during years of economic adversity while Treasury surpluses and the rapid retirement of the public debt will be planned for during years of prosperity. When a series of annual budgets is thus put together, the result is the balancing of the long-term budget with reference to economic cycle periods. The equilibrium between revenue and expenditures is thus intentionally struck over a period of years rather than annually.[38]

This rationale more than foreshadowed the compensatory fiscal theory. It is in essence the optimistic version of the compensatory doctrine that became popular a few years later.

Writing shortly before the election, Robert Murray Haig deplored the numerous assertions regarding deficits and fiscal soundness that were so widely disseminated. From December to July an apprehensive people had followed closely the struggle to balance the 1933 budget, and during the campaign the state of the finances, economy, and taxation were favorite subjects of partisan oratory. In Haig's opinion two propositions that underlay much of the discussion were es-

[37] *Ibid.*, p. 108.

[38] S. E. Leland and Others, *Balancing the Budget: Federal Fiscal Policy During Depression:* A Statement by a University of Chicago Round Table (January 1933), pp. 10–11. Sixteen suggestions in regard to budget and fiscal policy were offered. The fifth one follows: "We suggest that Congress and the President should adopt the policy of balancing the budget over a period of years, taking account of the swings of the business cycle, rather than attempt to balance each annual budget without reference to the effects of such policy on business and social welfare." The other ten signers included Paul H. Douglas, H. A. Millis, H. C. Simons, and Jacob Viner. Pp. 28–30.

pecially disturbing. First, the federal budget must be balanced forthwith. Second, a balanced budget could be achieved by imposing a sales tax. In his judgment both were debatable.[39]

Haig stressed the fact that the federal accounts were not so arranged as to reflect clearly the financial status of the government. The faults and limitations of the present report, he observed, are those of the cash account book. The "large figure currently quoted as federal deficit is, because of the shortcomings of governmental accounting, seriously misleading and practically worthless as a dependable measure of the true state of the finances." In a pointed challenge to those who regarded a balanced budget as the answer to the depression, Haig suggested that perhaps "no deficit at all now exists in the fundamental economic sense."[40]

The deflationary fiscal policy that seemed to be favored by the Hoover administration and an influential segment of public opinion was sharply questioned by Stuart Chase, a popular writer on economic subjects. Chase prefaced his analysis with the observation that those who had deflated wages were turning their attention to taxes. "It appears that strict economy on the part of the several governments, federal, state and local, and a drastic reduction of the 'crushing burden of taxation' are at once the royal road out of the depression, and a mandatory policy for the future." It is arguable that the wage deflation, "by annihilating a good many billions of purchasing power . . . has carried us appreciably backward. Will a wholesale deflation of government expenditures be any more successful?"[41]

Chase deplored the practice of using large aggregates without considering the nature of the components. He saw no "devastating trend" towards governmental extravagance

[39] Haig, "The State of the Federal Finances," *Yale Review*, New Series, Vol. 22, p. 234.

[40] *Ibid.*, pp. 237 ff.

[41] Chase, "Government Economy: An Impolite Survey," *Scribner's Magazine*, Vol. 92 (1932), p. 321.

and cited figures showing that compared with consumer expenditures taxes had made no appreciable advance. The drive for the deflation of taxes was identified as a phenomenon of the downswing of the cycle. Chase stressed the fact that governmental expenditures, in so far as they put purchasing power into circulation, may be vital not only to society at large, but also to business itself. Under conditions of depression public expenditures may have a balance-wheel function; the deflationists had not looked at them from this standpoint. It was concluded that from "the longer point of view, a programme of rigid government economy may turn out to be a mistake of the first order."[42]

A common feature of the thinking of the economists whose views we have cited was that they found unacceptable the assumptions of the balanced budget rationale, as expounded during the early 1930's. In particular, they questioned the idea that a balanced federal budget achieved through some combination of lower expenditures and higher taxes was essential for the restoration of confidence and a sustained recovery. To them balancing the budget in this manner was deflationary rather than expansionist in tendency. The central issue of fiscal policy was thus sharpened immeasurably. Perhaps their most valuable contribution was that they helped clarify the relation between governmental expenditures and the generation of income. All expenditures for goods and services and cash payments to the public such as relief payments and pensions became some one else's income. Another worthwhile service was that they effectively questioned the validity of the official deficit as a point of departure for the formulation of an appropriate fiscal policy. If there is one aspect of budget and fiscal policy of the early 1930's on which in retrospect all can agree, it is that the prevailing method of computing the deficit was conducive to exaggeration of the seriousness of the budget situation.

[42] *Ibid.*, pp. 322 ff.

The Budget As An Election Issue

Well before the nominating conventions it was apparent
that the state of the federal finances would be an issue in the
1932 election. On the basis of accepted standards the party
in power was clearly vulnerable. The budget had not been
brought into balance, and there seemed little likelihood that
a marked improvement in the fiscal situation would be
achieved during the summer and early autumn.

The need for a balanced federal budget continued to be
stressed as the presidential campaign gained momentum. On
September 10 President Hoover called for a reduction in expenditures of $500 million for the fiscal year 1934. This goal
for the budget then in preparation was said to be desirable not
merely for its own sake, but also because it would ease the
burden of taxes. A few days later the President called for
economies through the reorganization, consolidation, and re-
grouping of federal agencies and activities. The soldiers'
bonus agitation was the occasion for special concern; advance payment of the adjusted service certificates would add
more than $2 billion to expenditures and throw the budget
hopelessly out of balance. Mainly for this reason the President believed payment of the bonus would be a fatal threat
to the recovery program.[43]

Official demands for lower federal expenditures were
strongly seconded by private groups and individual citizens.
Prominent among the organizations concerned about the
federal budget was the National Economy League. Approximately six weeks before the election the League urged the
establishment of economy groups throughout the nation.
The initial objective would be to "force" a reduction of $452
million in federal expenditures.[44] A week later, the chairman

---

[43] New York Times (Sept. 11, 1932), p. 1; (Sept. 14, 1932), p. 6; (Sept. 15, 1932),
p. 1.
[44] Statement by Archibald Roosevelt, Secretary, National Economy League, ibid.
(Sept. 22, 1932), p. 3.

of the executive committee forecast that the National Economy League would have five to ten million voters as members and "organized like a national political party."[45] Speaking in New York before starting on a national tour in behalf of this program, the League's chairman warned of the need to organize to cut the burden of government waste. "Dangerous taxation affects every group and every class. The poor are often more disastrously affected than the well-to-do."[46]

Though the need for lower federal expenditures was stressed, the primary goal was a balanced federal budget. This objective required that unusual expenditures such as prepayment of the soldiers' bonus be avoided. Perhaps more important, it was deemed necessary that the relief problem be handled by private agencies and local and state governments. The official view was that private agencies should first do all they could, and that the federal government should not participate directly in the financing of relief.[47] In any case, this seemed to be the philosophy underlying the President's statement at the welfare and relief mobilization conference held in Washington in mid-September. On this occasion the President emphasized the responsibilities of local governments and the states during the coming winter, which he hoped would be "the last Winter of this great calamity." Any direct federal financing of relief that might be proposed would presumably have been regarded as objectionable, for the reason that it would constitute "cold and distant charity."[48]

[45] Address by Grenville Clark, *ibid.* (Sept. 30, 1932), p. 3.

[46] Address by Admiral Richard E. Byrd, *ibid.* (Oct. 4, 1932), p. 23.

[47] Following a discussion of how various groups were affected by the depression, Denis W. Brogan observes: "Against this background of differential suffering, it was hard to take calmly the refusal of the Federal Government to help alleviate such widespread misery. True, the Reconstruction Finance Corporation was authorized to lend money to states and other governmental units for relief work, but President Hoover stood firmly by the doctrine of local responsibility for relief, regardless of the insolvency of many cities and counties, of the reluctance of bankers to lend, and the frequent constitutional impotence of local governments to borrow." *The Era of Franklin D. Roosevelt* (1950), p. 14.

[48] *New York Times* (Sept. 16, 1932), pp. 1, 14. In a radio address a few days later Senator Simeon Fess of Ohio commended the "titanic struggle" of the President to

The attitude of the administration toward the financing of relief and other ameliorative expenditures was doubtless influenced by the view that federal activities and costs had been seriously overexpanded. In the opinion of one spokesman for business, too much spending—public and private—was the dominant cause of the depression.[49] An influential member of Congress equated the upward trend in public expenditures with socialism. "Unless the tide of increasing public expenditures begins to ebb, this Nation, originally dedicated to individualism, will increasingly become a socialistic state."[50] According to the most extreme interpretations, of which *The Federal Octopus* was typical, federal activities and expenditures had expanded to a point where the economy had been ruined by bureaucratic domination.[51]

Throughout the early years of the depression, it was frequently asserted that heavy or excessive tax burdens were a major reason for, if not the sole cause of, the unsatisfactory economic situation. As the depression deepened, the obvious remedy—according to this view—was to reduce taxes. This theme continued to be fairly prominent as the 1932 presi-

---

prevent "a dole system." The President's efforts "should be met with the profound gratitude of every citizen who respects the character and strength of our system of government." *Ibid.* (Sept. 20, 1932), p. 3.

[49] Statements by Magnus W. Alexander, President, the National Industrial Conference Board, *New York Times* (Sept. 3, 1931), p. 42; (April 16, 1932), p. 2. In the private sector Mr. Alexander emphasized overspending for capital outlays. In his judgment the need for governmental economies was especially urgent at the state and local levels.

[50] James M. Beck, *Our Wonderland of Bureaucracy* (1932), p. 85.

[51] Sterling E. Edmunds, *The Federal Octopus* (1932). The subtitle of this publication follows: "A Survey of the Destruction of Constitutional Government and of Civil and Economic Liberty in the United States and the Rise of an All-Embracing Federal Bureaucratic Despotism." In support of the "bureaucratic despotism" thesis, Mr. Edmunds pointed out that under the influence of the Agricultural Extension Service a large number of 4-H clubs had been established and more than 750,000 rural youths had been "enrolled as wards of the federal government. If Congress will furnish the money—and that is what the Department of Agriculture is striving for—the ten million or more rural children not yet enrolled will be similarly reduced to federal wardship." Pp. 2–3. Mr. Edmunds was a St. Louis attorney.

dential election approached.[52] However, tax reduction was
not generally regarded as an independent objective. A balanced budget achieved primarily through rigorous expenditure control was the primary goal.[53]

If the foregoing discussion mirrors the climate of opinion
with reasonable accuracy, the tack on the fiscal problem the
party seeking control of the government might be expected
to take becomes more or less obvious. The logical strategy for
the Democratic party was to assure the electorate that, if
granted the opportunity, it would soon place the finances of
the federal government on an even keel. Nevertheless, the
severity with which the incumbent administration was ac-
cused of mishandling the nation's finances was quite un-
expected.

In his major fiscal address delivered at Pittsburgh, Franklin D. Roosevelt indicted the Hoover administration "for
wrong action, for delayed action, for lack of frankness and
for lack of courage." It was clear that in the existing situation federal, state, and local expenditures must be reduced in
the interest of the nation as a whole. But federal expenditures
had actually been increasing; routine federal expenditures or
expenditures other than for debt service had increased by a
billion dollars from 1927 to 1931.[54]

The one sound foundation of permanent economic recov-

[52] Returning from a tour of over half the states, Major-General John F. O'Ryan
reported that he had found much suffering and blamed over-taxation for the
country's economic ills. *New York Times* (Sept. 10, 1932), p. 2. In the same vein,
John W. Davis asserted that taxes must be reduced and that all business would collapse unless the burden were lessened. "The present situation cannot continue";
taxes have become "prohibitive." *Ibid.* (Sept. 20, 1932), p. 3. A few weeks later Robert
R. McCormick, publisher of the *Chicago Tribune*, attacked public spending in a
radio address for the American Taxpayers' League. In his opinion the depression
had a single cause—high taxes. *Ibid.* (Oct. 9, 1932), sec. 1, p. 25.

[53] It was widely believed that a reasonable approach to public finance required
that state and local budgets also be balanced. For example, in a radio address
delivered early in October 1932, Nicholas Murray Butler stated: "We must insist
from this time that every public budget be balanced." *Ibid.* (Oct. 9, 1932), sec. 8,
p. 2.

[54] *Public Papers and Addresses of Franklin D. Roosevelt*, Vol. 1 (1938), pp. 789, 799,
804.

ery—a complete and honest balancing of the federal budget
—was lacking. In Roosevelt's opinion the problem was one
of making both ends meet, as in household finance. Prodi-
gality and extravagance, however, are especially dangerous
in the case of the federal government. Federal financial stability is basic to the stability of trade and employment, and
of the entire banking, savings, and insurance system. The
credit structure is impaired by the unorthodox financing
made necessary by the unprecedented magnitude of recent
federal deficits.[55]

On the basis of the deficit for the first quarter (July–September 1932), Roosevelt estimated that the deficit for the
fiscal year 1933 would be over $1.6 billion—"a deficit so
great that it makes us catch our breath." The appeal of the
Hoover administration "for applause for its soundness and
courage last winter is simply not based on facts. The budget
is not balanced and the whole job must be done over again in
the next session of Congress."[56] There is here more than a
suggestion that those charged with the responsibility lacked
both the ability and the will to place the nation's finances in
proper order.

The party in power defended its record. It did not desire
continued deficits and, for the most part, it did not try to
explain away those incurred in 1931 and 1932. Both parties
were steeped in fiscal orthodoxy, and the record of the Hoover
administration was vulnerable on the basis of traditional
standards. For the period of the campaign the Democratic
party became the self-appointed champion of what was accepted as fiscal conservatism. Its opponents were in effect
requested to defend their record, not because they had spent
too liberally, but because they had played fast and loose with
the nation's credit. Desiring to assume responsibility, the
party seeking control of the government made the most of

[55] *Ibid.*, pp. 796–98, 806–07.
[56] *Ibid.*, p. 805.

the "recklessness" of those who would tolerate continued unbalance in the federal accounts.

The numerous assertions and counterassertions regarding federal finances during the 1932 campaign made no recognizable contribution to fiscal thought. The resort to hyperbole was perhaps no greater than in earlier national elections. The unusual feature was that so large a portion of the preelection pyrotechnics was concerned with finance.[57]

The Interregnum, November 1932–March 1933

The 1934 budget submitted by the Hoover administration about a month after the election confirmed the fact that the budget remained unbalanced. The deficit for 1933 was officially estimated at over $1.1 billion (exclusive of debt retirements) and that for 1934 at more than $300 million. In the President's opinion such a situation could not be continued without disaster to the federal finances. In order to balance the 1934 budget, he recommended a uniform manufacturers' excise on articles other than food to be imposed at a rate of $2\frac{1}{4}$ per cent. He also proposed that the federal tax on gasoline be continued for the fiscal year 1934. The President believed that the additional revenues, together with the "drastic reductions in expenditures" recommended, would be sufficient to balance the accounts for 1934 "only if Congress will refrain from placing additional burdens upon the Federal Treasury."[58] The views expressed by others

[57] Writing during the campaign, Professor Robert M. Haig deplored the numerous assertions regarding deficits and fiscal soundness that were so widely disseminated. "In recent weeks, it has been impossible to page a newspaper or to twirl a radio dial without being assailed by dissertation, invective, and propaganda regarding federal expenditures, deficits, and taxes." "The State of the Federal Finances," *Yale Review*, Vol. 22, New Series, p. 234.

[58] *Message of the President of the United States Transmitting the Budget for the Service of the Fiscal Year Ending June 30, 1934*, pp. VII–VIII, XVII.

prominent in the administration conformed closely with those of the President. Deficits had to be eliminated if financial health was to be regained.[59]

A fiscal policy focused on the single objective of balancing the federal budget continued to be favored by influential segments of public opinion. At a symposium held at New York University in December 1932, a number of speakers took what was then regarded as a conservative view of the federal fiscal problem. Perhaps the most valuable of these addresses was presented by F. S. Baldwin, Director of Research for the National Industrial Conference Board, who endeavored to state the position of industry with respect to the proper scope of governmental activity.

In a paper moderate in tone Baldwin deplored the extremism of certain critics of governmental extravagance. "These critics have themselves been guilty of much extravagance." It is "foolish and futile to declaim about the rising cost of government" as something "entirely unjustifiable and utterly reprehensible and to condemn indiscriminately every increase in total public expenditures as extravagant and wasteful. The cost of government is bound to increase in a dynamic, progressive society."[60]

It was Baldwin's thesis that industry and the business community accepted a reasonable expansion of public activities. But in his analysis of the proper scope of governmental activity, he was unable to depart from traditional conceptions. Public works programs to provide employment and financed by bond issues are ill-advised at a time when the bond market is demoralized by business depression. It is one thing to talk about spending if you have any money to spend, or can borrow it without disastrous consequences. It is quite another thing to urge federal spending from borrowed

---

[59] See, for example, statements by Andrew Mellon and Ogden L. Mills, *Congressional Digest*, Vol. 11 (1933), p. 138.

[60] F. S. Baldwin, "The Viewpoint of Industry," *Current Problems in Public Finance* (1933), p. 25. The quotations from *Current Problems in Public Finance*, copyright 1932, are reprinted by permission of Commerce Clearing House, Inc., Chicago 46, Illinois.

funds that would complicate the problems of economic recovery. Two stock arguments were used to buttress this position: (1) income in private hands is likely to be expended to better advantage than income transferred by taxation to the government; and (2) the advocates of increased spending "ignore the paramount necessity of balancing the federal budget." In Baldwin's opinion, the "menace of a continued federal deficit" remained the greatest obstacle to business recovery.[61]

The need for economy in all public expenditures was stressed on the same occasion by the executive director of the National Economy League. The League, it was said, sees two outstanding features of the federal budget which should compel the early attention of the Congress, one of them good and the other bad. "The good feature is the big slice of pork which the President seeks to cut from the appropriations of public buildings, rivers and harbors and Federal-aid highways. . . . The bad feature is the negligible little whittling which is addressed to the wrongful payment of the people's money to veterans who came out of the war without a scratch or a sickness of any kind."[62]

In retrospect it seems inexplicable that anyone should have referred to federal appropriations for highways and public buildings as "pork" under 1932 conditions. However, economy was the need of the hour, according to one point of view, and all efforts to narrow the range of federal expenditures— by caricature or otherwise—were commendable. Veterans' benefits, especially those not justified by misfortunes while in the service, received the greatest scorn. The fight against such minorities "will be long, and tedious, and tough," but that should not deter us. "Shall the government of the people be for the benefit of all the people, or shall the American democracy be broken down by the pandering to privileged groups?"[63]

[61] *Ibid.*, pp. 30–31.
[62] Charles M. Mills, "The Vital Need for National Economy," *ibid.*, p. 155.
[63] *Ibid.*, pp. 155–57.

In the opinion of the chief of the United States Bureau of Efficiency, the cost of the federal government had reached a point where expenditures must be sharply curtailed. "This can and must be done." Reorganization and consolidation in the administrative departments would be helpful, but substantial reductions would require reductions in other than ordinary civil expenditures.[64] In addition to savings in so-called civil expenditures and those achieved by reorganization and more efficient management, this official recommended a cut of about $400 million in payments to veterans and the reduction of defense expenditures to the 1925 level, which would mean a saving of $94 million. He also proposed that the interest component of the sinking-fund appropriation be eliminated—a reduction in total expenditures of $174 million.[65] The latter saving of course would be purely nominal, especially under deficit financing.

In February 1933 a number of financial leaders testified before the Senate Committee on Finance on cures for the depression. Bernard Baruch stated at these hearings that a balanced federal budget was required if confidence in the nation's credit was to be retained and a serious inflation avoided. In his opinion inflation had been going on for three years on a vast scale, and it could not be continued indefinitely. Of the $5.5 billion increase in the federal debt attributable to depression deficits, $5 billion had been acquired by the Federal Reserve banks and the member banks. Delay in balancing the budget was courting disaster. Inflation, Baruch emphasized, is the enemy of the people. "I regard the condition of this country as the most serious in its history. It is worse than war. In war there is a definite enemy. We know

[64] Herbert D. Brown, "Economy Through Consolidation and Readjustments of Administrative Departments," *ibid.*, p. 145.

[65] Herbert D. Brown, "Government Economies," in *Essentials for Prosperity, Annals of the American Academy of Political and Social Science*, Vol. 165 (January 1933), p. 145. The "interest component," as here used, refers to the second part of the formula for determining the annual credit to the sinking fund. See footnote 8, p. 317.

what and where he is and how to fight him. . . . But this
enemy wears no uniform and takes no position on any
front."[66] The idea that an unbalanced federal budget and
inflation were synonymous continued to be widely held when
the low point in the deflationary process was reached early
in 1933. The contrary view that a degree of inflation or "refla-
tion" was necessary before a balanced budget might again
be possible had not yet gained wide acceptance.

To those who found the balanced budget rationale unacceptable, arguments such as those above were ineffective because they were based on incorrect premises. The assumption
that the extreme depression experienced in 1932–1933 was
an inevitable stage of the business cycle was sharply questioned. "The crisis is not principally cyclical at the present
time. . . . The crisis is composed mainly of straight-ahead
downward movements that have no return ticket attached."
Mistaken and destructive policies were followed during the
early years of the depression, especially in the financing of
relief. Federal expenditures were restricted instead of expanded. "The key to stabilized prosperity is the continuous
distribution of buying power; the key to distribution is the
diversion of money from unnecessary capital investment into
the market for services; the key to an immediate enlargement
of the market for services is the education of public opinion
toward an expanded program of Federal expenditure."[67]

A favorite argument of those who questioned the balanced
budget thesis was that the deficits of the early 1930's were
extremely small, when compared with those incurred during
World War I. It was presented in its most succinct form at
the New York University symposium. "During the war, the
budget was far more seriously unbalanced than it is today.
Nobody then worried about it: the main issue was winning
the War. Today the enemy is not Germany, but starvation.

[66] *New York Times* (Feb. 14, 1933), p. 1; (Feb. 19, 1933), sec. 8, p. 2.
[67] David Cushman Coyle, "The Viewpoint of an Engineer," *Current Problems in Public Finance*, pp. 33, 40.

It is far more important that we should win this war than the other."[68] On the same occasion it was observed: "This is a war, and the proper function of the National Government is to lead us with understanding and courage so that we may have a chance to win."[69]

The budget-cutting and tax-reduction approach to public finance was, in the opinion of one observer, a phase of the general social psychosis of fear and flight from reality that had affected every field of activity and was forcing the whole economic and social system into a retreat. The pressure of the deflation process was partly at fault. A second principal factor was the pressure of insidious propaganda designed to bring about the abolition of governmental agencies and activities. "The idea that taxpayers actually save anything by public economy during a period of general deflation is a delusion." As a start toward a rational approach to public finance,

. . . it is necessary that the economy leagues and other organizations interested in problems of public finance try first to clarify their conception of the strategy of attack on governmental extravagance. Let them abandon broadside condemnation of all public spending and blind blanket demands for tax reduction. Let them stop preaching economy in the fields affecting the other fellow's interests and unite to enforce efficient use of public funds in every field.[70]

Critics of the fiscal policies of the administration had lost confidence in the idea that the normal operation of economic forces would bring about a recovery. It was widely believed that, if permitted to follow its relentless course, there was no definable limit to the deflationary spiral. The idea that ultimately we would arrive at "some mysterious automatic equilibrium point" was regarded by those questioning the self-generating theory of recovery as little more than a pious

---

[68] Bruce Bliven, "The Progressive Viewpoint on Federal Expenditures," *ibid.*' p. 136.

[69] Coyle, "The Viewpoint of an Engineer," *ibid.*, p. 40.

[70] Virgil Jordan, "The Public Finance Problem as a General Observer Sees It," *ibid.*, pp. 5 ff.

hope. A fiscal policy that accentuated the deflationary trend was described as "a species of fiscal hysteria" and "a sort of public financial phobia."[71]

The economy was plainly suffering from an extreme dearth of purchasing power in late 1932 and early 1933. Almost every suggestion for dealing with the depression was designed to stimulate spending of one type or another. Yet, as one observer pointed out, "when attention is turned to government, nearly all efforts at present are aimed at restriction of expenditure." We are earnestly trying to force governments to buy less at a time when the great need is for more spending. It is clear from the clash of opinion that "the real difference concerns the question *who shall do the spending* more immediately than the question whether more shall be spent in the aggregate." In the prevailing situation and in the future, the two greatest duties of government "are concerned with the proper distribution of income, and with the enhancement of the income to be distributed, both qualitatively and quantitatively."[72]

The purchasing-power thesis had no stronger adherent than William Trufant Foster. From the beginning of the depression he believed that the government could have controlled the situation. The administration had made one psychological blunder after another. The fear of an unbalanced budget in official circles was in his opinion beyond all reason. To Foster the main reason for the prolonged depression was that consumer purchasing power had been reduced far below that required to sustain the economy. The efforts to balance the budget by means of a sales tax were misguided. "Nothing but an increased volume of consumer buying power can restore prosperity. The sales tax reduces the volume."[73]

[71] *Ibid.*, p. 5.

[72] George Soule, "The Progressive Viewpoint," *ibid.*, pp. 41 ff.

[73] Foster, "When a Horse Balks," *North American Review*, Vol. 234 (1932), pp. 7–9; "Wizards with Bootstraps," *ibid.*, Vol. 235 (1933), p. 367. The latter article was published in April 1933. It was in part a reply to Allen T. Treadway's arguments for a sales tax in the March 1933 issue. These articles were prepared just before and dnring the month in which President Hoover's term of office ended.

On the basis of traditional standards, the federal finances were in an unsatisfactory condition at the close of the Hoover administration. In a little more than two years the federal debt had increased by almost $6 billion. The budget remained out of balance, despite new taxes and higher rates for old taxes. The depression had caused additional demands for expenditures that more than offset the savings from economies in regular expenditures. In the opinion of leading public officials and influential citizens, this situation had to be corrected or dire consequences would ensue. From the vantage point of 1958, the importance then attached to balancing the federal budget may seem excessive. But there is one fact no objective analyst can ignore. The balanced budget rationale had been accepted doctrine from the beginning of the nation. In their appeals for a balanced budget, the President, other public officials, and private citizens were following the accepted principles of their times—the only principles then widely recognized and supported.

As inauguration day approached, those who favored substantial drafts on the federal credit for the purpose of overcoming the depression were in the minority. The thesis that an unbalanced federal budget should be accepted as an anti-deflation measure was contrary to tradition. Economists and others who advocated a positive federal program emphasized that a policy of drift might be disastrous; a reversal of the downward trend might never occur as a consequence of a favorable convergence of forces making for recovery. They, too, were acting in accordance with what they considered to be the welfare of the nation. The idea that in a period of economic adversity and large-scale unemployment there are more fundamental considerations than a balanced federal budget was in the ascendency.

CHAPTER V

The Emergence of Fiscal Policy: The Roosevelt Era

THE IMMEDIATE PROBLEM confronting the Roosevelt administration in the spring of 1933 was how to provide for relief and other emergency needs. The longer-range goal was a sustained recovery that would be followed by a period of prosperity. If at times the policies designed to achieve these objectives seemed inconsistent, it was perhaps understandable. Never before had the federal government assumed major responsibility for turning a depression into recovery and prosperity. The idea that the federal government should play a positive role in the economy had not yet gained wide acceptance. Letting go of conceptions that had enjoyed official and public approval for well over a century was not an easy matter.

Changing Focus of Budget Policy

The vigorous fiscal action presaged by the 1932 presidential campaign was not long in making its appearance. On March 10, 1933, just six days after the inauguration, the President sent a message to the Congress requesting economies in the federal pay roll and in veterans' pensions and

allowances. A major justification for this request was that
the budget remained out of balance. The combined deficits
for the four-year period ending June 30, 1934 were estimated
at $5 billion. The President summarized his views concern-
ing the deficit in the following language:

> With the utmost seriousness I point out to the Congress the pro-
> found effect of this fact upon our national economy. It has con-
> tributed to the recent collapse of our banking structure. It has
> accentuated the stagnation of the economic life of our people. It has
> added to the ranks of the unemployed. Our Government's house is
> not in order and for many reasons no effective action has been taken
> to restore it to order.[1]

The Economy Act of March 20, 1933 authorized the reductions in the compensation of federal employees and in
veterans' benefits desired by the administration.[2] In line with
its provisions, a reduction of 15 per cent in the compensation
of employees was made effective as of April 1 by executive
order; the payless furlough plan previously in effect was repealed. Savings under this act were estimated at upwards of
$500 million for a full fiscal year.[3] This large reduction was
justified on three grounds. First, a cut in the ordinary costs
of government was desirable in order that the federal credit
might remain unimpaired. "Too often in recent history
liberal governments have been wrecked on the rocks of loose
fiscal policy." Second, if appropriate economies were made
there was a reasonable prospect that within a year federal
income and expenditures would balance. Third, these economies represented the first step in the fulfillment of the
pledge in the 1932 Democratic platform to reduce federal
costs by not less than one fourth.[4]

---

[1] *Public Papers and Addresses of Franklin D. Roosevelt*, Vol. 2 (1938), p. 49.
[2] 48 Stat. 8.
[3] *New York Times* (March 11, 1933), p. 1; (March 21, 1933), p. 3. As evidence of
his budgetary intentions, the President refunded 15 per cent of his first month's
salary; the law applicable to March 1933 provided for a reduction of only 8⅓ per
cent. *Ibid.* (April 8, 1933), p. 15.
[4] *Public Papers and Addresses of Franklin D. Roosevelt*, Vol. 2, pp. 49–52.

THE FIRST TERM, 1933–1937

In the spring of 1933 it appeared that economy would remain the keynote of fiscal policy. In May the President placed the savings resulting from the Economy Act and other measures at $1 billion; it was estimated that the budget for 1934 was within $120 million of balancing.[5] To those not fully posted on fiscal developments, this seemed an extraordinary achievement. Considered by itself, however, the deficit that had been announced was misleading. Only general expenditures, or less than half of total expenditures, had been taken into account. Though the classifications "general" and "emergency" were not used in the financial statements of the Treasury until July 1, 1933, it had been reported in March that emergency expenditures might run to $8 billion and that they would be financed by long-term borrowings.[6]

Before the inauguration there had not been any suggestion that the proposed economies might be more than offset by emergency expenditures. Perhaps the main reason for the change in policy was that a balanced budget for 1934 did not seem even remotely attainable. Though some expenditures were sharply reduced, the reduction in "general" expenditures was far less than the additional outlays under the recovery program. Another possibility is that the magnitude of the appropriations and authorizations for recovery purposes suggested the desirability of their segregation.[7]

[5] *New York Times* (May 4, 1933), p. 31.

[6] *Ibid.* (March 25, 1933), p. 1. This policy was clearly in mind when Title II of the National Industrial Recovery Act was planned; this act was approved on June 16, 1933. It authorized $3.3 billion for public works, subject to certain allocations for other purposes. At the same time the capital-stock tax, the declared-value excess profits tax, and the excise on dividends were enacted and the rate on gasoline increased in order to provide the necessary funds to service the increase in indebtedness. Receipts from these taxes were not specifically earmarked for debt service. 48 Stat. 200, 206–10.

[7] J. W. Sundelson, "The Emergency Budget of the Federal Government," *American Economic Review*, Vol. 24 (1934), p. 61.

The Roosevelt administration was clearly committed to two opposing budget policies—contraction and expansion. The former was followed vigorously in the case of general expenditures. On the other hand, the expansionist theory, which "proposes the use of public credit to increase expenditures for capital improvements and to aid in the planned extension of private production," was accepted only with respect to emergency expenditures.[8] This dual budget system was a new phenomenon in our fiscal annals. A principal justification was that it was possible to show approximately the extent to which federal expenditures were an outgrowth of the depression.[9] A major objection was that it suggested a qualitative differentiation that often seemed more apparent than real.[10] No consistent theory of public expenditure was applied.[11]

When the revised budget estimates were announced in January 1934, expenditures for the fiscal year 1934 were placed at $10.5 billion and the deficit at $7.3 billion, as shown in the table on page 179.[12] These figures were above expecta-

[8] A. E. Buck, "Public Budgeting," *The Nation*, Vol. 139 (1934), p. 472.

[9] In the fireside chat of July 24, 1933 the President stated: "It may seem inconsistent for a government to cut down its regular expenses and at the same time to borrow and spend billions for an emergency. But it is not inconsistent because a large portion of the emergency money has been paid out in the form of sound loans which will be repaid to the Treasury over a period of years; and to cover the rest of the emergency money we have imposed taxes to pay the interest and the installments on that part of the debt." *Public Papers and Addresses of Franklin D. Roosevelt*, Vol. 2, p. 296.

[10] Curtailment of the regular or established activities of government while emergency or make-work projects were undertaken at times seemed lacking in justification. For example, the Bureau of the Census sharply curtailed its work on the annual compilations of financial statistics of states and cities at the same time that an extensive study of property tax delinquency, among other emergency projects, was being developed.

[11] Referring to the dual budget policy of 1933–1934, Paul A. Samuelson states: "Two pools of money with widely different net utilities at the margin violates all rational principles of allocation." "Principles and Rules in Modern Fiscal Policy: A Neo-Classical Reformulation," in *Money, Trade, and Economic Growth: In Honor of John Henry Williams* (1951), p. 169.

[12] The figure of $10.5 billion, which excludes debt retirements, is about $1.2 billion larger than the total shown in the detailed tables in the 1935 budget. It includes "additional expenditures which will be made out of additional authorizations and appropriations here recommended."

tions. The large excess of expenditures over revenues, the President stated, "has been rendered necessary to bring the country to a sound condition after the unexampled crisis which we encountered last spring. It is a large amount, but the immeasurable benefits justify the cost."[13]

The tone of this budget message (January 3, 1934) was decidedly optimistic. The "results of expenditures already

Estimated and Actual Budget Expenditures and Deficits
Fiscal Years 1934–1937[a]

(In millions of dollars)

Fiscal Year	Expenditures			Deficit		
	Initial Estimate	Revised Estimate	Actual	Initial Estimate	Revised Estimate	Actual
1934............	3,202	10,500	6,694	494	7,309	3,630
1935............	5,903	7,940	6,521	1,986	4,297	2,791
1936............	7,819	7,046	8,494	3,892	2,683	4,425
1937............	6,123[b]	7,803	7,756	518	2,248	2,777

[a] Estimated expenditures and deficits computed from data in the federal budget. Figures for completed years from *Annual Report of the Secretary of the Treasury on the State of the Finances for the Fiscal Year Ended June 30, 1956*, p. 323; the figures in the Treasury Department's historical series do not correspond precisely with those for completed years derived from the federal budget. Expenditures exclude tax refunds and transfers to the old-age reserve account and the railroad retirement account.
[b] Does not include work relief except for expenditures covered from unexpended balances.

made show themselves in concrete form in better prices for farm commodities, in renewed business activity, in increased employment, in reopening of and restored confidence in banks, and in well-organized relief." The size of relief and other emergency expenditures did not dampen the President's optimism. In his opinion powerful forces for recovery existed. "It is by laying a foundation of confidence in the

[13] *Message of the President of the United States Transmitting the Budget for the Service of the Fiscal Year Ending June 30, 1935*, pp. VIII–IX.

present and faith in the future that the upturn which we
have so far seen will become cumulative. The cornerstone of
this foundation is the good credit of the government." The
proper course was to "plan to have a definitely balanced
budget for the third year of recovery and from that time on
seek a continuing reduction of the national debt."[14] These
observations suggest that the President was thinking in terms
of a broad recovery policy based mainly on the federal
credit.[15]

When the emergency program was announced, there was
reason to doubt that expenditures for the fiscal year 1934
would reach the $10 billion level. The Civil Works Adminis-
tration program had been improvised, mainly because of the
slowness with which the public works program authorized
the previous June was getting under way. It seemed improbable, however, that this program would bring federal
expenditures to a much higher level. When the figures for
the completed year became available, expenditures for 1934
were $6.7 billion or almost $4 billion less than the revised
estimate released in January. Expenditures were closer to
the original 1934 estimate submitted by President Hoover
than to the revised figure announced one year later by the
new administration.

The budget message of January 3, 1935 was less optimistic
than the preceding one. Despite the substantial measure of
recovery, unemployment was still large, and the federal
government was financing a large proportion of relief costs.
For this reason "we have not yet reached a point at which a
complete balance of the Budget can be obtained." Instead of
"a definitely balanced budget for the third year of recovery,"

[14] *Ibid.*, pp. v, viii, xi.

[15] Despite the large estimated deficits caused by emergency expenditures, the
President held to the view that the federal credit had been strengthened by the reduction in regular or ordinary expenditures. In the annual message submitted the
same day as the 1935 budget he stated: The "credit of the Government has been
fortified by drastic reduction in the cost of its permanent agencies through the
Economy Act." *Public Papers and Addresses of Franklin D. Roosevelt*, Vol. 3 (1938),
p. 9.

the stated goal a year earlier, the objective should be to cover all expenditures from current receipts, "except for expenditures to give work to the unemployed."[16] Expenditures and the deficit for 1935, as estimated in this budget, are shown in the table on page 179.

Renewed confidence in the recovery program was expressed in the next budget message (January 3, 1936). It is "a cause for congratulation within our own Nation to realize that a consistent, broad national policy, adopted nearly three years ago by the Congress and the President, has thus far moved steadily, effectively, and successfully toward its objective." There is no doubt concerning the "fundamental soundness" of the policy adopted in 1933. "Our policy is succeeding. The figures prove it. Secure in the knowledge that steadily decreasing deficits will turn in time into steadily increasing surpluses, and that it is the deficit of today which is making possible the surplus of tomorrow, let us pursue the course that we have mapped." The President reported that the revised estimates for the fiscal year 1936 indicated that "the results with respect to both expenditures and receipts have surpassed expectations." Expenditures for 1936 were revised downward—from $7.8 billion to $7 billion.[17] The budget for 1937 was reported in balance, except for recovery and relief.[18]

[16] *Budget of the United States Government for the Fiscal Year Ending June 30, 1936*, p. x. When the accounts for the fiscal year 1935 became available, expenditures were only $6.5 billion. For the second straight year the original estimate released approximately six months before the beginning of the fiscal year was closer to actual expenditures than the revised estimate released one year later, or at the middle of the year to which the figures relate.

[17] Because of the Adjusted Compensation Payment Act (49 Stat. 1099) approved in January 1936, expenditures for the year were well above the revised estimate. Actual expenditures were $8.4 billion, of which $1.7 billion or one fifth was accounted for by the soldiers' bonus legislation.

[18] *Budget of the United States Government for the Fiscal Year Ending June 30, 1937*, pp. v–ix. Expenditures for the fiscal year 1937 were initially estimated at $6.1 billion. This estimate, however, could scarcely be considered adequate, since provision was not made for work relief in excess of unexpended balances of about $1.1 billion. When the budget for 1938 was released, expenditures for the full year 1937 were placed at $7.8 billion—including work relief. See the table on p. 179.

Confidence in the eventual success of the recovery program was again expressed in the budget message of January 5, 1937.

The programs inaugurated during the last four years to combat the depression and to initiate many needed reforms have cost large sums of money, but the benefits obtained from them are far outweighing all their costs. We shall soon be reaping the full benefits of those programs and shall have at the same time a balanced budget that will also include provision for reduction of the public debt.[19]

This statement contrasts rather sharply with the first budget message submitted by President Roosevelt, which promised a balanced budget in the third year of recovery. A fully balanced budget was now assured only in the indefinite but apparently not-too-distant future.

The foregoing analysis indicates that a balanced budget was abandoned as a short-run objective during the early days of the Roosevelt administration. Restoring the economy, which above all else required a reduction in unemployment to a reasonable minimum, became a primary objective of public policy. Since this goal and a balanced budget were apparently irreconcilable, the proper course seemed to be to accept an unbalanced budget and make substantial drafts on the federal credit. In accepting an unbalanced budget for a period of years the administration was breaking with tradition; yet the break was by no means complete. Every effort was made to leave the impression that long-range fiscal policy would remain firmly anchored to the balanced budget.

The deficits of the early Roosevelt years were not planned deficits. At no time was it decided to incur a deficit of a given magnitude and adjust specific programs with a view to achieving the proposed deficit. Rather, the deficits were a reflection of the fiscal impact of a wide variety of policies that had as

[19] *Budget of the United States Government for the Fiscal Year Ending June 30, 1938*, p. v.

their common goal the financing of relief and recovery needs. Since the budget was far out of balance in March 1933, the question whether the Roosevelt administration deliberately unbalanced the budget is largely academic. The main difference between the administration and the preceding one was that during the Hoover years an annually balanced federal budget never lost caste as a policy objective. The Roosevelt administration, on the other hand, was not many weeks old before it became clear that short-run adherence to the balanced budget formula was no longer an element of policy.

Though the budget messages and other pronouncements exuded optimism, they frequently seemed lacking in assurance. The promise of a balanced budget in the future at times seemed to receive greater emphasis than the benefits flowing from federal expenditures in the present. An important contributory factor was that no one seemed to have a clear idea of the amount of federal spending or deficit financing needed in order to produce the desired stimulus.[20] Improvisation and trial-and-error were the order of the day. It was never claimed that the relief and recovery program, as it evolved in 1933–1934, was geared to the needs of the economy.[21]

When the recession of 1937–1938 set in, it appeared to many that emergency federal spending for relief and recovery purposes would not in itself restore the economy to a going-concern basis. The extraordinary sharpness of the decline, together with the fact that the recession occurred before any part of the debt incurred had been retired, was accepted by the balanced budget adherents as proof that the expectation that federal spending might make a major contribution to

[20] In June 1934 J. M. Keynes suggested that loan-financed federal expenditures of $400 million per month were desirable. (See p. 206). There is no reason to believe that the idea that the federal government should strive to increase the deficit to a specified average figure received more than perfunctory consideration at the highest official level.

[21] The early months of the Roosevelt administration have been aptly described as "crisis government." Edward A. Williams, *Federal Aid for Relief* (1939), p. 58.

recovery was little more than a pious hope. The preceding recovery seemed to many to lack a sound foundation. To exponents of the public-spending approach to recovery this view was unacceptable. They emphasized the unusual conditions that had prevailed during the period 1933–1937. Whether public spending could serve as an offset for the dearth in private spending had neither been proved nor disproved.[22] According to this view, it was hazardous to reduce sharply the federal "net contribution to purchasing power" while trying to bring the budget into balance, unless there was assurance that other spending—preferably private capital expenditures—would take up the slack.[23]

THE YEARS 1938–1940

When economic conditions remained unsatisfactory during the autumn and early winter of 1937–1938, it soon became apparent that the federal government would endeavor to mitigate the harsher effects of the recession. A broad expenditure program focused largely on work relief was officially forecast at the turn of the year 1938. In the budget

[22] E. Cary Brown concludes that fiscal policy "seems to have been an unsuccessful recovery device in the thirties—not because it did not work, but because it was not tried." He found that in the calendar years 1930 through 1937, the "direct effects on aggregate full-employment demand of the fiscal policy undertaken by all three levels of government" was clearly relatively stronger than in 1929 in only the two years—1931 and 1936—when large payments were made under the veterans adjusted compensation programs. "Fiscal Policy in the Thirties: A Reappraisal," *American Economic Review*, Vol. 46 (1956), pp. 863–66.

[23] The federal "net contribution to purchasing power" declined sharply before the recession set in. Federal cash outgo was actually less than cash income for the nine months July 1937–March 1938. For the July–September 1937 quarter the excess of cash income was $58 million; for the October–December quarter outgo exceeded income by $32 million; and for the January–March 1938 period cash income exceeded outgo by $130 million. Computed from data in *Bulletin of the Treasury Department*.

The difference between budget expenditures and cash expenditures did not become important until the 1930's. In recent years cash expenditures have exceeded budget expenditures by a wide margin. The difference between the administrative budget and the cash or cash-consolidated budget is explained in the Appendix. See p. 322.

message of January 3 the President stated that if the economic
situation did not improve "I expect the .approval of Congress and the public for additional appropriations if they become necessary to save thousands of American families from
dire need."[24] In the annual message submitted the same day
the President said that he was "as anxious as any banker or
industrialist or business man or investor or economist that
the budget . . . be brought into balance as quickly as possible." But the times imposed certain priorities; in particular,
the needy must be cared for through work relief programs.[25]

An extensive work relief and public works program in line
with the January forecast was announced on April 14. In a
special message to the Congress the President proposed three
groups of measures to "help to start an upward spiral." The
first consisted of appropriations for the "maintenance of
relief." The largest item in this category was a recommendation of $1,250 million for the Works Progress Administra-
tion, to be used during the seven months beginning July 1,
1938; other appropriations in this group totaled $300 million.
The second group of measures related to the expansion of
credit. Additional bank resources would be made available
through the de-sterilization of about $1.4 billion of Treasury
gold and a reduction of member-bank reserve requirements
by some $750 million. The third proposal related "solely to
definite additions to the purchasing power of the Nation by
providing new work." Total expenditures from the Treasury
for work, including maintenance of relief and new work, were
placed at $2,062 million. In addition, $950 million would be
available on a loan basis through the Public Works Administration, the Farm Security Administration, and the United
States Housing Authority.[26]

[24] Budget of the United States Government for the Fiscal Year Ending June 30, 1939,
p. IX.
[25] Public Papers and Addresses of Franklin D. Roosevelt, 1938 Vol. (1941), p. 8.
[26] Ibid., pp. 226–30.

Probably the most important feature of this message was the President's reaffirmation of federal responsibility under adverse economic conditions. "The prosperity of the United States is of necessity a primary concern of Government. Current events, if allowed to run undisturbed, will continue to threaten the security of our people and the stability of our economic life." The economy had operated adversely for half a year and "we owe it to ourselves to turn it in the other direction before the situation becomes more definitely serious." The budget and spending policies of the first term were not rated a failure. The administration, it was asserted, had established reservoirs of credit, put purchasing power in the hands of the consuming public, and secured a more equitable distribution of the national income. "Thus the downward spiral was stopped—and not merely stopped, but started on an upward course—a trend lasting through four years and a half." The national income had increased each year after 1932—including 1937.[27]

The Work Relief and Public Works Appropriation Act of 1938 enacted to carry out the President's recommendations was approved on June 21.[28] Title I appropriated a little over $1.7 billion for the Works Progress Administration and other agencies such as the National Youth Administration and the Farm Security Administration. Title II made available $965 million to the Federal Emergency Administration of Public Works for projects that could be commenced before January 1, 1939 and substantially completed by June 30, 1940.[29]

The net effect of the recession and the legislation enacted to cope with it was to increase both expenditures and the deficits for the next few years. The figures for the fiscal years 1938, 1939, and 1940 are presented in the table on page 187.

[27] *Ibid.*, pp. 221–22.
[28] 52 Stat. 809. No legislation was necessary to implement the measures designed to expand credit.
[29] 52 Stat. 810, 816.

The expenditures shown include work relief and other emergency expenditures financed by later appropriations.[30]

The budget and other messages submitted during the period 1938–1940 suggest that the President and his principal advisers were thinking in terms of an expansionist fiscal policy. In the annual message of January 3, 1938, it was

Estimated and Actual Budget Expenditures and Deficits
Fiscal Years 1938–1940[a]

(*In millions of dollars*)

Fiscal Year	Expenditures			Deficit		
	Initial Estimate	Revised Estimate	Actual	Initial Estimate	Revised Estimate	Actual
1938............	5,164[b]	6,838	6,792	1,537[c]	1,088	1,177
1939............	6,226	8,816	8,858	950	3,972	3,862
1940............	8,240	8,909	9,062	3,326	3,933	3,918

[a] Estimated expenditures and deficits computed from data in the federal budget. Figures for completed years from *Annual Report of the Secretary of the Treasury on the State of the Finances for the Fiscal Year Ended June 30, 1956*, p. 323; the figures in the Treasury Department's historical series do not correspond precisely with those for completed years derived from the federal budget. Expenditures exclude tax refunds and transfers to the federal old-age and survivors trust fund (or old-age reserve account) and the railroad retirement account.

[b] The original budget estimates for 1938 did not include work relief, except for expenditures covered from unexpended balances.

[c] Surplus.

pointed out that one of the essential conditions or priorities was "to raise the purchasing power of the Nation to the point that the taxes on this purchasing power—or, in other words, on the nation's income—will be sufficient to meet the necessary expenditures of the national government." Estimated federal requirements were placed at about $7 billion annually.

[30] See, for example, the discussion of later appropriations in *Public Papers and Addresses of Franklin D. Roosevelt*, 1939 Vol. (1941), pp. 59, 164.

"That sum can be raised and will be cheerfully provided by the American people, if we can increase the Nation's income to a point well beyond the present level." About six weeks later the President stated: "This Administration has from the beginning pursued a policy designed to promote full employment of our human and material resources. That continues to be our policy."[31]

The expansionist theme was reiterated in the next annual message (January 4, 1939). "We suffer from a great unemployment of capital. . . . We want to get enough capital and labor at work to give us a total turnover of business, a total national income, of at least eighty billion dollars a year." At that figure federal revenues "will be sufficient to balance the current level of cash expenditures on the basis of the existing tax structure."[32] The budget message submitted the previous day included a tabulation showing the estimated yield of the existing federal tax structure with the national income at $70 billion, $80 billion, and $90 billion; all three figures were higher than the national income of about $67 billion for the calendar year 1938. The desirability of stimulating the national income was clearly suggested. There was no intimation, however, that the national income would be forced to a high level, regardless of the amount of deficit financing required. Roosevelt merely expressed the hope that in times of prosperity current revenues would provide a surplus which could be "applied against the public debt that the government must incur in lean years."[33]

In the next budget message (January 3, 1940) it was observed that in the early 1930's "fiscal policy was exceedingly simple in theory and extraordinarily disastrous in practice."

[31] *Ibid.*, 1938 Vol., pp. 8, 113.

[32] *Ibid.*, 1939 Vol., p. 8. The President emphasized that "the entire debt of our national economic system, public and private together, is no larger today than it was in 1929, and the interest thereon is far less than it was in 1929."

[33] *Budget of the United States Government for the Fiscal Year Ending June 30, 1940,* pp. VI, XII.

On the other hand, following 1933 the fiscal policy of the government "was more realistically adapted to the needs of the people." The deliberate use of government funds and of government credit, in the opinion of the President, had a profound effect both on government income and on private incomes. The experience of 1938–1939 "should remove any doubt as to the effectiveness of a fiscal policy related to economic need." But at this point the following observation was added: "The wise exercise of such a fiscal policy imposes grave responsibility on the Government. Government must have the wisdom to use its credit to sustain economic activity in periods of economic recession and the courage to withhold it and retire debt in periods of economic prosperity."[34]

The above analysis suggests that the administration never lost confidence in the belief that the work relief and other emergency programs financed with borrowed funds would have a beneficial effect on the national income. In the second inaugural address (January 20, 1937) the President had stated that we had "sensed the truth that democratic government has innate capacity to protect its people against disasters once considered inevitable, to solve problems once considered unsolvable. We would not admit that we could not solve economic epidemics. . . . We refused to leave the problems of our common welfare to be solved by the winds of chance and the hurricanes of disaster."[35] The recession of 1937–1938 brought no change in this philosophy. On numerous occasions the President stated that government was responsible for providing for the unemployed and the needy. At the same time, it was held that these and other governmental expenditures would contribute to rising income levels and increases in private employment.

[34] *Budget of the United States Government for the Fiscal Year Ending June 30, 1941.* pp. V–VII.

[35] *Public Papers and Addresses of Franklin D. Roosevelt,* 1937 Vol. (1941), p. 1.

The Search for a New Budget Theory

The frank admission during the first year of the Roosevelt administration that deficits would be incurred for at least several years required no little courage. Because of the scope of the relief problem and the unsatisfactory condition of the finances of numerous state and local governments, some federal borrowing to meet urgent needs found general acceptance. But the idea that a broad-gauged program based on a liberal use of the federal credit would restore the economy to a going-concern basis ran directly counter to accepted thought. To influential sectors of the electorate, an annually balanced federal budget was an article of faith fortified by long experience—one not to be taken lightly. In 1932 spokesmen for both major political parties had claimed that a balanced federal budget was a prime essential for recovery and prosperity. Recovery was being delayed, it was then argued, because of the abandonment of the canons of orthodox finance, among which a balanced budget was paramount. If the opposite view—that an unbalanced budget was a necessity—were to be acceptable, it could not be justified solely on the ground of expediency. A convincing theory or rationale was needed.

THE WAR ANALOGY

The analogy between depression financing and war finance, which had been drawn during 1932 by various observers, continued to be offered in support of deficit finance. In his first inaugural address, Roosevelt stated that if the Congress did not take appropriate action he would ask for "broad Executive power to wage a war against the emergency, as great as the power that would be given to me if we were in fact invaded by a foreign foe."[36] On several occasions the President

[36] *Ibid.*, Vol. 2, p. 15.

expressed the view that peacetime emergency costs were to be funded, as was our war outlay.[37] The inference was that the depression should be recognized as a serious emergency, which if not akin to war, at least justified recourse to the federal credit.

Prominent members of the administration employed the war analogy. Toward the end of 1933 a leading advocate of spending for recovery asserted that "5 billions of dollars is not a great price to pay for recovery. We cheerfully and without criticism raised some 20 billions of dollars in two years to fight a war in 1917–1918, and no one ever questioned its repayment."[38] In like vein, another official said: "The money expended in these great constructive efforts is, of course, far less than the cost of one year of participation in the World War with its vast destruction of life and property. It has been a small price to pay for a great gain."[39] A former Under Secretary of State pointed out early in 1934 that the total cost of the "war against the depression" will be $15 billion, an amount well below the $25 billion cost of the great war.[40]

The war analogy also enjoyed a degree of popularity in the Congress. For example, the Chairman of the House Committee on Appropriations pointed out that the cost of World War I had been $23.4 billion, after deducting loans to allied governments and ordinary peacetime expenses. The great depression should also be treated as a serious emergency. "We are engaged in a different kind of war at this time, but one just as important to the people of this nation. If the cost

[37] Sundelson, "The Emergency Budget of the Federal Government," *American Economic Review*, Vol. 24, p. 59.

[38] Rexford G. Tugwell, "How Shall We Pay for All This," *American Magazine*, Vol. 116 (1933), p. 87.

[39] Statement by Donald Richberg, quoted from Raymond Clapper, "Paying the New Deal Bill," *Review of Reviews*, Vol. 90 (October 1934), p. 33.

[40] Statement by Raymond Moley, *New York Times* (Jan. 6, 1934), p. 8. Referring to deficit spending, Mr. Moley continued: "It will leave us with new roads, bridges, forests, housing, and other substantial evidences of national wealth. It will stimulate normal private enterprise and expenditures which will take up the slack. These are material results." Mr. Moley resigned as Under Secretary in September 1933.

of defeating this depression should approximate one fourth our cost of the World War, it would be money well expended. A new United States will emerge from this era, one with greater hope, greater opportunity, greater vision, and a greater soul."[41]

The war analogy was not offered as a theory of deficit finance. Considered by itself, it was scarcely an adequate rationalization of deficit spending. It was in fact little more than an effort to dramatize a difficult situation. Viewed in this light, the war analogy was not without justification. Certainly at no time during World War I were the finances of state and local governments in anything like their condition in 1933. The point brought home by this analogy was that the depression had assumed proportions so serious that the full financial resources of the federal government were required. As in wartime, the federal credit was too valuable and powerful a weapon "to be idly cast aside."[42]

THE PUMP-PRIMING THEORY

The pump-priming theory was the first advanced in support of the the federal deficits incurred during the depression. The key thought suggested by pump priming is that a program of public spending will get the economy off the dead center of a depression and stimulate revival and recovery. There is the implication that "a certain volume of public spending, varying under different conditions, will have the effect of setting the economy going on the way toward full utilization of resources on its own power, without further aid from governmental spending."[43] The pump-priming idea was

[41] Statement by James P. Buchanan, *Review of Reviews*, Vol. 90 (October 1934), p. 33. The analogy between war and the depression was criticized by opponents of deficit spending. See, for example, Dan T. Smith, *Deficits and Depressions* (1936), p. 85; Lewis W. Douglas, "The Danger of Mounting Deficits," *Atlantic Monthly*, Vol. 156 (1935), p. 566.

[42] "Credit is too powerful a war weapon to be idly cast aside." C. C. Plehn, *Introduction to Public Finance* (1920), p. 405.

[43] Alvin H. Hansen, *Fiscal Policy and Business Cycles* (1941), p. 262.

clearly in the minds of Foster and Catchings, Slichter, and other economists who had advocated a positive federal program during the Hoover years. The stimulation of consumer purchasing power through loan-financed public expenditures, it will be recalled, was a basic element in the approach of the leading critics of the Hoover budget policies.[44]

In discussions of pump priming the emergency expenditures were usually assumed to be loan-financed. But this is not the most vital element of the theory. The basic requirement is that the funds used be derived from inactive sources—that they do not represent a subtraction from active purchasing power. In most circumstances, loan-financed expenditures meet this requirement in greater degree and are more expansionist in tendency than those financed by any other means.

The stimulative effect on national income will ordinarily be greater than the priming expenditures, because of the multiplier principle. In the early 1930's the induced income effect was usually assumed to be two or more times the original expenditure.[45] This multiplying effect is a consequence of expenditures by later recipients of the funds injected into the purchasing-power stream. A multiplier of two or slightly

[44] See pp. 153 ff. Throughout the 1920's Foster and Catchings, among others, had emphasized the compensatory role of expenditures for public works. When the national income sank (they would prefer "was permitted to sink") to the low levels of 1932–1933, their proposals for dealing with the situation then confronting the nation were more nearly akin to pump priming than to compensatory spending.

[45] The multiplier principle may be stated as the principle that an initial addition to expenditure will generate an increase in total expenditure and income greater than itself because it will induce increases in expenditures by its recipients, which in turn will induce increases in expenditures by their recipients, and so on in an infinite but diminishing series. Thus, suppose that in a recession the federal government employs a number of available unemployed persons on a public works project which is financed from borrowings. The typical person who thus obtains employment we shall assume is paid $60 per week, of which $45 is spent for consumer goods and services and $15 is saved. In turn, if those who receive the $45 maintain the same proportion between spending and saving, they will account for additional consumer purchases of $33.75. Applying the same proportion at the next two stages, the additions to consumption become $25.31 and $18.98. Since $123.04 (45+33.75+25.31 +18.98) is slightly over 2 times the initial expenditure of $60, a multiplier of 2 plus is obtained when only the first four stages are considered.

more makes allowance for substantial leakages, or funds held or withdrawn from active purchasing power and not directed toward consumption.[46]

The pump-priming analogy suggests that if the priming operation is properly done, further doses of stimulative expenditures will not be necessary—at least until a similar situation arises in the future. However, the theory as it evolved during the 1930's did not assume that the priming expenditures would be limited to a brief period of a few weeks or a month. Discussions of pump priming uniformly assumed that the initial expenditure would be a continuing stream extending over successive income periods. The higher level of total public and private spending thus attained, it was believed, would in time become self-perpetuating as a consequence of the stimulative effect of emergency public spending on the economy.

The pump-priming theory assumes that recovery will be hastened and that production will increase because resources that are unused will be brought into use by increased governmental expenditures. It further assumes that recovery or prosperity will continue after the priming expenditures have ceased; private spending will continue to rise or remain high on its own power. The emergency expenditure is not viewed as permanent or continuing or as needed indefinitely to offset subnormal expenditures in other areas.

The pump-priming theory does not provide specifically for the retirement of the debt incurred while the pump is being primed. In a nation that had long looked with favor on a policy of rapid reduction of public debt, a theory of deficit finance would be more palatable if some reference were

[46] The development of multiplier theory stems from an article by R. F. Kahn, "The Relation of Home Investment to Unemployment," *Economic Journal*, Vol. 41 (1931), pp. 173 ff. A detailed discussion and elaboration of the multiplier principle is that of J. M. Keynes, *The General Theory of Employment, Interest and Money* (1936), Chapter 10. A less technical discussion will be found in Hansen, *Fiscal Policy and Business Cycles*, Chapter 12.

made to the retirement of the debt incurred in connection with the priming program. Perhaps with this in mind, President Roosevelt stated in his first budget message that after the third year of recovery the government should seek "a continuing reduction of the national debt." Other officials were more definite as to how the debt incurred to prime the pump would be handled. For example, it was said that the "country as a whole will pay its debts out of the profits it will make by spending now the money it is borrowing."[47] Replying to an inquiry as to whether emergency relief expenses could be paid off in taxes before another depression, the administrator of the relief program said: "Certainly, and a whole lot more will be taken care of."[48] These observations suggest that official thought in regard to deficit spending was veering away from pump priming in the literal sense and in the direction of compensatory fiscal action.[49]

COMPENSATORY FISCAL THEORY

The principle of compensatory fiscal action is that in formulating governmental expenditure and tax policies, attention shall be given primarily to the economic situation and existing trends. In contrast with pump priming, which is a temporary expedient, compensatory fiscal theory stresses that the guiding consideration *at all times* shall be the state of the economy. If private spending—individual and busi-

[47] Rexford G. Tugwell, "How Shall We Pay for All This?" *American Magazine*, Vol. 116 (December 1933), pp. 11 ff. Mr. Tugwell continued: "If we can spend 5 billions of dollars and make our economic machine operate so that we can turn our national income back toward 80 billions a year, instead of 40, the costs will be more than offset; our nation will profit 40 billions a year."

[48] Statement by Harry Hopkins, quoted from Raymond Clapper, "Paying the New Deal Bill," *Review of Reviews*, Vol. 90 (October 1934), p. 33. Mr. Hopkins further observed that "taxes on real estate are stiff, but income taxes are light comparatively. We do not know what real heavy taxation is."

[49] In the early Roosevelt years the distinction between pump priming and compensatory fiscal action was less sharply drawn than in later years. A clear-cut differentiation will be found in Hansen, *Fiscal Policy and Business Cycles*, pp. 261–64.

ness—declines, public spending should be increased or taxes reduced with a view to stimulating private expenditures. In some situations both facets of the compensatory policy—increased expenditures and lower taxes—might be applied simultaneously. The converse of course is that public expenditures should be reduced or taxes increased (or both) as the volume of private spending increases.

The basic idea underlying the compensatory fiscal doctrine is considerably older than the theory itself. All earlier proposals for expanding public works in periods of economic adversity were based on the compensatory principle. From one viewpoint, the compensatory theory as it evolved during the 1930's may be regarded as a logical extension of the ideas embraced in the countercyclical public works proposals and programs of preceding decades.[50] A more accurate statement is that compensatory fiscal theory resulted from the coming together of a number of strands of thought. Prominent among these are the principle of the multiplier, which had been clearly presented by R. F. Kahn in 1931.[51] The ideas in his famous article were a major influence in the development of Keynesian theory.[52] The development of Keynes' theoretical structure, as is pointed out later, was an essential step in the process by which the compensatory fiscal doctrine became a part of accepted thought.[53] A third strand is the idea that borrowing by the central government to meet emergency needs other than those incident to war is entirely justified. Historically, this view is probably as old as government itself. It figured prominently in the German literature of the

[50] See Otto T. Mallery, "The Long-Range Planning of Public Works," in *Business Cycles and Unemployment* (1923), pp. 231 ff.

[51] Kahn, "The Relation of Home Investment to Unemployment," *Economic Journal*, Vol. 41, pp. 173 ff. See p. 193 of this study.

[52] "The ideas in this article had a crucial influence on Keynes' subsequent thinking." The close relationship of Kahn and Keynes during the early 1930's was an important factor in the evolution of Keynesian theory. R. A. Harrod, *Life of John Maynard Keynes* (1951), pp. 434, 451.

[53] See pp. 207 ff.

late nineteenth century. In this country it gained a number of adherents during the Hoover administration.[54]

In the context of the 1930's leading exponents of the compensatory fiscal theory placed major emphasis on the compensating effects of public expenditures in excess of revenues. Compensatory fiscal action was viewed as embracing deficit spending, which would be tapered off during the upswing, combined with a policy of retiring during prosperity the debt thus incurred. Compensatory theory was frequently couched in narrower terms. The central idea was that public expenditures should be increased in order to compensate for the dearth of private investment, which was widely regarded as the one factor most responsible for prolonging the depression. Money savings of the community that were not flowing into customary investment outlets were at the heart of the problem. The compensatory fiscal theory in effect proposed that loan-financed public expenditures be used to absorb, or serve as an offset for, these money savings.

Perhaps the best statement of how governmental spending and taxing policies should be used to maintain economic balance was that of Marriner Eccles, Chairman of the Board of Governors of the Federal Reserve System:

Fiscal policy may be directed not only toward moderating and off-setting a decline in general business activity but also toward moderating the rate of expansion. Just as an excess of federal expenditures over tax collections tends to increase incomes, enables banks to expand their investments, and, in so far as it results in the creation of new deposits, produces new buying power, so, contrariwise, an excess of tax collections over expenditures tends to

[54] Writing in 1934, Walter Lippmann pointed out that the compensated economy is "a conception which is not spun out of abstract theory. It is rather an induction from many experiments actually undertaken." The oldest example of the method, according to Lippmann, is to be found in the operation of a highly developed central bank which is supposed to contract credit when member banks show a tendency to over-expand credit, and to make credit abundant when they are making it scarce. *The Method of Freedom* (1934), p. 51. From this viewpoint, the development of the compensatory fiscal rationale is an extension from monetary theory.

restrain the growth of spending and to offset the expansion of private bank credit. Hence a full acceptance of the compensatory fiscal policy implies a willingness to run counter to private business behavior not only on the downswing but also on the upswing.[55]

Large governmental expenditures during the depression were favored by Eccles, but in the spring of 1937 he advocated debt reduction. Both attitudes, he observed, are part and parcel of the same principle of compensatory action. Though he believed the changed business picture then called for a different policy, both policies were designed to achieve a common end—moderating and offsetting the effects of fluctuations in private business activity. Surveying the economic scene, it was concluded that some time in 1936 or early 1937 increased private expenditures in the production of durable goods became the factor of major importance, and at this point recovery became self-generating and proceeded under its own momentum.[56]

The excerpt from Eccles' article suggests that compensatory fiscal action may be appropriately viewed as a device for keeping the economy on an even keel. The compensatory theory presupposes prompt and continuous fiscal action as the state of the economy may require. In brief, public spending and taxation should be so adjusted as to prevent a recession from becoming a severe depression, and conversely to slow down a boom that might threaten the continuance of prosperity. Under the most optimistic version of the theory, the debt incurred during revival and recovery would be paid off during the ensuing period of prosperity. The budget would be balanced over a complete business cycle.

The theory just outlined is properly described as optimistic. It assumes that when increases in public spending or tax reductions become necessary, the appropriate amounts are readily determinable. Conversely, when a reversal of policy

[55] Marriner S. Eccles, "Controlling Booms and Depressions," *Fortune*, Vol. 15 (April 1937), p. 88d.
[56] *Ibid.*, pp. 88c–88d.

is called for, the theory assumes that public spending can be tapered off or taxes increased as may be required. Critics of the compensatory fiscal theory have taken the position that from a practical standpoint these assumptions were unwarranted. The recession of 1937–1938, it was claimed, afforded ample proof that the federal government could not manage a program of deficit financing in such a manner that private investment could be stimulated to a level where the deficit could be eliminated, with recovery continuing under its own momentum. Though the administration appeared to take the opposite tack, the issue was never sharply joined. A variant of the compensatory theory—one more pessimistic in outlook—was presently advanced and became the center of discussion.

The pessimistic version of the compensatory theory assumes that private demands for capital are unable to absorb all the savings generated by the economy. Government, it is said, must *permanently* take up the slack by spending in excess of its income.[57] In contrast with the Eccles version, it is not assumed that—as a consequence of public spending—private investment will be raised to a point where deficit financing can be suspended, with the retirement of the debt previously incurred following more or less automatically. The emphasis is "not on stimulating private investment, temporarily depressed, but on compensating for the lack of it."[58] Under conditions such as those prevailing in 1937–1938, deficit financing should be undertaken in substantial volume until approximately full employment is attained. When this goal is

---

[57] As here used, *permanently* does not imply that government must spend in excess of its income in every month or year. Though the tendency toward stagnation was usually assumed to be strong, some fiscal theorists held that it might be possible occasionally to get along for short periods without the benefit of deficit financing. An occasional balanced budget would have the effect of making the upward trend in the public debt less steep than it otherwise would be; the long-run trend would never be completely flattened out or reversed.

[58] John H. Williams, "Deficit Spending," *American Economic Review*, Supplement, Vol. 30 (1941), p. 58.

reached, the amount of public expenditure in excess of revenues (net public investment) should be whatever is necessary to maintain employment and the utilization of resources at high levels.

The tendency of the economy to generate savings in excess of private investment and hence the need for more or less continuous public investment, according to the theory, is a consequence of factors such as (1) shrinkages in private demand for capital; and (2) the fact that economies such as that of the United States tend to develop a large and increasing flow of current saving at levels of income corresponding to full employment. Shrinkages in private demands for capital, it is claimed, are a direct outgrowth of economic maturity and secular stagnation, phenomena attributable primarily to the decline in the rate of population growth and the end of the extensive frontier. The dearth of important new industries during the 1930's was a major reason for the low private demand for capital. In earlier periods the railroad, automobile, and electrical industries, among others, provided outlets for large amounts of capital. For the future the development of new industries would continue to be of first-rate importance. But the rise of new industries does not occur at a uniform pace; rather, it tends to be discontinuous and jerky. The stimulus of technology—both of the new product and cost-reducing varieties—on investment would have to be sufficient to compensate for the decline in the rate of population growth and the passing of the extensive frontier.[59] A related development is the tendency of relatively mature enterprises to finance their capital needs from earned depreciation and obsolescence allowances. The consequence is that it would become increasingly necessary for government to take an active part in directing the flow of saving into investment channels.

Most advocates of the compensatory or deficit finance ap-

---

[59] Hansen, *Fiscal Policy and Business Cycles*, pp. 362–64.

proach to the economic problem stressed investments in public works, such as roads, dams, water-power projects, public buildings, and housing developments.[60] But this is not the most basic aspect of the theory. The primary objective is to offset saving in excess of private investment at full employment with net governmental borrowings of comparable amount. The theory assumes that with appropriate deficits a growth trend for the economy can be maintained with the labor force approximately fully employed. The deficits would of course decline in size when private investment was rising; occasional surpluses might occur when full employment was attained temporarily on the basis of private demand.

Though the great depression was the principal manifestation of converging forces making for stagnation, in the opinion of the leading exponents of the compensatory doctrine the conditions calling for deficit spending did not develop during the 1930's. Some of the forces making for secular stagnation, it was claimed, began to develop toward the end of the nineteenth century. Because of the paucity of outlets for savings and the declining rate of population growth, it was asserted that the problem of secular stagnation may well overshadow that of the business cycle. Against this background, governmental expenditures take on a new significance. "From being purely a cyclical compensatory device, designed to stimulate consumption, public expenditures may come to be used increasingly as a means of directing the flow of savings into real investment."[61]

Acceptance of this philosophy presupposes a willingness to assign a broader economic role to government, together with

---

[60] One well-known author stated that public works may be broadly interpreted to include "not only physical things that are built, but also services rendered in the public interest and administered by the government." Stuart Chase, *Goals for America: A Budget of Our Needs and Resources* (1942), p. 101. Services mentioned by Mr. Chase include a program for adult education, a federal arts project, dental clinics, and research projects.

[61] Alvin H. Hansen, "The Consequences of Reducing Expenditures," *Proceedings of the Academy of Political Science*, Vol. 17 (January 1938), p. 72; *Full Recovery and Stagnation* (1938), pp. 288–89.

greater responsibilities than were previously assumed. A group of Harvard and Tufts economists stated the matter in these terms: "The government must assume responsibility for maintaining the national income at a sufficiently high level to assure full and effective utilization of our human and material resources if needless hardship and suffering are to be averted. . . . The notion that public spending can safely be resorted to only as a temporary, emergency device must be abandoned. A program must be developed which recognizes the necessity for permanent public investment."[62]

The authors of this statement based the case for continued deficit financing firmly on the existence of secular stagnation. Writing in 1938, they divided the economic history of the United States into two periods. The first period was one of economic expansion; it began with the colonization of the eastern seaboard shortly after 1600 and "came to a dramatic close with the collapse of 1929." The second period, dating from 1929 or 1930, "has so far been one of economic stagnation."[63]

Leading advocates of the deficit finance or public investment approach to economic stability took the position that it may be desirable to extend the economic area controlled by the state. For example, it was said that "a dual economy in which railroads and public utilities operate under state enterprise, leaving trade, manufacturing, and finance under private management, would offer certain advantages from the standpoint of stability and full employment of resources." With this division, perhaps one third of the total national income "would spring from governmental expenditures," which can be regularized much more readily than expenditures by private competitive business.[64]

The significance of the new rationale could scarcely be

[62] Richard V. Gilbert and Others, *An Economic Program for American Democracy* (1938), p. 40.

[63] *Ibid.*, p. 15.

[64] Hansen, *Fiscal Policy and Business Cycles*, p. 404.

overemphasized. Up to 1937 it had been assumed that the economic problem was essentially a cyclical problem. According to the later version of the compensatory theory that emphasized the continuing role of public investment, this view was erroneous. The problem was basically a secular one. From the standpoint of the public credit and debt management, the difference between the two explanations of the need for deficit financing is of great importance. The former implies that there will be little, if any, long-run increase in the public debt. The public investment offset to secular stagnation presupposes a continuous upward trend in public debt. The secular upward trend, however, would not necessarily mean a rise in the debt burden. The growth in debt resulting from more or less continuous deficits might conceivably be at a slower rate than the rise in the national income; constant interest rates are assumed.[65]

The compensatory fiscal theory as outlined above was not regarded as satisfactory by all the economists who believed that fiscal policy could play a major role in bringing about economic recovery and stability. Though this theory set forth the principles by which appropriate governmental action can maintain prosperity, there was a tendency—intentional or otherwise—to compromise with orthodox ideas in economics and finance. Any attempt to force the principles of deficit spending into the old framework was said to be necessarily awkward and undesirable. The pure theory of deficit spending, it was asserted, should be based on the idea of functional finance, which is described as the "principle of judging fiscal measures by the way they work or function in the economy."[66]

The first financial responsibility of the government, ac-

[65] Evsey D. Domar, "The 'Burden of the Debt' and the National Income," *American Economic Review*, Vol. 34 (1944), pp. 798ff.

[66] Abba P. Lerner, "Functional Finance and the Federal Debt," *Social Research*, Vol. 10 (February 1943), p. 39. The article in which functional finance was first expounded appeared more than a year after the entry of the United States into World War II.

cording to functional finance, is to keep the total rate of spending on goods and services at the rate which will buy the maximum that can be produced at current prices. Taxing is never to be undertaken merely because the government needs to make money payments, but only when it is necessary to reduce private spending. There are just two main effects of taxation: the taxpayer has less money to spend and the government has more. Since the second effect can be brought about much more easily by printing the money, only the first one is important. Government should borrow only when it is desirable that the public should have less money and more government bonds. "When taxing, spending, borrowing and lending (or repaying loans) are governed by the principles of Functional Finance, any excess of money outlays over money revenues, if it cannot be met out of money hoards, must be met by printing new money, and any excess of revenues over outlays can be destroyed or used to replenish hoards." The sole consideration guiding fiscal policy and decisions concerning spending and taxing shall be "the results . . . on the economy."[67]

Fiscal Theory and Economic Theory

The compensatory theory in its several variants provided theoretical support for the deficits incurred by the Roosevelt administration. It also bolstered the reasoning of those economists who during the Hoover administration took the position that an unbalanced budget should be accepted.[68] On the other hand, this theory was unsatisfactory to those imbued with the idea that the economy was self-regulating. From the viewpoint of traditional economics, the appropriate

[67] *Ibid.*, pp. 39–41. See also Lerner, *Economics of Control* (1944), pp. 302 ff.
[68] See pp. 153 ff.

policy was to see that conditions conducive to a full recovery through the operation of "natural" economic forces were established. A depression—no matter how severe—was merely a transitory phenomenon.

In the early years of the depression only a small minority of economists held rigidly to the belief that reliance for recovery should be placed solely on the operation of the forces on which the consistency of the classical theory depends. The idea of countercyclical public works had long since attained respectability and more adherents were gained as the depression deepened. The near collapse of the economy, together with the apparent inability to achieve a recovery, led to no little soul-searching. Answers to policy questions based on the assumption that a tendency toward equilibrium at full employment was operative and that the economy would soon be going forward at full vigor were unconvincing. Yet there was no alternative body of economic theory that might be helpful as a guide to policy.

How in fact does the economy operate? Are there weak links in the theory which points to equilibrium at full employment as the norm? Has something disrupted the automaticity of the economic process implicit in traditional theory? If the annually balanced budget formula should be discarded, is the traditional approach to recovery vulnerable in other respects? The intellectual ferment of the times cast up questions such as these, and economists were trying to find the answers.

As is often the case, practice preceded theory. The intervention by the Hoover administration—the lending operations of the Reconstruction Finance Corporation and the like —was equivalent to recognition that reliance could not be placed solely on "natural" economic forces. In proposing much higher federal expenditures and substantial borrowings for 1934 and 1935, Roosevelt was in effect repudiating the traditional approach that emphasized economy in federal expenditures and a balanced budget as prime essentials for re-

vival and recovery. The President and other high officials
hoped that the unemployment problem would be solved
mainly by a strong business recovery. But no one was able
to foresee clearly how or when the "normal" forces making
for recovery would appear.

When J. M. Keynes proposed in June 1934 that federal
expenditures from borrowed funds in the amount of $400
million monthly were needed to speed recovery, no attempt
was made to reconcile this proposal with accepted economic
theory. It was merely asserted that large-scale loan-financed
federal spending was necessary, pending a return of business
confidence. Three questions were raised by Keynes: "How
soon will normal business enterprise come to the rescue?
What measures can be taken to hasten the return of normal
enterprise? On what scale, by which expedients and for how
long is abnormal government expenditure advisable in the
meantime?"[69] The first two questions suggested that for the
long run major reliance should be placed on private enterprise for the generation of income and substantially full
employment. The third question assumed that large federal
expenditures were desirable as long as the depression continued.

To Keynes and others who favored increased public spending, traditional theory that started from the side of production and posited a complete system with little or no analysis
of aggregate consumption was obviously inadequate. By
1933–1934 it was quite apparent that the purchasing power
or consuming power essential for its operation had been cut
from under the economy. Both consumer and business spending had been reduced to levels at which the tendency toward
equilibrium, if any, appeared to be toward one far short of
full employment. Keynes' policy recommendations of June
1934 showed the direction of his thinking. His theory of

[69] *New York Times* (June 10, 1934), sec. 4, pp. 1, 6.

how the economy operates was being perfected in this period, and he was lecturing on it at Cambridge University.[70]

The General Theory of Employment, Interest and Money published in 1936 presented this theory.[71] Economists were provided with a more realistic theory of effective demand that allowed for and explained the possibility that involuntary unemployment could persist without setting in motion forces that would restore full employment. The key role of investment in determining the level of total income and output, and therefore—in the short run—of employment, was delineated. There were numerous new insights concerning the parts played by money and interest. Perhaps most important, *The General Theory* provided a new rationale that caused economists to re-examine accepted doctrines and their underlying premises. From the standpoint of the present study, the vital feature of Keynes' work is that it compelled economists of varying persuasions to reconsider their preconceptions concerning the role of public expenditures and governmental activities in the economy.

The General Theory represented a new and refreshing approach to the economic process. The emphasis is on the level of aggregate expenditure, or effective demand, which is the source of income and determines the volume of output and employment. A decline in demand means a decline in income. The fundamental economic problem is to maintain income at a level that will ensure full or high utilization of resources. Since income is derived from demand, it is necessary to examine the components of a country's aggregate demand if one is to understand how the economy operates. They are:

[70] "By the end of 1934 the first draft of *The General Theory of Employment, Interest and Money* was complete. The following year was spent in revision and the conduct of correspondence with commentators." Harrod, *Life of John Maynard Keynes*, p. 451.

[71] In the discussion that follows no attempt is made to present a complete résumé of Keynesian theory. The sole purpose is to show the relationship between Keynes' theory and the fiscal theories considered in the preceding section.

(1) consumers' demand for goods and services; (2) the demand of government and public agencies for goods and services; (3) private investment—the demand for new capital goods, including additions to inventories; and (4) the "net foreign balance"; that is, the net excess of exports over imports of goods and services.[72] A first requirement for policy is to watch these components, for a decline in any one will cause a fall in aggregate demand and income—unless it is offset by increases in one or more of the other components.

The approach to the operation of the economy from the side of effective demand or expenditure was a revolutionary development. In making the theory of effective demand a principal element in the formulation of his theoretical system, Keynes was striking indirectly at one of the weakest links in traditional economics.[73] What he was saying was that aggregate effective demand determines not only the volume of output or the volume of goods and services produced, but also—given the state of technology and capital development —employment. In Keynesian economics aggregate supply and demand may be in equilibrium at outputs that yield less than full employment. Keynes held that aggregate demand is partly independent of aggregate supply. This was tantamount to a repudiation of Say's law, which asserts that aggregate supply and aggregate demand are necessarily equal

---

[72] International transactions must be taken into account, since exports are not in the first three categories (but are reflected in domestic income and employment), and some of the expenditures in these categories are for imports that are not reflected in domestic income and employment. It is customary to allow for the latter fact by deducting imports from exports and taking into account only the net effect of international transactions on domestic income and employment.

[73] "The Principle of Effective Demand" is discussed in Chapter 3 of *The General Theory of Employment, Interest and Money*, pp. 23 ff. The first chapter is a one-page statement concerning *The General Theory* and the direction of the argument, and Chapter 2 is concerned with "The Postulates of the Classical Economics." The classical economists, as mentioned previously, regarded full-employment equilibrium as the normal situation in the economy; any departure from this norm brought forces into play that tended to restore it. See p. 53. In sharp contrast, Keynes regarded full employment as a special case; his analysis led to the conclusion that there may be any number of equilibrium positions, of which only one corresponded with the norm stressed by the classicists.

at all levels of employment and therefore that output will tend to be at a full-employment level.

In Keynesian economics income is the primary determinant of consumption. In contrast, the neoclassical economists made aggregate consumption a function of the interest rate in a highly developed theory of interest and saving. A rise in the rate of interest, it was reasoned, made saving more attractive and increased the proportion of income that was saved, thereby reducing consumption in relation to income. Conversely, a decline in the rate of interest was reflected in lower saving and a rise in consumption. Adjustments of savings and investment were therefore brought about by movements of the interest rate rather than by changes in income. Long before *The General Theory* the idea that interest rates and saving always moved in the same direction had come to be regarded as unrealistic. Keynes not only denied the validity of this view and the theory of consumption that it implied; he developed entirely new theories of interest and consumption.[74]

In the Keynesian system total income equals the sum of private consumption expenditures, private investment, government expenditure, and the export surplus. Consumption demand depends on the level of income. Keynes assumed that, given the tax structure, the functional relation between consumption and income, which he called the "propensity to consume," is relatively stable over short periods; that is, that private consumption varies in a regular manner with income.[75] He further assumed that this variation is of such a nature that when income changes, consump-

[74] Fifty years before Keynes' *General Theory* was published, Simon N. Patten stated that "correct ideas about the consumption of wealth are a necessary factor in the solution of any economic problem." "The Effect of the Consumption of Wealth on the Economic Welfare of Society," *Science Economic Discussion* (1886), p. 123.

[75] Keynes, *The General Theory of Employment, Interest and Money*, pp. 63, 89 ff. The propensity to consume may be viewed in either aggregate or individual terms. Viewed in aggregate terms, consumption depends on the amount of aggregate income after taxes, and on its distribution among individuals with different propensities to consume.

tion changes in the same direction but by a smaller amount.

By investment expenditure Keynes meant purchases of real capital goods. The level of private investment is determined by the relationship between expected net returns from additional capital goods and interest rates. Leaving aside the factors influencing these two determinants of investment, it is clear that if the national income at full employment consists of goods and services worth $400 billion, and if at this level of national income $300 billion is spent on consumption, the output at full employment can be sold as long as the level of investment and government expenditure is maintained at $100 billion. Under these conditions, there is a market for $400 billion worth of goods and services.[76]

If, however, the expected profitability of investment declines so that investment falls by $20 billion, bringing investment plus government expenditure down from $100 billion to $80 billion, the equilibrium level of output must fall below the $400 billion that corresponds to full employment. Moreover, it will fall by more than $20 billion, the amount of the decline in investment. This sharper decline is due to the decline in consumption demand, which is in addition to the fall in investment. With income below $400 billion, the level of consumption will be less than $300 billion. Let us assume that consumption declines by half of the decline in income. With income at $380 billion, consumption will be $10 billion lower or only $290 billion. This amount, together with the $80 billion of investment and government expenditure, will buy only $370 billion of goods and services, leaving $10 billion of output unsold. Output will be further reduced and income will decline further, even if investment plus government expenditure remains at $80 billion. With their sum at $80 billion, income will reach a new equilibrium only when it has declined by $40 billion or to $360 billion.[77] At this point—

---

[76] For the present analysis, the export surplus may conveniently be disregarded. That is, we in effect assume an isolated economy.

[77] At this level consumption expenditure will have declined by $20 billion (one half of the $40 billion decline in income) to a level of $280 billion ($300 billion less

and only at this point—a new equilibrium of income, output, and employment is established. Thus the $20 billion decline of investment expenditure has a multiplied effect on income, causing a decline of $40 billion in national income and a corresponding decline in employment.

Keynes recognized that the decline in income would tend to cause lower interest rates, but he did not believe they would suffice to restore full employment. Even if the decline in income were accompanied by lower interest rates, the change in rates would not offset the expected decline in the profitability of investment and therefore would not restore investment to its original level. In a deteriorating situation Keynes regarded it as far from certain that interest rates would decline, in the absence of aggressive policy measures. In fact, a point might eventually be reached at which even such policy measures could not force interest rates down. In his view interest rates are influenced by the demand for money for all purposes. An increased desire for liquidity in a depression may offset the effect on interest rates of the decline in the demand for money to finance investment and other transactions.[78]

What can be done in such a situation? The decline in income and employment might be halted before it becomes serious if the interest rate can be reduced enough to offset part or all of the decline in private investment demand at the initial rate of interest. This approach has serious limitations, however. In practice it may not be possible to gauge the changes in the profitability of investment (marginal efficiency of capital) in advance and adjust interest rates accordingly. Nor is it possible to foresee all the factors that may affect

---

$20 billion). This amount plus the $80 billion of combined investment and government expenditure will just suffice to permit the sale of $360 billion of goods and services.

[78] This oversimplified account is perhaps sufficient to show that Keynes' theory did not support most of the orthodox remedies for depression, other than measures to reduce interest rates and ease credit conditions. Keynesian analysis suggested that traditional budget policy was perverse in its effects. Efforts to cut government expenditures in order to balance the budget would not only fail to revive private investment but would tend to cause a lower level of income.

business expectations adversely. But the most important factor, according to Keynesian theory, is that there may be a rate level below which interest rates cannot be reduced by an increase in the money supply because of liquidity preference. At this interest rate potential investors will prefer to hold the additional money rather than use it to increase investment.

The remaining means of filling the gap attributable to the decline in private investment is through increased consumption or public expenditure. If aggregate consumption could be increased by the amount by which investment declines, this would fill the gap. Given the level of national income, an increase in consumption might be attained by a tax cut which increases income after taxes at the initial level of national income. The increase in government expenditure may take the form of relief payments or subsidies for current educational purposes, as well as desirable public works. In some circumstances public expenditures might advantageously be increased by the full amount of the desired addition to income. In other instances a reduction in taxes may be preferable; with public expenditures constant the tax reduction would mean increased consumption and would also tend to stimulate private investment. In still others an increase in expenditures combined with a reduction in taxes might be the preferred course.

The link between the compensatory fiscal theory and the "new economics" is thus clearly established. Public spending attained a new respectability. Keynes' theory demonstrated that there is not necessarily a tendency for market forces to restore full employment in a relatively brief period of time. In the absence of governmental action unemployed resources would not be used. It was also shown that the funds used to finance public spending need not be obtained at the expense of funds required to finance private spending. The resources brought into use as a result of additional public spending when there is involuntary unemployment constitute a net addition to resource use and output. It follows that the additional public spending is not wasteful, in the sense of substituting an inferior use of resources for a superior use.

Ideas with respect to fiscal and public expenditure policy not only became a part of economic thought. Keynes' theory supported the view that in certain circumstances an appropriate fiscal policy may be the important factor in achieving or maintaining tolerable levels of income and employment. It provided theoretical support for both variants of the compensatory fiscal theory discussed in the preceding section. It is true that Keynes developed his theory during a world-wide depression, and that he pointed out certain characteristics of maturing economies such as the tendency to generate an increasing volume of saving. But on the question whether the depression was cyclical in nature or a phenomenon attributable mainly to secular stagnation, the theory itself is neutral and impartial.

Keynes' theory had an immediate impact on economic thought. To numerous economists—especially members of the younger generation—who found important elements of traditional doctrine unacceptable, it provided both a rallying ground and a basing point for the analysis of economic problems. The reasons for the great appeal of Keynesian economics have been well stated by J. M. Clark. It "takes hold of the problem which the interwar experience drove home deep in the feelings of mankind as the major sickness of Western economic society, and it does so with an analysis that commands standing as objectively scientific, centering in a formula of the way in which the economic mechanism operates, the analysis being translatable into statistically observable quantities."[79]

Acceptance of Keynes' theory was by no means instantaneous. Some economists found the exposition confusing.

[79] J. M. Clark, *Economic Institutions and Human Welfare* (1957), p. 14.

Others regarded Keynes' theory with skepticism because they felt that the suggested policy tended to establish too strong a presumption in favor of governmental spending. Some economists and numerous other people believed any marked increase in public expenditures would result in a qualitative deterioration of the national income or would be undesirable on social grounds.[80]

Nevertheless, by 1940 there were few economists whose thinking was not influenced in some degree by Keynes' theory of how the economy functions. Literally "hundreds of economists and government policy planners had come . . . to accept the Keynesian analysis as the new orthodoxy."[81] Even those economists who had held that economic theory, at least in its broad outlines, was virtually complete were compelled to re-examine received doctrine and the underlying premises. Though the reactions to Keynes' theory covered the widest possible range, *The General Theory* had not been available for many months before one fact was quite evident. Economics would never be the same again.

The Theories and Budget Policy of the 1930's

At no time during the period 1933–1937 was the compensatory fiscal theory officially accepted as a basis for public policy. Relief and other emergency needs, as previously stated, were the dominant influence during these years. It was the urgency of these needs that compelled the temporary abandonment of the annually balanced budget as a policy goal.

---

[80] At the time *The General Theory* appeared the idea that the private or market sector of the economy supports all public activities financed from revenues other than fees and charges still enjoyed a wide vogue. See, for example, Paul F. Cadman, *National Income and Deficit Financing* (1939), p. 11.

[81] Stephen K. Bailey, *Congress Makes a Law* (1950), p. 20.

They did not lead to the immediate adoption of an alternative theory as a guide for policy. If for no other reason, the reluctance of the administration to accept an alternative theory could be justified on the basis of the maxim that public policy should not run too far ahead of, or diverge too greatly from, public opinion.[82] But there was a more compelling reason. Up to 1937 President Roosevelt himself believed in a balanced budget.[83]

When in 1933–1934 the President and other officials took the position that large-scale loan-financed federal expenditures were required to restore the economy to a sound condition, they were in effect advocating the pump-priming approach to recovery. For the longer run no departure from traditional budget policy was contemplated. It was merely planned to use the federal credit as the cornerstone in laying the foundation for recovery; a "definitely balanced budget for the third year of recovery" was part of the plan. From the standpoint of the pump-priming theory, a period of something like three years was perhaps unduly long for the priming operation. In official circles, however, the emergency program was viewed as a continuing or composite operation and, to this extent, it met the requirements of the theory.

The basic assumption underlying pump priming is that private investment can be stimulated to a point where deficit financing can be discontinued. Bridging the gap between deficit spending and private investment assumes the existence of a resilient economy capable of response to a priming operation. To many thoughtful students it seemed that a basic need was to see that any operational or structural barriers impeding an independent revival of private investment

---

[82] Full and unqualified acceptance of compensatory fiscal theory would have been construed as a revolutionary break with tradition. The public, as pointed out in earlier chapters, had long been accustomed to a purely financial approach to the federal budget. During the 1920's the virtues of the annually balanced budget had been extolled to a greater extent than ever before.

[83] Roy Blough, *The Federal Taxing Process* (1952), pp. 240–42.

were removed or minimized. Little was done in this direction. In the opinion of some observers, the pursuit of conflicting recovery and reform objectives lessened the possibility that the transition from deficit spending to adequate private investment would be achieved.[84]

Two examples will suffice. First, the investigations of investment methods and practices, together with the legislation enacted in 1933 and 1934, unsettled the investment climate.[85] That reforms were necessary is recognized, but it was not so much the reforms as the zeal of the reformers that had an unsettling influence.[86] Second, in formulating tax policy, little or no consideration was given to the impact of the tax structure on investment. Taxes on investment income became heavier than at any time after World War I. Sight was lost of the fact that high income taxes may act as a deterrent to investment—that "taxation, especially taxation of income, shifts the odds against the risk taker."[87]

A certain amount of working at cross purposes was doubtless inevitable, as long as the administration held to the view that recovery and reform could be pursued simultaneously.[88]

[84] "If prosperity is to flourish, people must have confidence in their own economic future and that of their country. This basic truth was temporarily lost sight of during the 1930's in the process of grafting new economic ideas and practices onto the old." Arthur F. Burns, *Prosperity Without Inflation* (1957), p. 27. "After the collapse of 1932–1933 a New Deal of some sort was imperative. But not everything that has been dealt out was imperative. That has depended upon the temperament, the prejudices, the quick judgments of the dealers." Lippmann, *The Method of Freedom*, p. 25.

[85] The reference here is to the Securities Act of 1933 and the Securities Exchange Act of 1934 (48 Stat. 74, 881) and the investigations that preceded their enactment.

[86] For an overseas view, see T. Balogh, "Chaos or Recovery?" *Nineteenth Century and After*, Vol. 114 (1933), pp. 540 ff.

[87] Carl Shoup, Milton Friedman, and Ruth P. Mack, *Taxing to Prevent Inflation* (1943), p. 76. According to one school of thought, taxes were not the major reason private investment remained sluggish during the 1930's. Nearly all sectors of the economy were operating far below capacity. Under these conditions, it was held, little more investment in additional productive capacity than occurred could have been expected without a revival of consumption—irrespective of tax rates and reform measures.

[88] The President did not accept the view that reform should be subordinated to recovery. See, for example, the introduction to *Public Papers and Addresses of Franklin D. Roosevelt*, Vol. 2, pp. 3–10.

That these two goals required radically different approaches was emphasized by J. M. Keynes, among others. "For the first, speed and quick results are essential. The second may be urgent too, but haste will be injurious, and the wisdom of long-range purpose is more necessary than immediate achievement. It will be through raising high the prestige of your administration by success in short-range recovery that you will have the driving force to accomplish long-range reform."[89] This advice was not heeded.

It would be easy to overemphasize the role played by the pump-priming philosophy during Roosevelt's first term. Pump priming "was not one of the principal methods relied on to bring about recovery. Monetary experiments and the controls of production and competition in the NRA and AAA were the major recovery programs."[90] In this sense, pump priming was not even a secondary "method" of bringing about recovery. Realistically viewed, the pump-priming doctrine merely provided theoretical justification for federal expenditures in excess of revenues under adverse economic conditions. The deficits incurred were "more the unintentional results of policies designed to give direct relief to farmers, home owners, business, and unemployed workers, than the conscious aim of a recovery policy through deficit spending."[91]

Prior to the recession of 1937–1938 whatever influence the pump-priming and compensatory fiscal theories may have had on policy was indirect. Though these ideas were advanced in informal discussions, at no time was any group or committee assigned the task of ascertaining how the newer budget theories might be implemented. The most that can be said is that the relief and recovery programs had pump-

---

[89] An Open Letter to the President, *New York Times* (Dec. 31, 1933), sec. 8, p. 2.
[90] Blough, *The Federal Taxing Process*, p. 241.
[91] Gerhard Colm, "Fiscal Policy," in *The New Economics*, Seymour Harris, ed. (1947), p. 451. In Colm's opinion, it "is likely that, without a line written by economists on deficit spending, we would have had the same policy."

priming overtones, and that officially a balanced budget remained the goal of fiscal policy—though a deferred one.

It was not until after the recession of 1937–1938 set in that a comprehensive recovery program was formulated and discussed by a top government committee on monetary and fiscal policy. Referring to the work of this committee, Colm states that its program "was, broadly speaking, in line with Keynes' recommendations for a national investment policy."[92] Members of the committee were well grounded in Keynes' theory and regarded his policy recommendations favorably. In turn, the efforts of the committee strongly influenced the President's message of April 14, 1938.[93]

For the first time, there was a clear affirmation that the federal government should do whatever is necessary to bring the national income to a tolerable level of about $80 billion. It was pointed out that "today's purchasing power—the citizens' income of today—is not sufficient to drive the economic system at higher speed." The President then stated: "Responsibility of government requires us at this time to supplement the normal processes and in so supplementing them to make sure that the addition is adequate."[94]

The idea that the federal government should endeavor to bring the national income to a high level and then do whatever was necessary to maintain a suitable growth trend was not accepted by the Congress. Though the appropriations requested in April 1938 were approved, there is no evidence that the Congress had any real interest in any theory of deficit finance or the new concept of public investment. The combined executive and congressional effort was predicated on the assumption that the unemployment problem was essentially a cyclical problem. It was hoped that in time the economy would go forward without the aid of deficit spending. In

[92] *Ibid.*
[93] See p. 185.
[94] *Public Papers and Addresses of Franklin D. Roosevelt,* 1938 Vol., p. 230.

a sense, this was equivalent to a denial of the validity of the stagnation thesis, which assumed that the problem was primarily a secular one and that deficit finance would be necessary on a continuing basis, except in unusual circumstances.

Only in retrospect is it possible to say that the federal program of 1938–1940 conformed with any theory. Thus viewed, the entire effort might appropriately be classified under pump priming. In taking this position, one author emphasizes both the size of the program and the phraseology of the special message of April 14, 1938.[95] Perhaps the best way of putting the matter is that the program, as proposed in April 1938, was a work relief program with pump-priming and compensatory fiscal overtones. The program in its entirety was justified by the President in the budget messages of January 1939 and January 1940 on the basis of what we have called the optimistic version of the compensatory fiscal theory. It was appraised by some economists who accepted the stagnation thesis and recommended permanent deficit financing (public investment) as a solution.[96] But no one took the position that it represented a full-fledged commitment to incur more or less continuous deficits if they should appear necessary in order to keep the economy operating at or near full employment.

In the period 1938–1940 there was a fairly pronounced upward trend in business activity and income payments. How-

[95] Sherwood M. Fine, *Public Spending and Postwar Economic Policy* (1944), pp. 118–19.

[96] These economists believed there was little hope that private investment could be stimulated and deficit spending discontinued. A "new conception of the problem" was said to be needed. "The government should announce its intention to spend as long and as fast as necessary to get the national income to a satisfactory level, let us say $100 billion as an immediate goal. Then it should announce its intention to keep it there." "Public Spending, Its Tasks and Limits," discussion by Paul Sweezy in *Social Research*, Vol. 6 (1939), pp. 230–31. Though the goal of a $100 billion national income is here described as "an immediate goal," the next sentence suggests a lack of perception of the growth factor. Observations that seemed to assume the economy had lost all capacity for future growth were fairly common during the 1930's.

ever, the large volume of unemployment at the middle of 1940, when the defense program was instituted, indicated that the economic problem was far from solved. To the advocates of compensatory fiscal policy the reason was obvious. As a nation, we had not adopted a real expansionist program.[97] It was because of inadequate public spending that employment and national income remained at unsatisfactory levels. In brief, neither the new aim of fiscal policy—ensuring the full employment of the factors of production—nor Keynesian theory with which it is closely allied had been fully accepted.[98]

The foregoing discussion does not imply that the federal spending programs of the 1930's were not justified. Under the conditions of 1933–1934 and 1937–1938 large-scale relief and recovery expenditures were inevitable.[99] Programs such as those of the Civil Works Administration, the Public Works Administration, and the Works Progress Administration not only mitigated the worst consequences of unemployment; they also had a stimulative effect on the economy. A marked rise in employment occurred during Roosevelt's first term, and again in 1938–1939.[100] Perhaps the only important basis for criticism was that recovery and reform objectives

[97] "It is, it seems, politically impossible for a capitalistic democracy to organize expenditures on the scale necessary to make the grand experiment which would prove my case—except in war conditions." J. M. Keynes, "The United States and the Keynes Plan," *New Republic*, Vol. 103 (1940), p. 158.

[98] Those who criticized federal spending on the ground that it was inadequate perhaps did not give suitable recognition to three factors: (1) the compensatory fiscal theory and Keynes' theory of how the economy operates were comparatively new developments; (2) it requires considerable time for any theory—no matter how convincing—to attain acceptance at the policy-making level; and (3) any theory that becomes the basis for public policy must be implemented in a political environment.

[99] "Regardless of the candidate elected to the Presidency in 1932, an expansionist budgetary policy was inevitable." Fine, *Public Spending and Postwar Economic Policy*, p. 88.

[100] A factor frequently overlooked in discussions of employment and unemployment in the 1930's is the increase in the labor force. Reduction in unemployment to a tolerable level required not only re-employment of those who had lost their jobs, but also finding employment for the annual addition to the labor force.

were pursued at the same time. Though they were a response to the challenge of popular discontent, the reform measures "were not dictated by the emergency and might have been imposed later and in more leisurely fashion."[101]

The Public View on Deficits and Fiscal Policy

In the early 1930's the balanced budget idea remained firmly embedded in the social fabric. For almost a century and a half an annually balanced federal budget had been equated with fiscal solvency and sound finance. In the depth of the depression a majority of citizens who had any interest in governmental finance continued to have an "almost instinctive and intuitive belief in the sanctity of balanced budgets."[102] Whatever direction budget and fiscal policy might take, it was apparent that the balanced budget philosophy would not soon disappear as a social force.

When in the summer and autumn of 1933 it became clear that for a few years no attempt would be made to balance the budget, the reaction was immediate. Senator Dickinson was reflecting an influential segment of public opinion when he said that the government "is overwhelmed with debt." Spending for relief and recovery that resulted in substantial deficits was not an appropriate policy for the times. "Instead of putting our financial house in order, we are facing the

---

[101] Walter Lippmann, "The Permanent New Deal," *Yale Review*, New Series, Vol. 24 (1935), p. 661. In Lippmann's opinion the distinction between recovery and reform should not be too sharply drawn. "In one sense the most radical of all the reforms are these very recovery measures themselves." The "acceptance by the government of responsibility for recovery, and the corollaries," such as the resort to monetary management, the use of government credit, and the expansion of government enterprise "mark great changes in a political system which until 1929 was committed to the general doctrine of *laissez faire*."

[102] Smith, *Deficits and Depressions*, p. 170.

other way by adding billions of debt to the already crushing load." The debt outstanding plus present commitments and authorizations would mean a debt of "approximately $30 billion, a peak of all time, and a load that would break the back of the nation." The proper course is to return to "sane living as a government as well as a people."[103]

A return to normalcy in public finance was urgently required, according to one publicist who endeavored to influence public opinion. The "fantastic spending of the money of the people" by the Democratic Congress was one of the "powerful issues for the opponents of the New Deal." We are not "a normal country." The abnormality arose because of attempts at planning and the prevailing levels of spending and taxes. The real issue was said to be taxes, which the people understand more readily than public spending. "Taxes are a necessary and inevitable concomitant of government, and the people are educated to pay them, grudgingly, perhaps; or pay them, if possible, to escape penalties the laws have set for nonpayers. Taxes are the bane of every country and every people, but there they are, and there is no escaping them."[104]

The fear of unbalanced budgets was based in part on the belief that they would lead to inflation. According to the traditional view, a balanced budget was both a weapon against depression and a guarantee against inflation. It is a powerful anti-depression weapon because "it gives absolute security to the currency. Thus it develops an atmosphere of confidence in which capital, with a pent-up demand for improvements and expansion, can reasonably seek invest-

[103] L. J. Dickinson, "The Drift in Federal Finance," *Review of Reviews and World's Work*, Vol. 88 (December 1933), pp. 17, 58.

[104] Samuel G. Blythe, "The Real Issue," *Saturday Evening Post*, Vol. 208 (Nov. 30, 1935), pp. 5–6. The program of the Roosevelt administration had been previously referred to in the same journal as the third great spending spree. "The first of these sprees began when we tried to make the world safe for Democracy; the second when we tried to make it safe for speculators. In the third . . . Government is trying to make it safe for everyone except those who have saved." "Our Three Great Spending Sprees," an editorial, *ibid.*, Vol. 206 (Jan. 20, 1934), p. 22.

ment."[105] Unbalanced budgets inevitably lead to inflation. "History demonstrates without exception that whenever a government continuously spends more than it takes in the social consequences are tragic." The American colonies, it was pointed out, had destroyed their currency and impoverished their people, and France had experienced an extreme inflation about the same time. The Civil War inflation in the United States and the post-World War I inflation in France were other outstanding examples. The reason for the universal experience resides in two powers of government. "The first is the power to appropriate and to expend money. The second is the power to manufacture money."[106]

The fate of the Roosevelt administration, it was said, would be determined in large part by whether federal expenditures could be met without an excessive rise in prices. The other major consideration was whether the taxes required to bring the budget into balance could be held within bearable limits. The relief question was "the crux of the federal financial problem." Concrete plans were necessary in order "to deal with the relief problem within the limits of the people's capacity." No one denies "the obligation to protect the unemployed. But more economical methods must plainly be pursued through the return of responsibility to local communities, through tightened administration, and through less expensive methods of relief."[107]

The federal finances, it was asserted, were not being handled in a manner conforming with the traditional virtues of thrift, prudence, and common sense. One author believed that "those traits which are traditionally feminine should be given a chance in our national housekeeping. . . ." These

---

[105] Lewis W. Douglas, "Recovery by Balanced Budget," *Review of Reviews*, Vol. 91 (January 1935), pp. 25, 69.

[106] Douglas, "Over the Hill to the Poorhouse," *ibid.*, Vol. 91 (June 1935), p. 23.

[107] Grenville Clark, "Federal Finances and the New Deal," *Atlantic Monthly*, Vol. 154 (1934), pp. 755 ff. The belief that the federal budget must be balanced to avoid inflation was held by numerous persons well versed in finance. See, for example, the statement by Russell C. Leffingwell, *New York Times* (March 22, 1934), p. 16.

traits are "thrift, carefulness, simple common sense, the ability to face things as they are." Their exercise "would mean that we would get more for our money. . . . The Nation . . . can, if it will, draw upon women for the strength and shrewdness that life has developed in them."[108] These observations are suggestive of the household analogy that had long been used to support the annually balanced budget formula.

The attitudes of the public toward deficit finance thus far considered reflect what was generally regarded as a conservative outlook on federal finance. Though there is no reason to believe that the alleged deficiencies of budget policy weighed heavily on the public at large, any suggestion that these attitudes were found only among an ultra-conservative minority would be unwarranted. For example, in March 1933 Alvin Johnson, a moderate or liberal economist, discussed the perils of excessive debt. "If one re-reads with modern eyes Cicero's and Sallust's analyses of Cataline's following, or the diatribes of the orators preceding the French Revolution, he will agree that the way of excessive debt is, for a state, the way to the Devil."[109]

The apparent inability of the Roosevelt administration to develop a well-rounded budget policy was criticized by people of widely divergent views. Thus, the editors of *The Nation* observed that the failure to formulate a consistent policy was dangerous because it presented an invitation to pressure groups to launch "new raids" on the Treasury. "Billions of the taxpayers' dollars have been handed out to organized

---

[108] Henrietta Ripperger, "What This Country Needs is a Woman," *Harper's Magazine*, Vol. 172 (1936), pp. 373, 376. The same idea had been advanced at the time of the 1932 campaign. The "right kind of woman" could govern the country effectively. The "dominant trait of the best women is realism—an educated insight into values, a cool remorseless discrimination between what you want and what you can get." Elmer Davis, "The Collapse of Politics," *Harper's Magazine*, Vol. 165 (1932), p. 393.

[109] Alvin Johnson, "Debt and the Devil," *Yale Review*, New Series, Vol. 22 (1933), pp. 450 ff.

groups merely because the Administration was unable to present Congress with a carefully worked-out program." The silver interests were mentioned as an example. "The tragedy is that once the money has been distributed to these pressure groups there is none left for such socially necessary projects as slum clearance, social security, or adequate public-health activities."[110]

The record for the period 1933–1936 supports the charge of inadequate fiscal planning. Yet curiously a major charge against the Roosevelt administration was that the intention was to establish a planned economy. For example, Frank Knox believed that federal deficits would lead to a regimented economy.[111] According to a leading authority on banking, by 1936 we had "already gone beyond the limit, both of taxation and borrowing, that is safe and wise for the nation as a whole." If this limit is to be extended, "we must make up our minds to great changes, both in average consumption or in cost of living and in conditions of employment."[112] These observations were typical of the comments made before and during the election campaign of 1936. They did not go unchallenged.

The opposite tack was taken by Robert H. Jackson, then Assistant Attorney-General in charge of the Tax Division of the Department of Justice. As a nation, we had only begun to draw on our resources. The campaign opens with the cry of "Wolf," and the candidate for Vice President talks of "a rendezvous with a receiver for the Treasury." In pungent language Jackson continued: "Opposition leaders who promise a tight financial policy in loose language and seek to impress the country with their patriotism by slandering the

[110] "The Budget in Chaos," *The Nation*, Vol. 142 (Feb. 19, 1936), p. 209.

[111] The "one sure way to bring Fascism to this country is through prolonged government spending of large sums of borrowed money." Frank Knox, *We Planned It That Way* (1938), p. 41.

[112] H. Parker Willis, "Up to Our Neck in Debt," *The Forum*, Vol. 96 (1936), p. 108.

nation's credit are trying to capitalize an honest anxiety which Mr. Willis expresses and many share."[113]

The sharp difference of opinion evidenced by the debate between Willis and Jackson may seem to suggest that there was little unanimity of opinion concerning the consequences of deficit finance and the increase in debt. But Jackson was closely identified with the Roosevelt administration, and his views were far from typical. In 1936 the sheer bulk of the $30 billion debt, together with the fact that it was "the epic obligation of human history," had considerable emotional impact. Yet deficits and the rising public debt were not particularly effective as campaign issues. Those who believed that the federal debt was the greatest of all evils, basing their case on the canons of fiscal orthodoxy, were in the minority.

The opinion most commonly held during the mid-1930's was that continued deficits were undesirable, but large-scale unemployment was intolerable. An increasing number of people, particularly in the middle- and low-income groups, regarded the deficits and the rising federal debt in a spirit of tolerance. This was true of the unemployed and W.P.A. workers in particular. Farmers and others who had been saved from economic disaster by federal programs reacted similarly. There is also reason to believe that the younger generation took a more optimistic view of federal finances than did their elders. To them the large and increasing federal debt did not appear prohibitive if the economy could be set aright.[114] The deficits incurred had not resulted in disaster. If the administration had not succeeded in effecting a full-scale recovery, it had at least faced up to the relief problem and attempted to "shore up" the economy.

Yet to even a casual observer it was apparent that the balanced budget rationale and the belief that in time of peace

[113] Robert H. Jackson, "America Has Only Scratched Her Resources," *The Forum*, Vol. 96 (1936), p. 108. The candidate for Vice President here referred to was Frank Knox.

[114] Duncan Aikman, "America Talks Debt," *Harper's Magazine*, Vol. 174 (December 1936), pp. 92–96.

a rising public debt was an evil remained firmly embedded in our financial folklore. To numerous persons in all strata of society the balanced budget idea remained a basic tenet of what is perhaps best described as dogmatic financial ortho-doxy.[115] At no time during the 1930's could it be said that deficit finance had attained popularity in itself. The popu-larity of the Roosevelt administration, as shown by the 1936 election, did not mean that unbalanced budgets were both acceptable and popular among the people generally. To the extent that deficit finance was accepted by the public, it was for the most part regarded with misgivings. The conse-quences, it was believed, were less objectionable than those that might follow a hastily balanced budget and the adjust-ment of other policies in conformity with this objective.

The evidence that deficit finance was accepted with reluc-tance is quite definite, especially with respect to the late 1930's. Early in 1939 a survey conducted by Elmo Roper for *Fortune* included this question: "If you were a member of the incoming Congress, would you vote yes or no on a bill to reduce federal spending to a point where the national budget is balanced?" The distribution of the replies is shown in the following table.

	Yes	No	Don't Know
Total............	61.3%	17.4%	21.3%
Prosperous........	76.3	11.1	12.6
Upper middle class..	67.1	17.8	15.1
Lower middle class..	62.2	17.8	20.0
Poor.............	54.8	18.3	26.9

Only 17.4 per cent of those polled would not attempt to bal-ance the budget. At the same time *Fortune* reported that 63.5 per cent regarded the President—and presumably his

---

[115] The moral connotation of indebtedness did not vanish during the depression· At best the influence of so-called "moral precepts" receded gradually. See, for exam-ple, Duncan Aikman's account of his visit with a lady living in the Ozark Mountains just before the 1936 election. *Ibid.*, p. 97.

administration—favorably. Among those classified as "poor" the figures are even more remarkable—18 per cent would not attempt to balance the budget through reduced spending and 74 per cent regarded the President favorably.[116]

In their interpretation of the answers to the question about balancing the budget, the editors of *Fortune* suggested that "at the very moment that President Roosevelt was defending deficit spending and reiterating the theory that balancing the budget is the least of our problems, a wave of deflationary sentiment suddenly swept across his path."[117] To one who followed federal fiscal developments continuously from 1929, "a wave of deflationary sentiment" seems an exaggeration. That there were changes in popular attitudes goes without saying. But they were at best gradual and in- fluenced by changes in the economic tide. Numerous persons who in 1933–1934 and again in 1937–1938 were willing to accept an unbalanced budget did so with a feeling of uncer- tainty. In some instances no more than a change in personal fortunes was required to place them in the opposite camp. It was not a case of apostates coming back to the ancient faith, but a return of those who had not strayed very far away.

[116] "The Fortune Survey: XIX," *Fortune*, Vol. 19 (March 1939), pp. 66, 135.

[117] *Ibid.*, p. 135. The references to public expenditures and debts in the message of January 4, 1939 on the State of the Union were interpreted by the editors of *Fortune* as indicating a continuance of "the free-spending philosophy."

CHAPTER VI

Fiscal Policy Since 1940

THE SECOND WORLD WAR had a revolutionary effect on the American economy and on public finance. In a comparatively brief period a nation seemingly unable to solve the unemployment problem was operating at forced draft. Under the impetus of wartime demands, federal expenditures rose from about $9 billion for 1940 to a peak of almost $100 billion in 1945. In the same period revenues rose from $5 billion to about $45 billion.[1] When the war ended the federal debt exceeded $250 billion—a figure approximately six times as large as the federal debt in 1940 and ten times that at the close of the First World War.[2]

Changing Role of Fiscal Policy

During World War II, as in all major wars, the level of federal expenditures was determined by the force of circumstances. For a few months the curtailment of nondefense expenditures was a subject of controversy, but this issue soon

[1] The budgetary record of the war years is summarized in the Appendix table at p. 320. The proportion of expenditures covered by receipts was higher than during the Civil War and World War I. See the tables in the Appendix, pp. 316, 317, and 320.

[2] Debt-management problems in connection with the World War II debt are considered in Henry C. Murphy, *The National Debt in War and Transition* (1950) and Charles C. Abbott, *The Federal Debt: Structure and Impact* (1953).

shaded into the background. From the beginning of the defense effort, the central issue of budget policy related to the
extent to which taxes should be increased.

The World War II experience was in some respects unique.
To a far greater extent than in earlier war periods, it was
recognized that the goal of wartime taxation is not confined
to the raising of revenues. An excess profits tax became an
absolute essential. The principle that business should not
profit unduly from the war effort was applied several months
before Pearl Harbor.[3] With this exception, the emphasis on
additional taxes was relatively mild during the defense build-
up and the early stages of the war. Priority was given to the
mobilization of idle resources, but at the same time restrictive tax policies were being prepared for use when full employment was reached.[4] In formulating tax policy the avoidance of unnecessary shock to the economic system was a
guiding consideration.[5]

From 1942 on the emphasis was on the largest possible increase in taxes. The wartime tax system became "the instrument of raising huge amounts of revenue; but, more than
that, it . . . played a major role in restricting war profiteering
and curbing inflation." Reductions in personal exemptions
and increases in rates for the individual income tax were
made effective with a view to controlling inflation. The tax

[3] "The Excess Profits Tax Act of 1940" was enacted as Title II of the *Second
Revenue Act of 1940*, which was approved on October 8, 1940. This tax applied to
"adjusted excess profits tax net incomes" of corporations for taxable years beginning
after December 31, 1939. The initial rates were graduated from 25 per cent to 50 per
cent. 54 Stat. 975.

[4] *Budget of the United States Government for the Fiscal Year Ending June 30, 1942*,
p. xii; this budget message is dated January 3, 1941. *Budget of the United States
Government for the Fiscal Year Ending June 30, 1943*, pp. xi–xv; this budget message
is dated January 5, 1942.

[5] The view that priority should be given to the mobilization of idle resources and
that restrictive tax policies should be made effective only after full employment was
reached was not generally accepted outside the government. This approach was
championed mainly by the younger economists, especially a small group who were
working for the federal government. These conflicting views were discussed with
Keynes during his visit to Washington in June 1941. R. F. Harrod, *Life of John
Maynard Keynes* (1951), pp. 508–09.

program "effectively supported the economic stabilization program by removing billions of dollars of excess spending power from the hands of civilians." These high taxes helped to control civilian demand and eased the strain imposed on the direct controls—wages, prices, and priorities. The excess profits tax was a key element in this program. By limiting the financial gains from the war, this tax helped gain acceptance of the direct controls that were necessary. Tax policy became "an integral part of our wartime economic policy designed to promote the maximum war effort while protecting minimum living standards."[6]

The most important wartime innovation was the adoption in 1943 of withholding of income taxes on salaries and wages. In recommending a system of withholding in 1941 and 1942, the stated objectives of the Treasury were "to ease the payment problems of taxpayers" and to remove "the spectre of overhanging tax liabilities for earnings in a prior year."[7] From a longer-range viewpoint, the fact that withholding involved a basic change in collection and administrative procedures was of secondary importance. Withholding was essential if fiscal policy was to become an effective component of a peacetime stabilization program.

One other phase of wartime finance and financial policy should be mentioned briefly. Federal, state, and local cooperation reached a high level of effectiveness. It would be an exaggeration to say that we have ever achieved complete national unity in fiscal policy. But during the war years we

[6] "Report to Congress by Secretary Morgenthau," in *Annual Report of the Secretary of the Treasury on the State of the Finances for the Fiscal Year Ended June 30, 1945*, pp. 400–01. Debt policy was focused on the same objectives, especially the control of inflation. "In April of 1942 . . . it was determined that war bonds should be sold with a view to minimizing the inflationary effect of governmental expenditures. This meant that every effort would be made to sell bonds to individuals rather than to banks, and that sales would be made under conditions which would discourage private expenditure on goods and services in short supply. . . . The populace was urged to buy war bonds *and* cut down consumer expenditures." Jesse Burkhead, *Government Budgeting* (1956), p. 63.

[7] "Report to Congress by Secretary Morgenthau," p. 401.

came closer to this goal than at any time during the 1930's. The states in general maintained tax rates, thus helping to control effective demand, and set aside unneeded revenues as postwar reserves. In turn, some of these funds were invested in federal debt obligations, thereby aiding in financing the war effort. Co-operation was not a one-way affair. Wherever possible, the federal government tried to take into account the impact of the defense effort on local finance. For reasons such as these, it is accurate to say that "during the war we approached a truly national fiscal policy on all levels of government."[8]

POSTWAR PLANNING DURING THE WAR YEARS

The United States had scarcely become an active participant in World War II before the impact of the war on the postwar economy became a subject for serious consideration.[9] World War I had been followed by a sharp recession, and it was widely believed that an even more troublesome period of adjustment after World War II was inevitable. Heavy unemployment during demobilization could be avoided, it was reasoned, only if government stepped in with a large-scale public works program, among other measures. Presumably the immediate postwar period would be a real test for fiscal policy.

On January 5, 1942—just four weeks after Pearl Harbor —President Roosevelt stated that our "capacity to carry a large debt in a post-war period without undue hardship depends mainly on our ability to maintain a high level of employment and income." The sharp recession of 1920–1921

[8] Harold D. Smith, "National Unity in Fiscal Policy," *American City*, Vol. 60 (October 1945), p. 89. *Budget of the United States Government for the Fiscal Year Ending June 30, 1943*, p. x.

[9] There were frequent references to the post-defense period during the defense build-up of 1940–1941. In some instances it was assumed that World War II would end without the United States becoming a participant. See, for example, Carl Shoup, *Federal Finances in the Coming Decade* (1941), p. 13.

and the thought that the maladjustments caused by World War I were largely responsible for the depression of the 1930's were doubtless in mind when he added: "I am confident that by prompt action we shall control the price development now and that we shall prevent the recurrence of a deep depression in the post-war period. There need be no fiscal barriers to our war effort and to victory."[10]

Fiscal and other policies that would be appropriate for the reconversion and postwar periods received increasing attention as the war effort gained momentum. In January 1944— approximately five months before the Normandy invasion— Roosevelt stated that the peacetime objective "must be a permanently high level of national income and a correspondingly high standard of living." To achieve this end, "a well-planned demobilization program" is necessary. Many "inter-related adjustments of fiscal policy, production policy, price policy, and labor policy" will be required. "Our reconversion policy should have as a major aim the stimulation of private investment and employment." At the same time, there will be "an urgent need for certain public works" because of the postponement of normal construction. Timing of their construction in accordance with employment requirements is desirable. We have a "responsibility to prepare for victory and for peace. Let us make sure that the Budget, the Government's work plan, serves both ends."[11]

Postwar planning became a leading interest of the Congress. The Special Committee on Post-War Economic Policy and Planning of the Senate held hearings on a number of subjects, including fiscal requirements and the probable level of national income. A similar committee—the so-called

---

[10] *Budget of the United States Government for the Fiscal Year Ending June 30, 1943*, p. XVIII. A year later the President said: "The economic stabilization program, although born of war necessity, will greatly facilitate post-war reconstruction," *Budget of the United States Government for the Fiscal Year Ending June 30, 1944*, p. XVIII.

[11] *Budget of the United States Government for the Fiscal Year Ending June 30, 1945*, pp. X, XIII, XXV.

Colmer Committee—was created by the House of Representatives.[12] Establishment of these committees reflected the
public concern about probable developments after the cessation of hostilities. The war had shown that, given adequate
effective demand, the economy could be brought to a high
peak of productive effort. The problem soon to be faced was
how to bring the economy from the forced-draft status of the
war years to a relatively stable peacetime basis at or near
full employment.

The budget message of January 3, 1945 was a milestone in
the evolution of fiscal and economic planning. After pointing
out that the huge war expenditures had brought full employment, President Roosevelt asked: "What will the outlook be
when Federal expenditures are 50 and 25 billion dollars in the
period of demobilization and thereafter?" As background for
consideration of this question, a table entitled "The Government's Budget and the Nation's Budget" was presented.
Receipts and expenditures for the calendar years 1939 and
1944 were shown for four "economic groups": consumers,
business, the federal government, and state and local governments.[13] This table was the point of departure for a discussion
of the changes in peacetime demand that would be required
to offset postwar reductions in war demands. The President
observed that "full employment in peacetime can be assured
only when the reduction in war demand is approximately offset by additional peacetime demand from millions of consumers, businesses, and farmers, and by Federal, State, and

[12] The Senate committee was established pursuant to S. Res. 102, 78 Cong. 1 sess.
Its members included Senators George, Chairman, O'Mahoney, Taft, and Vanden-
berg. The House committee was established pursuant to H. Res. 408, 78 Cong. 2
sess. The Office of War Mobilization and Reconversion was established in 1944
pursuant to legislation enacted by Congress; 58 Stat. 785.

[13] For the business group, only undistributed profits and reserves were included
under receipts and gross capital formation under expenditures. In this way, it was
possible to show the combined receipts and expenditures for the four groups in
balance at the estimated gross national product—$88.6 billion for 1939 and $197.5
billion for 1944.

local governments." It was suggested that "consumers' expenditures and business investments must increase by about
50 per cent, measured in constant prices, above the level of
the year 1939 if full employment is to be provided by private
enterprise."[14]

"The Government's Budget and the Nation's Budget," together with the accompanying discussion, was a logical outgrowth of an earlier statement by the President in January
1941. "The Budget of the United States presents our national program. It is a preview of our work plan, a forecast of
things to come. It charts the course of the Nation."[15] During
the late 1930's and early 1940's the budget was rapidly becoming an important instrument in the formation of economic policy. What had been added by 1945 was official recognition of the idea that the federal budget should be formulated and appraised in relation to the total national economy.

A similar table was included in President Truman's first
budget message dated January 14, 1946. The figures were for
the calendar year 1944 and the October–December 1945
quarter—the first quarter of reconversion—with the latter
shown in seasonally adjusted annual rates.

> Government programs [the President said] are of such importance
> in the development of production and employment opportunities
> ... that it has become essential to formulate and consider the
> Federal Budget in the light of the Nation's budget as a whole. . . .
> Considering the whole Nation, total expenditures must equal the
> total receipts, because what any individual or group spends be-
> comes receipts of other individuals or groups. Such equality can be

[14] *Budget of the United States Government for the Fiscal Year Ending June 30, 1946*,
pp. xxiv–xxv. The table here referred to was little more than a summary or skeleton
table. Its use in the budget released in January 1945 followed by more than a year
the publication of the article "A Budget for the Nation" by Grover W. Ensley
(*Social Research*, Vol. 10 (1943), pp. 280 ff). The underlying conceptions of this article, which in turn directly influenced the table in the 1946 budget, were developed
in consultation with Gerhard Colm. J. Weldon Jones and Arthur Smithies helped
clarify the basic ideas.

[15] *Budget of the United States Government for the Fiscal Year Ending June 30, 1942*,
p. xiv.

achieved on either a high level of incomes or on a low depression level of incomes.[16]

The discussion of "The Government's Budget and the Nation's Budget" reflected the trend of official thought at the highest executive level. When this table was first published, federal policy commitments for the postwar period were being debated. In January 1946 full employment bills had been passed by the Senate and the House of Representatives, and the conference committee was soon to iron out the version that became the Employment Act of 1946.

The foregoing summary of postwar planning during the war years has been based almost exclusively on official pronouncements. It may leave the impression that postwar planning was of interest mainly to officials at the highest executive and legislative levels. To a large extent, official concern with the problems that would arise after the cessation of hostilities stemmed from the efforts of economists and others employed by the federal government during the war. Informal discussion groups, consisting in part of individuals studying reconversion and demobilization problems but mainly of persons engaged in other tasks, helped maintain a continuing interest in the question: What will the economy be like after the war? For the most part, these people were advocates of compensatory action or were sympathetic toward compensatory fiscal ideas. Nominally the Employment Act of 1946 came into being through the efforts of Congress aided by the executive branch. A more realistic view is that it was a product of the intellectual ferment of the times.[17]

[16] *Budget of the United States Government for the Fiscal Year Ending June 30, 1947*, pp. L–LI. The table showing the federal budget and the nation's budget was not continued in later budgets. However, a table entitled "The Nation's Economic Budget," together with the accompanying discussion, became a feature of the *Economic Report of the President*.

[17] An interesting account of the work of an informal committee in molding a full employment bill is presented in Stephen K. Bailey, *Congress Makes a Law* (1950), p. 45.

THE EMPLOYMENT ACT OF 1946

The Employment Act of 1946 was a landmark in federal economic legislation. The declaration of policy in this law was agreed upon after a great deal of discussion. Because of its role in shaping the direction of postwar economic and fiscal policies, this declaration is presented in full:

The Congress hereby declares that it is the continuing policy and responsibility of the Federal Government to use all practicable means consistent with its needs and obligations and other essential considerations of national policy, with the assistance and cooperation of industry, agriculture, labor, and State and local governments, to coordinate and utilize all its plans, functions, and resources for the purpose of creating and maintaining, in a manner calculated to foster and promote free competitive enterprise and the general welfare, conditions under which there will be afforded useful employment opportunities, including self-employment, for those willing, and seeking to work, and to promote maximum employment, production, and purchasing power.[18]

The Employment Act requires the President to transmit an economic report to the Congress at the beginning of each regular session. The mandatory content includes: (1) levels of employment, production, and purchasing power obtaining in the United States; (2) current and foreseeable trends in the levels of employment, production, and purchasing power; (3) reviews of the federal economic program and economic conditions affecting employment; and (4) a program for carrying out the policy set forth in the declaration above. Supplemental reports may be transmitted to the Congress from time to time, if the President desires.[19]

To help carry out the objectives of the act, a Council of Economic Advisers was created in the Executive Office of the President. The council consists of three members appointed

---

[18] The Employment Act was approved by President Truman on February 20, 1946. Its antecedents are well presented in Edwin G. Nourse, *Economics in the Public Service* (1953), Chapters 4, 5, and 6; and Bailey, *Congress Makes a Law* (1950), Chapters 1 and 2. Its legislative history is fully considered in Bailey, Chapters 3-12.

[19] 60 Stat. 24, 838.

by the President, with the consent of the Senate. Its function
is to assist the President. It is an advisory body, not an administrative agency. In theory at least, the council influences
the policy-making process only indirectly. A primary duty is
to assist and advise the President in the preparation of the
economic report. It is authorized to employ such specialists
and advisers as may be necessary in carrying out its functions. The council and its staff in effect comprise a continuing study group. In the performance of its duties, it may
constitute advisory committees and consult with representatives of industry, agriculture, labor, consumers, state and
local governments, and other groups.[20]

A Joint Committee on the Economic Report (now the
Joint Economic Committee) consisting of seven members of
the Senate and seven members of the House of Representatives was also created. A major function of this committee is
to make a continuing study of matters relating to the President's economic report and to study means of co-ordinating
programs in order to further the policy of the Employment
Act. The Joint Committee is given the authority to employ
its own staff and to hold such hearings as it may deem advisable.[21]

Underlying the Employment Act was an awareness that
the federal government, as then constituted, was not well
equipped either to discern emerging economic problems or to
deal with them intelligently. It is properly described as a
moderate approach to economic stability. If this act seems
to make the President the "Manager of Prosperity," it does
so in a manner that few would find objectionable.[22] In the

[20] 60 Stat. 24. Edwin G. Nourse and Bertram M. Gross, "The Role of the Council
of Economic Advisers," *American Political Science Review*, Vol. 42 (1948), pp. 287–
89.

[21] 60 Stat. 25.

[22] Clinton Rossiter has suggested that the President has ten clearly discernible
functions, of which the newest is "Manager of Prosperity." *The American Presidency* (1956), pp. 21–23, 94. A not unimportant consequence of this legislation is
that the President and influential members of the Congress are better informed on
economic matters, including the interrelationships between the federal government
and other sectors of the economy.

words of the first chairman of the council, the Employment
Act "constituted a formal recognition of the integral character of the economics of the economy." It makes "a vigorous
reaffirmation of the principle of 'free competitive enterprise'
and, at the same time, a positive declaration of enlarged Federal responsibility in the economic sphere."[23] The "mandate
to maintain high employment and economic stability was
written indelibly into public policy and became the continuing concern of government."[24] The act makes clear that the
federal government is necessarily concerned with the total
economic process.

A principal motivation of the Employment Act was the
belief that a sharp recession or depression would occur soon
after the cessation of hostilities. The events of the 1930's
were of recent memory, and there was apprehension lest
there might be another depression of comparable severity.
The question whether a suitable federal policy for coping
with a sharp recession during reconversion could be formulated proved to be largely academic. The dreaded period of
deflation and unemployment did not materialize. The
strength of pent-up demands emanating from both the private and public sectors had been misgauged, as had also the
time required for reconversion and the importance of accumulations of liquid assets. As a consequence, the efficacy of
fiscal policy as a component of stabilization policy under the
trying conditions of a postwar deflation was not put to the
test. The forecasts of a serious recession, however, contributed indirectly to a re-examination of the role of fiscal policy.
If economic forecasts could be so wide of the mark, could an
effective peacetime policy be devised?

To sophisticated observers it was apparent that adapting
fiscal policy to the requirements of postwar stabilization policy was something markedly different from devising a policy
for dealing with the harsher effects of a depression. The con-

[23] Nourse, *Economics in the Public Service*, pp. 16, 29.
[24] Donald K. David, Chairman, Committee for Economic Development, "An-
nouncement of a National Commission on Money and Credit" (1957), p. 6.

cept of fiscal policy, as it evolved during the 1930's, was characterized by its simplicity. What has come to be known as fiscal policy was originally proposed as a means to overcome depressions.[25] In the prewar years expansionist fiscal and other policies were clearly in order; the need for stimulating income and employment was unquestioned. The usefulness of fiscal policy after the war would depend in larger measure on the reliability of economic forecasts, especially the ability to judge the direction and intensity of economic trends. The methods and techniques required would obviously differ from those employed in fashioning appropriate lines of action during the great depression.

The Employment Act, together with the hearings and discussion preceding its enactment, made clear that fiscal policy was merely one aspect of public economic policy. This does not mean that a conscious effort was made to minimize the role of fiscal policy. Rather, fiscal policy merely began to assume its place as a component of what it was hoped would be a co-ordinated economic policy. In the development of such a policy, an essential first step was to recognize that, however vital the role of fiscal policy may be in the long run, at certain times monetary and other policies might loom more important. In laying the groundwork for an effective stabilization program, the only possible approach was to regard fiscal policy as one component of public economic policy. Public economic or stabilization policy necessarily consists of many ingredients.[26]

THE YEARS 1946–1958

The first postwar budget message (January 14, 1946) reflected the concern of the government with economic instability. Peacetime prosperity, Truman said, "will be based on

[25] Gerhard Colm, "Fiscal Policy and the Federal Budget," in *Income Stabilization for a Developing Democracy*, Max F. Millikan, ed. (1953), pp. 213–14.

[26] There "is no clear line to divide fiscal policy from public finance, from monetary policy, or from government economic policy." Burkhead, *Government Budgeting*, p. 60.

the private enterprise system," but government can and. must assist in many ways. The operations of government affect the whole economy, and its total program must be geared to the achievement "of full production and full employment." The goals of wartime stabilization policy must be reversed; the economy will be dependent on adequate purchasing power. "The best protection of purchasing power is a policy of full production and full employment opportunities."[27]

The trend of official thought is illustrated by the President's observation that the government, "acting on behalf of all the people, must assume the ultimate responsibility for the economic health of the Nation. There is no other agency that can." It "will require determined action to keep our Federal Budget in order and to relate our fiscal policies to the requirements of an expanding economy." The annually balanced budget was no longer the keynote of fiscal policy. But it "is good to move toward a balanced budget and a start on the retirement of the debt at a time when demand for goods is strong and the business outlook is good." Tax reduction should not be considered as long as powerful forces are "working in the direction of inflation."[28] The following year the President stated: "As long as business, employment, and national income continue high, we should maintain tax revenues at levels that will not only meet current expenditures but also leave a surplus for retirement of the public debt."[29] The influence of the compensatory fiscal rationale is apparent.

[27] *Budget of the United States Government for the Fiscal Year Ending June 30, 1947*, pp. VI, X, XXII, XXV.

[28] *Ibid.*, pp. XXV, LVI. The same thought was expressed by Secretary John W. Snyder. "We cannot afford a general reduction of tax rates so long as the economy is confronted with strong inflationary pressures." When "these pressures subside, we should maintain tax rates high enough to effect as rapid a reduction in the public debt as is consistent with the maintenance of a high-production, high-employment economy." *Annual Report of the Secretary of the Treasury on the State of the Finances for the Fiscal Year Ended June 30, 1946*, p. 1.

[29] *Budget of the United States Government for the Fiscal Year Ending June 30, 1948*, p. M5.

The idea that government has the ultimate responsibility is implicit in Truman's first economic report. "The job at hand today is to see to it that America is not ravaged by recurring depressions and long periods of unemployment. . . ." Prosperity in the United States is important not only to the American people. "It is the foundation of world prosperity and world peace." In a statement exuding a great deal of confidence, the President said: "I reject, and I know the American people reject, the notion that we must have another depression. I am not referring to minor detours and bumps in the road ahead—these we know we shall have. I am referring to economic collapse and stagnation such as started in 1929. This need not happen again, and *must* not happen again."[30] This statement helped set the tone for federal postwar stabilization policy. An occasional minor swing in the economic pendulum was to be expected; a serious and prolonged depression must not be permitted to occur.

Without in any way denying the usefulness of fiscal policy, the first Council of Economic Advisers at times seemed to assign it a smaller role than it enjoyed in the budget messages and other official pronouncements. Fiscal measures, the council asserted, cannot in themselves solve problems that arise because of structural maladjustments, lagging or declining industries, and imbalances in specific price, wage, and profit relationships. The "internal relationships of business must be carefully adjusted by business participants themselves within an institutional atmosphere made favorable by government. . . ." Nevertheless, the council believed that government has a complementary role to play. To an increasing extent, it will be a "stimulative and guiding element in the economy." The "timing, volume, and distribution" of federal expenditures must be considered in relation to those of private business and state and local governments.[31]

The complementary nature of public and private activities

---

[30] *Economic Report of the President* (Jan. 8, 1947), p. VII.
[31] *First Annual Report to the President* (December 1946), pp. 12–14, 17.

was reaffirmed in the discussion of the nation's economic budget in the *Economic Report of the President*. The economic budget "indicates whether a given level of economic activity is being achieved mainly by private expenditures, or by public expenditures, and in what proportion." This budget, it was said, is primarily a device for measurement of our economic activity; the use of this device "is not wedded to any particular economic theory."[32]

The postwar budget messages, together with the economic reports, show conclusively that the approach to the federal budget was no longer solely—or even primarily—in terms of money costs. For example, it was stated that the 1949 budget reveals the magnitude of the problems with which the federal government must deal. "It demonstrates alike the heavy responsibilities of our international position and our concern for the maintenance of a sound domestic economy." It "would be gratifying if I could say . . . that our existing programs fulfill our national requirements. But this is not the case. Our national and international responsibilities demand that we undertake new activities and expand some activities in which we are already engaged."[33] Two years later it was stated that the budget "is an expression, in financial terms, of the actions this Government can and should take at this time to build toward economic growth and the expansion of human freedom, in our own country and in the world." Federal expenditures are of fundamental importance to our prospects for steady economic growth. The budget then submitted, it was said, "meets the obligations of our Government to nourish and support the economic and social health of our Nation." Economic growth "must be matched by comparable development in the social well-being and living standards of all our people."[34] One is reminded of Fillmore's

[32] *Economic Report of the President* (Jan. 8, 1947), p. 5.

[33] *Budget of the United States Government for the Fiscal Year Ending June 30, 1949*, pp. M5–M8.

[34] *Budget of the United States Government for the Fiscal Year Ending June 30, 1951*, pp. M5, M8, M12, M86.

observation a century earlier that government must keep pace with the progress of the people.

The role of fiscal policy in combating inflation was explicitly recognized by the President and the council. In July 1947 Truman stated that it is necessary to use the fiscal powers of the government as "a safeguard against inflationary possibilities which still exist. A policy of budget surplus and debt redemption is imperative under present conditions." Tax reduction would add to inflationary pressures. A "policy of restraint at the present time will enable us to use fiscal policies effectively if they are required at a later time to lend support to the economy. . . . The purpose of fiscal policy must be to facilitate, rather than to hinder, the basic adjustments in the private economy which will be necessary for continued high employment and production."[35] Six months later it was pointed out that a substantial excess of government receipts over expenditures is counterinflationary. Though a large cash surplus was forecast for the calendar year 1948, with "inflationary pressures a major threat to the stability of the American economy, no action should be taken now to reduce this excess." Federal, state, and local public works should be deferred wherever feasible, but "drawings and specifications for public-works projects to be undertaken when needed" should be prepared.[36] Despite the President's

[35] *Midyear Economic Report of the President* (July 21, 1947), p. 37.

[36] *Economic Report of the President* (Jan. 14, 1948), pp. 47, 89. The budget surplus for the fiscal year 1948, more than half of which had elapsed at the time of this report, was $8.4 billion. On a cash basis, the surplus was $8.8 billion. *Budget of the United States Government for the Fiscal Year Ending June 30, 1950*, pp. A4, A123. To those who held that inflation was in the main a consequence of an unbalanced budget, continuation of inflation in the face of a large surplus posed a dilemma. The Republican majority of the Joint Committee on the Economic Report stated that "the inflationary condition is due to our attempt to accomplish more than is possible at our present capacity for production." Our people and our government "may well be criticized for trying to carry on at the same time so many large programs. . . . Liberal credit policies on the part of private and public agencies alike, and the maintenance of low interest rates have encouraged the expansion of these programs." The "attempt to carry them all on at once, with very little restraint in the field of consumer spending and liberal credit policies, is the basic reason for inflation, which otherwise could hardly coincide with a large Government surplus." S. Rept. 1358, 80 Cong. 2 sess., pp. 3–4.

admonition, taxes were reduced. This reduction, the Council of Economic Advisers stated, "sharply reduces the large surplus at a time when inflationary forces are still present and thereby removes our principal protection against the strengthening of these forces."[37]

On January 7, 1949 the President recommended a tax increase of $4 billion, together with an increase in social security contributions.[38] It soon became apparent, however, that a recession had begun during the last few months of 1948, and the need for a change in policy was recognized. The fact that governmental expenditures—federal, state, and local—were running at a rate of close to $60 billion a year was "an element of great stability" during the recession. The official position was that government fiscal transactions were "a source of support against other factors making for decline" in the economy. The moderate cash deficit was not a cause for alarm. There are "economic and social deficits" that would be far more serious than a temporary federal deficit. The situation did not call for an immediate and sweeping expansion of public works, but plans should be made to cope with a more serious business decline if one should occur.[39]

Early in 1950 the President reported that the test of the readjustment had been met. Federal policies were credited with a major assist in reversing the economic trend. "The relatively safe passage from inflation to greater stability was no accident." Businessmen, workers, and farmers "were aided by public policies which had been developed over the years and had been improved by experience. Government measures in fields such as credit and banking, social insurance, and agricultural price supports, proved their worth in cushioning the downswing and lending strong support to the recovery movement." Government fiscal transactions had helped to stabilize the economy; cash payments by all gov-

---

[37] *The Economic Situation at Midyear 1948*, A Report to the President by the Council of Economic Advisers (July 22, 1948), p. 42.

[38] *Economic Report of the President* (Jan. 7, 1949), p. 10.

[39] *Midyear Economic Report of the President* (July 11, 1949), pp. 1–4, 8, 11–12.

ernments for the calendar year 1949 were $8 billion higher than in 1948. Though the government was currently running a deficit, the fiscal position was basically strong.[40]

With the outbreak of the Korean War in the summer of 1950, fiscal policy was strongly influenced by defense requirements. Fiscal policy was centered on the requirements of an economy partially mobilized for war. Increased taxes were recommended by the President; a tax reduction bill under consideration was converted into a revenue-increasing measure.[41] The Korean War meant a marked change in the pattern of private and public investment. Private capital expansion necessary for the defense build-up was given preference over other investment in the allocation of scarce materials, and was also supported by the government through various forms of financial assistance. Less essential forms of public investment were curtailed.[42]

Several observations in Truman's last budget message reflect the changing approach to the budget after World War II. The financial program of the federal government, said the President, "cannot be planned in terms of a single fiscal year. It must be planned in the light of security, economic, and budgetary goals—not just for the ensuing year but for three and even four years ahead." That is to say, an annual budget may be necessary for practical reasons, but the major functions and programs of government are necessarily continuous. Budget and fiscal policies, the President added, "are

[40] *Economic Report of the President* (Jan. 6, 1950), pp. 1, 5, 11. A number of editors took issue with the President's interpretation. "The public policies to which Mr. Truman is apparently alluding do not represent anything new in Government. . . . It is not possible to say to what degree, if at all, these policies contributed to the 1949 readjustment." Editorial, *New York Times* (Jan. 7, 1950), p. 16.

[41] 64 Stat. 906. The Revenue Act of 1950 was approved on September 23, 1950. The Excess Profits Tax Act of 1950 (64 Stat. 1137) was approved on January 3, 1951. As a result of the Korean War, federal expenditures rose from a level of about $40 billion for the fiscal years 1949 and 1950 to $65 billion for 1952 and almost $75 billion for 1953. *Annual Report of the Secretary of the Treasury on the State of the Finances for the Fiscal Year Ended June 30, 1956*, p. 323.

[42] *Economic Report of the President* (Jan. 16, 1952), pp. 108–12.

tools of national policy. As such they are the subjects of controversy and evolution."[43]

When Eisenhower assumed office in January 1953, the federal government was operating at a substantial deficit. The new administration endeavored to chart a course that would reduce the deficits and gradually bring the budget into balance. During the early months inflation appeared to be a danger and the appropriate fiscal policy required that tax rates be maintained and expenditures curtailed. In a special message on the budget sent to the Congress on May 20 the President called for full maintenance of all taxes during 1953, but suggested that "a reduction in personal income taxes can and should be made effective next January 1."[44] However, when the 1953–1954 recession set in, there was a change in tack. There was a "muting of emphasis on balancing the budget."[45]

In September the Secretary of the Treasury announced that the administration would not seek to postpone the termination date (December 31, 1953) of the increase in personal income taxes and the excess profits tax enacted early in the Korean War. The reduction in revenues was placed at $5 billion for a full year. In the economic report the President stated: "This unequivocal promise of tax relief to both families and business firms bolstered confidence at a time when trade and employment were slipping slightly. In coming months these well-timed tax reductions are likely to give substantial support to consumer and investment markets."[46] The Excise Tax Reduction Act of 1954 approved on March 31 reduced revenues by an amount estimated at $1 billion a

[43] *Budget of the United States Government for the Fiscal Year Ending June 30, 1954*, pp. M54–M55.

[44] *Congressional Record*, Vol. 99, Pt. 4, pp. 5277–79.

[45] Robert J. Donovan, *Eisenhower: The Inside Story* (1956), p. 214. The author states that the President and the Cabinet were determined "to undertake an extensive public-works program if necessary and to prevent a serious depression at any cost."

[46] *Economic Report of the President* (Jan. 28, 1954), p. 52.

year.[47] In addition, the revision of the Internal Revenue Code enacted in August 1954 resulted in a loss of revenue estimated at $1.4 billion for the fiscal year 1955.[48]

The change in administration did not mean an ultra-conservative approach to budgetary matters. In his first budget message President Eisenhower reiterated his pledge of a fiscal and economic policy that would reduce the federal deficits and bring the budget into balance. But a balanced budget was not promised by a particular date.[49] A balanced federal budget was not placed above all other considerations. The importance of government's role in the economy was recognized explicitly. "Government must play a vital role in maintaining economic growth and stability." Progressive economic growth, in the President's opinion, would be fostered by continuing emphasis on efficiency and economy in government, reduced public expenditures, and lower taxes.[50] Though it "is desirable to bring down the scale of Government, our society has become so complicated that, quite apart from the large and continuing needs for defense, the Government now properly assumes obligations unknown to earlier generations."[51]

With the transition from recession to recovery successfully achieved, full credit was taken by the administration. "Fiscal and monetary measures fostered an expectation of improving economic conditions and encouraged people to maintain

[47] 68 Stat. 37.

[48] 68 A Stat. (The Internal Revenue Code was published as a separate volume.) *Annual Report of the Secretary of the Treasury on the State of the Finances for the Fiscal Year Ended June 30, 1954*, p. 44. The combined reductions here shown amount to $7.4 billion on an annual basis. After allowing for an increase of $1.3 billion in social security contributions, the net reduction in revenues was $6.1 billion.

[49] *Budget of the United States Government for the Fiscal Year Ending June 30, 1955*, pp. M5–M6, M104. It was the expressed desire of the administration to shift to state and local governments and private enterprise those activities which can be "more appropriately and more efficiently carried on in that way." By making necessity rather than desirability the test for expenditures, it will be possible to reduce "the share of the national income which is spent by the Government." It is desirable to leave the largest possible share with individuals. P. M14.

[50] *Ibid.*, p. M14.

[51] *Economic Report of the President* (Jan. 28, 1954), p. 56.

a high rate of expenditure." The reduction in military and other outlays after the ending of the Korean conflict had been effected without serious disruption of the economy. Among the lessons learned in "our latest encounter with the business cycle" were (1) "wise and early action by Government can stave off serious difficulties later," and (2) "contraction may be stopped in its tracks even when governmental expenditures and budget deficits are declining, provided effective means are taken for building confidence."[52]

The situation at the beginning of 1955 required that the government direct its program principally toward fostering long-term economic growth rather than toward imparting "an immediate upward thrust to economic activity." Within its proper sphere, government must be ready to act. The role of government in economic progress should be a constructive one. In the 1953-1954 recession "definite and deliberate steps" had been taken to promote a stable prosperity. The government's role should be an active one rather than a passive one. Budget and fiscal policies can help to promote economic expansion and stable economic growth. Expansion of public works—federal, state, and local—is necessary in order that the economy may grow without hindrance.[53]

The federal government, in the President's opinion, could play a constructive and facilitating role in the economy and at the same time maintain budget discipline. In the budget message of January 1955 he expressed the determination of the administration to keep working toward a balanced budget. The goal of a balanced budget "provides the discipline

---

[52] *Economic Report of the President* (Jan. 20, 1955), pp. IV, 7, 17, 22. During the 1953-1954 recession "no responsible persons in either political party came forward . . . to suggest that the built-in stabilizers of our system be vitiated by the perverse discretionary action of raising tax rates in order to avoid budget unbalance. As a result of our built-in stabilizers and reinforcing discretionary actions, a more than 10 per cent drop in production was not permitted to have any net reducing effects upon disposable incomes." Paul A. Samuelson, "The Economics of Eisenhower, A Symposium," *Review of Economics and Statistics*, Vol. 38 (1956), p. 372.

[53] *Economic Report of the President* (Jan. 20, 1955), pp. V, 4, 19, 48-49, 61.

essential for wise and efficient management of the public business." At no time, however, was sight lost of other objectives. The government "must do its part to advance human welfare and encourage economic growth with constructive actions, but only where our people cannot take the necessary actions for themselves."[54]

The role of the federal government in maintaining prosperity was considered at some length early in 1956. As a nation, we have come to believe that the government has "the capacity to moderate economic fluctuations without becoming a dominant factor in our economy." The "early recognition of a need for monetary and fiscal caution" and the "policy of restraint" applied during the greater part of 1955 had contributed to the "achievement and maintenance of prosperity without price inflation." Action by the government in the long-run interest and approval by the people of fiscal and monetary restraints "testify to our increasing maturity as a Nation in dealing with the problem of economic instability." The administration looked with favor on the extension of the "automatic workings" of the fiscal system that tend to offset or cushion changes in income. However, the recital of the positive steps taken at the time of the 1953–1954 recession showed that the administration did not side with the view that reliance should be placed solely, or even primarily, on the so-called "built-in stabilizers."[55]

With a balanced budget in sight for the fiscal years 1956 and 1957, the President stressed the relation between a balanced federal budget and fiscal integrity. We "strengthen our financial position by a balanced budget." We "must make sure that we do not undermine our financial strength by laying the groundwork for future budget deficits."[56] But no

---

[54] *Budget of the United States Government for the Fiscal Year Ending June 30, 1956*, p. M6.

[55] *Economic Report of the President* (Jan. 24, 1956), pp. III–IV, 6, 10, 41–43, 72–73.

[56] *Budget of the United States Government for the Fiscal Year Ending June 30, 1957*, p. M7. At times the President's budget philosophy seemed to combine the household analogy and the idea that net federal borrowing is always inflationary. "Over

commitment was made to balance the budget every year. A
balance over a term of a few years was deemed satisfactory.[57]
Though a balanced budget was assumed to be desirable, the
importance of numerous other goals was recognized. The
budget, it was said, is a comprehensive plan for meeting our
national objectives. It reflects "the general responsibilities of
a Government which will be serving 172 million people in the
fiscal year 1958."[58]

Faced with increasing inflationary pressures early in 1957,
the administration did not lose confidence in fiscal and monetary policy. The 1953–1954 experience had demonstrated the
usefulness of well-timed fiscal and monetary actions; they
have a basic role to play "if the excesses that often accompany prosperity are to be avoided." But "experience suggests that fiscal and monetary policies must be supported by
appropriate private policies to assure both a high level of
economic activity and a stable dollar." Though fiscal and
monetary policy would not do the whole job, the administration remained committed to a flexible fiscal policy, one that
relates "the budget as far as feasible to economic conditions,
helping to counteract inflationary or deflationary tendencies
as the situation requires."[59]

An appropriate policy with respect to capital outlays was
deemed especially important. "We must move forward in
some areas of investment while we hold back in others. For
example, the needs for schools, highways, and homes are so
urgent that I am proposing to move ahead with programs to
help our States, cities, and people undertake such construc-

---

the long term, a balanced budget is a sure index to thrifty management—in a home,
in a business, or in the Federal Government. When achievement of a balanced
budget is for long put off in a business or home, bankruptcy is the result. But in
similar circumstances a Government resorts to inflation of the money supply."
Message on the State of the Union, January 5, 1956, *Congressional Record*, Vol. 102,
Pt. 1, p. 140.

[57] *Economic Report of the President* (Jan. 24, 1956), p. 73.

[58] *Budget of the United States Government for the Fiscal Year Ending June 30, 1958,*
pp. M5–M6.

[59] *Economic Report of the President* (Jan. 23, 1957), pp. v, 2–3, 18–19, 44, 47–48.

tion at a prudent rate." Because of active competition for labor, materials, and equipment, other desirable construction projects could not be recommended.[60] The complementary nature of federal, state, and local investment, as well as total public and private investment, is implied.

The paramount task during most of 1957 was to restrain inflationary tendencies. Money rates were maintained at high levels, and fiscal policy was directed toward restraining inflation. Federal expenditure programs, the President reported, "were closely reviewed to effect economies wherever such action was consistent with essential program objectives."[61] A major reason for this review was that the unused margin of borrowing power under the $275 billion debt limit had become extremely small. There is also some evidence that payments were made less promptly than usual, because of the near-impingement on the debt limit.[62]

With a change in the economic trend, money rates were eased. At the turn of the year 1958 the President reported that the over-all decline had been moderate, despite rather sharp reductions in inventories and in industrial production. There was an awareness that, if the recession continued, definite policies to cope with it might soon be necessary. Fiscal policies, the President said, "can contribute significantly to the attainment of national economic objectives or can impede their accomplishment. It is crucial . . . that they be attuned to the times and so designed as to promote the long-run as well as the immediate economic welfare of the Nation."[63]

[60] *Budget of the United States Government for the Fiscal Year Ending June 30, 1958*, pp. M6–M7.

[61] *Economic Report of the President* (Jan. 20, 1958), pp. 6–7.

[62] The federal government, "noting that continuation of the existing uptrend of defense expenditures would carry outlays far above the budget estimate for the fiscal year 1957–58, and seeking to remain within the authorized debt limit, curtailed new contract placements, cancelled some existing contracts, and accomplished a small reduction in the actual rate of expenditures." *Anti-Recession Policy for 1958*, A Statement by the Program Committee of the Committee for Economic Development (March 1958), p. 10.

[63] *Economic Report of the President* (Jan. 20, 1958), pp. 8, 38–39, 55–56.

In the early months of 1958 unemployment continued to rise. It appeared that the recession might become deeper and be of longer duration than either of the two preceding postwar recessions. The merits of a reduction in taxes, together with the conditions under which a tax cut would become imperative, were widely discussed. Though the administration did not propose a tax cut, the possibility that it might do so was not ruled out. Official pronouncements gave the impression that this and other fiscal-policy measures were being held in reserve. The usefulness of a positive fiscal policy was not denied. At no time was there any suggestion that first priority would be given to maintaining a balanced budget.[64]

The position of the administration during the first half of 1958 was that the recession had not become serious enough to warrant a broad program of governmental action. The official policy was one of wait-and-see. On a number of occasions the President stated that he would look with favor on a tax cut if the need should arise.[65] A seven-point anti-recession program announced on March 8 suggested that the approach to the recession was not entirely passive. This program could hardly qualify as a vigorous effort to control the recession, but it did constitute positive action of a sort.[66]

[64] In mid-January Eisenhower stated that under prevailing conditions a moderate deficit would be preferable to a tax increase. *New York Times* (Jan. 16, 1958), p. 1. Though the President did not commit himself definitely, it was widely recognized by economists and others within the administration that a deficit might be good public policy under the prevailing conditions.

[65] In February Eisenhower stated that the administration might favor a tax cut to cope with the recession. In March he said that his administration would propose a tax cut to fight the recession, if this step became desirable and necessary. In April the President saw no immediate need for a tax cut. *New York Times* (Feb. 6, 1958), p. 1; (March 19, 1958), p. 1; (April 10, 1958), p. 1.

[66] *New York Times* (March 9, 1958), p. 1. The seven points included: (1) acceleration of public works projects for which funds had been appropriated; (2) an early start on certain reclamation projects; (3) stimulation of construction of homes for people of modest means; (4) an amendment to the highway act suspending certain expenditure limitations for three years; (5) giving preference to labor-surplus areas, and especially small business, in awarding military procurement contracts; (6) making funds more readily available to veterans for the purchase of homes; and (7) spe-

Within limits, the wait-and-see attitude was no doubt justified. The role of the built-in stabilizers had long been stressed by economists and public officials. From its inception the automatic stabilizers were working against the developing recession. To place major reliance on this facet of fiscal policy and monetary policy was not illogical, at least up to the point where unemployment reached a level that one associates with a serious recession.[67] By the middle of the year it was clear that the course of fiscal policy had been strongly influenced by inertia.[68] Apparently little consideration was given to the fact that the effectiveness of fiscal policies may depend on the belief that they will be consistently pursued. The principal tax reductions enacted resulted from the repeal of certain taxes on transportation, effective August 31, 1958. Included were the general tax of 3 per cent on the transportation of property, the tax of 4.5 per cent on the transport of oil by pipeline, and the tax on coal shipments imposed at a rate of 4 cents per short ton.[69] The revenues derived from these taxes amounted to approximately $500 million a year. The financial plight of the railroads was the major reason for their repeal.[70] Additional reductions

cial grants for payments to unemployed persons who had exhausted their benefits under state employment compensation laws. (*Ibid.*, p. 54.) A number of other measures qualified as positive or discretionary action. See, for example, the list in *Newsweek* (March 31, 1958), p. 25.

[67] The administration approved the positive steps taken to ease credit. Reductions in the rediscount rates and other efforts to make funds available on more favorable terms, it was hoped, might be influential in effecting a reversal of the economic trend.

[68] "Nothing in our economic policy is so deeply ingrained, and so little reckoned with by economists, as our tendency to wait and see if things do not improve by themselves." John Kenneth Galbraith, *The Affluent Society* (1958), p. 207.

[69] A curious feature of these reductions was that they were made by "The Tax Rate Extension Act of 1958" approved June 30, 1958 (72 Stat. 259). The purpose of this act was to continue the rates for the corporate income tax and certain excises at existing levels.

[70] The contrast between tax policy during the 1953–1954 recession and that during the 1957–1958 recession was too marked to escape notice. See, for example, Walter Lippmann, "Today and Tomorrow," *Washington Post* (May 6, 1958), p. A17.

were made by the revisions for the benefit of small business and the excise tax revisions approved on September 2, 1958.[71]

The continuing rise in prices was a complicating factor. The cost-of-living index was edging upwards at the very time when the unemployment and other indexes showed that the recession had become more severe than the earlier postwar recessions. Those who regarded a reduction in taxes with disfavor stressed the dangers of inflation.[72] From the viewpoint of fiscal policy, a tax increase is a major weapon for dealing with inflation, though not necessarily a moderate rise in the price level strongly influenced by higher food costs. On the other hand, those who advocated a tax cut held that the slight upward trend in prices was not an adequate reason for delaying appropriate fiscal action. The trend in prices during the first half of 1958, it was pointed out, was not a consequence of fiscal and monetary factors.

Another troublesome matter was the federal debt limit, which seemed to stand in the way of a positive fiscal policy. The statutory debt limit in effect at the turn of the year was $275 billion. When the Secretary of the Treasury requested an increase in January, the debt was over $274 billion. The Treasury "had little or no margin for contingencies." Included among these contingencies was the possibility that the current recession would continue, which might mean a fairly sharp decline in receipts. In addition, there was "the possibility of a technological breakthrough" of some kind that would call for a speed-up in military spending.[73] Whatever fiscal policy might be deemed appropriate presumably had to be applied within the strait jacket im-

[71] 72 Stat. 1275, 1606; *New York Times* (Sept. 3, 1958), p. 22.

[72] See, for example, the statement by Bernard Baruch, *New York Times* (April 2, 1958), p. 18. The core of Baruch's argument was that any action that would raise the debt would spur inflation and weaken the federal credit.

[73] *Debt Limit of the United States*, Hearing Before the Committee on Ways and Means, 85 Cong. 2 sess., pp. 2, 29; *New York Times* (Jan. 18, 1958), p. 1.

posed by the statutory debt limit. After considerable debate a *temporary* increase in the debt limit from $275 billion to $280 billion for the period beginning February 26, 1958 and ending June 30, 1959 was approved in late February.[74] The margin of borrowing power thus created solved the immediate problem of the Treasury, but it was scarcely ample to meet the needs of a continuing recession. Later in the summer the *permanent* debt limit was increased from $275 to $283 billion.[75] Including the temporary increase of $5 billion approved earlier in the year, the debt limit thus became $288 billion until June 30, 1959 when it reverts to $283 billion.

To those who favored greater reliance on fiscal measures, the administration seemed to lack assurance in dealing with the recession. Divided counsel within the administration, according to one view, militated against the adoption of a more vigorous policy. A more plausible explanation is that in the spring of 1958 it appeared that a large deficit would be incurred for the fiscal year ending June 30, 1959. The size of the impending deficit, which was later officially estimated at $12.2 billion ($13.7 billion on a cash basis), acted as a restraining influence.[76] A deficit of this size would require borrowings in excess of the amounts permissible under the statutory debt limit.

Under the deficit projected for 1959, the automatic stabilizers presumably would play a more important role than in the two earlier postwar recessions. Because of the numerous forces that were operative, the influence of the automatic stabilizers in helping to arrest and reverse the downward trend in economic activity is necessarily indeterminate. But

[74] 72 Stat. 27.
[75] 72 Stat. 1758.
[76] The revised estimates for 1959 are from *The 1959 Federal Budget—Midyear Review* (Sept. 11, 1958), pp. 7, 19. The indicated deficit was well above any previously incurred in time of peace.

the fact that the change in the economic trend occurred at almost the same time that the federal government began running a fairly large cash deficit suggests that their influence may have been substantial.[77]

By autumn the recovery appeared to be well under way.[78] A gradual reduction of the deficit to a point where the annual figure might be smaller than the September estimate seemed probable, but a balanced budget in the near future seemed unlikely. Nevertheless, in December—almost a month before the release of the budget—the President proposed a balanced budget of $77 billion for the fiscal year 1960.[79] To students of fiscal policy, this development was of major interest. A balanced budget for 1960 would mean that the stimulative effect of the automatic stabilizers would be restricted mainly to the fiscal year 1959. The President's expressed desire for a balanced budget in 1960 showed conclusively that the balanced budget idea continued to be influential in shaping public policy.

Fiscal theory was far from dormant during the period covered by the preceding review of events and policies since 1940. New ideas were advanced and earlier doctrines were undergoing a process of refinement. In economics and public finance, as in other areas, new ideas tend to stimulate thought. To an indeterminate extent official acceptance of modern conceptions contributed to the further evolution of the theory of fiscal policy.

---

[77] The cash deficit for July 1958 was $4.1 billion, and that for the July-September quarter was $4.8 billion. For the April-June quarter there was a cash surplus of $1.4 billion. *Treasury Bulletin* (November 1958), p. 17.

[78] The low point in the index of industrial production was reached in April but it was not until June or July that a moderate upward trend was clearly discernible. Similarly the low point in personal income was reached in the spring; by mid-summer it seemed clear that an upward trend was under way.

[79] *Washington Post* (Dec. 23, 1958), p. 1.

Developments in Fiscal Theory

Compensatory fiscal theory, as it evolved during the 1930's, emphasized expenditures financed from public borrowings as a means of stimulating employment and the national income. The central idea was that governmental deficits should offset any savings generated by the economy at high levels of employment that were not siphoned into private capital formation. It was also recognized that in an economy with a tendency towards high saving, an increase in public expenditures covered by progressive taxes might lead to higher consumption for the economy as a whole and a rise in national income, with private investment remaining at the same level.

Though Keynes and others stressed additional public expenditures—public works, adequate relief payments, and the like—it soon became apparent that a stimulative fiscal policy does not necessarily depend on increased expenditures. A reduction of taxes, it was reasoned, might be just as effective as, and in some circumstances perhaps more effective than, a loan-financed rise in public expenditures in increasing national income. If savings were not being fully invested in private undertakings, the primary goal of fiscal policy was to ensure that net public borrowing absorbed the excess. This objective might be achieved by tax reduction as well as by increased expenditure.

Alternative methods of securing full employment through fiscal policies have been suggested by Nicholas Kaldor, among others. There are many ways, said Kaldor, of so regulating the fiscal policies of the state as "to ensure adequate total outlay for the community as a whole; but they can all be reduced to four distinct types." They are (1) by increased public expenditure covered by loans; (2) by increased public expenditure covered by taxation; (3) by increased private spending brought about through remission of taxation; and (4) by increased private spending brought about through changing the incidence of taxation or imposing a combined system of taxation and subsidies.[80] Of these, only the first and third imply deficit financing. With respect to the third method, Kaldor pointed out that the simple device of reducing taxation relatively to a given rate of expenditure will increase employment, since it converts the ordinary expenditure of the government into loan expenditure, which is an offset to savings. However, since some portion of the tax remissions will be saved, the net deficit would have to be larger than in the case of increased public outlay.[81]

The idea that stimulative fiscal action is not limited to expenditures covered from borrowings, together with reduction or redistribution of taxes, was an important development in the evolution of fiscal theory. The first reference to this idea in the modern literature appears to be that of Jörgen Gelting, a Danish economist. "When the public sector collects more taxes from the private sector and uses the revenue for increased outlays," he wrote in 1941, "total employment will be increased exactly by an amount corresponding to the increase in outlays. This at least holds true when the marginal propensity to consume as well as productivity in the private sector are unaffected."[82]

[80] Nicholas Kaldor, "The Quantitative Aspects of the Full Employment Problem in Britain," Appendix C in William H. Beveridge, *Full Employment in a Free Society* (1945), pp. 345 ff. The fourth method, Sir William stated, presents extreme practical difficulties. Accordingly, it was not included in his discussion of alternative routes to peacetime full employment in the report.

[81] *Ibid.*, p. 347. Kaldor's second method is considered at p. 261.

[82] P. N. Rasmussen, "A Note on the History of the Balanced-Budget Multiplier," *Economic Journal*, Vol. 68 (March 1958), p. 155. The translation is from an article in Danish on the problem of financing public activities. *Nationalokonomisk Tidsskrift*, 79 Bind, 5 hefte (1941), p. 295. The balanced budget theorem was further considered in a book in Danish by Kjeld Philip published in the spring of 1942. (*Ibid.*, p. 156.) Rasmussen states that Gelting did not regard his idea as original and that it perhaps stems from Ricardo. The first analysis in English was probably that of William A. Salant. His unpublished memorandum of June 30, 1942 is referred to by Wallich in the article considered in this section. The present discussion is intended to show the

Writing in 1944, Hansen and Perloff pointed out that "an increase in useful governmental expenditures (the initial expenditure being financed by borrowing) will tend to raise the national income even though subsequently financed from consumption taxes." When the additional government expenditures are paid out to the public, the income receipts of individuals are increased. If a consumption tax is then imposed equivalent to the enlarged income, it follows that private expenditures after taxes remain as before. "The Gross National Product is increased by the amount of the new government spending while private expenditures remain the same."[83] Obviously, an increase in total national product such as here envisioned is possible only when available productive resources are not fully utilized. At full employment the addition of new public expenditures would merely divert resources from the private to the public sector.

A similar conclusion was reached by Wallich. His analysis is concerned with the effects of a nonprogressive balanced increase in the budget, without regard to the progressiveness of the basic budget. In developing the argument, Wallich posited a national income of $130 billion and assumed that at this level there are unemployed resources capable of producing additional goods and services worth $10 billion. Suppose the personal income tax is raised to yield an extra $10 billion, which is used to build more roads and to provide more free education, the previously idle resources thereby finding employment. Incremental taxes and expenditures are so adjusted that the consumption and saving habits of taxpayers as a group are the same as those of the newly employed who are the recipients of incremental government expenditures. Though the additional tax reduces by $10 billion

development of the balanced budget theorem and its significance. No attempt is made to present a complete coverage of the literature or to explore all the refinements of this theorem.

[83] Alvin H. Hansen and Harvey S. Perloff, *State and Local Finance in the National Economy* (1944), pp. 244–45.

the purchasing power of those who "are employed to begin with," this purchasing power is not destroyed but merely transferred to the hands of the newly employed. "Since in their joint effect the additional taxes and expenditures are, by assumption, nonprogressive, the consumption demand exercised by the newly employed will be the same as that which would have been exercised by the initially employed, had they not had to pay the tax." Aggregate private demand and private output therefore remain unchanged, but meanwhile there is an increase in government purchases equal to the $10 billion produced by the previously unemployed, which is paid for out of taxes and therefore is not dependent on the level of aggregate demand. Thus national income has been raised to a total of $140 billion.[84]

Wallich states that the reason national income can increase, without an increase in investment and without a redistribution of income, is that the additional income financed by the government does not give rise to new net saving. The people who were unemployed will save part of their additional income, but an equal volume of savings of the initially employed is absorbed by the additional tax. Since the two groups are assumed to be similar, the savings of the one group are offset by the reduction in the savings of the other. He then adds: "By absorbing part of originally existing income and respending it in its entirety, the Government prevents some fraction of this amount from being saved, as it otherwise would be."[85]

Nicholas Kaldor also took the position that full employment could be secured by means of increased public outlay, even though the expenditure is fully covered by taxation.

[84] Henry C. Wallich, "Income-Generating Effects of a Balanced Budget," *Quarterly Journal of Economics*, Vol. 59 (1944–1945), pp. 78–80.

[85] *Ibid.*, p. 80. The increase in national income occasioned by the larger budget, it is emphasized, "comes about through an increase in government output." The additional goods and services are not necessarily produced by the government; they must be available through the government. P. 82.

The reason given is that "an increase in taxation is not likely to reduce private outlay by the full amount of the taxes paid." All taxes, it may be assumed, have some influence on saving. Taxes which fall on the poor "have a relatively large effect on consumption and a relatively small effect on savings; with taxes paid by the rich it is probably the other way round." It follows that an increase in public expenditure will cause a net addition to the total outlay of the community, even if it is covered by taxation; and "this net addition is likely to be all the greater, the more progressive is the incidence of the extra taxation raised to cover it."[86] In Kaldor's analysis the stimulative effect on employment is attributed solely to the fact that the increased taxes imposed to finance the rise in expenditures are covered in part from funds that otherwise would be saved.

The stimulative effects of a tax-financed rise in public expenditures, with the budget remaining in balance, were carefully examined by Trygve Haavelmo. The core of his argument follows:

Extra public expenditure covered, simultaneously, by taxes can obviously be added to the existing gross income in such a way that it will leave the people with exactly the same amount of net income, and hence will leave the private demand at exactly the same level as before the tax was imposed (provided the tax policy does not lead to a change in the distribution of net incomes and, thereby, to a change in the marginal propensity to consume of the society as a whole). But, while the government collects the tax money without any direct compensation to the individual taxpayer, the government requires goods and services from the public in return for money expenditures. Now, if there were already full employment before the tax was imposed, the result would be that the public as a whole would have to work partly for the government *instead* of working for their own direct benefit. Then they could not pay the taxes by working more. If, however, there is a sufficient amount of idle manpower and resources the amount of employment

[86] Kaldor, "The Quantitative Aspects of the Full Employment Problem in Britain," Appendix C in Beveridge, *Full Employment in a Free Society*, pp. 346–47.

and productive services required by the government will come forth in *addition* to what is wanted by the private sector of the economy. The gross income, i.e. the money value of all goods and services produced (for private as well as public needs) will have increased, although the net income has remained unchanged. In fact, from an employment point of view, the result for the society as a whole will be exactly the same as if the government had ordered idle manpower and resources to work without any direct compensation.[87]

Haavelmo presented a mathematical analysis of the multiplier effects that might be generated by public spending on goods and services balanced by taxes. This portion of the analysis he describes as "a more accurate demonstration" of the "simple conclusion" above. Stated in briefest form, the conclusion is that such a balanced increase in the budget "has a direct multiplier effect, with a multiplier equal to 1 in *addition* to whatever (positive or negative) effects there might be from a redistribution of income."[88]

Haavelmo's conclusion is comparable to that of Hansen and Perloff and Wallich. However, he believes that the Hansen-Perloff assumption that the initial expenditure must be financed by borrowing is unnecessary. Kaldor's argument, it is pointed out, hinges on the assumption that an increase in taxation is not likely to reduce private expenditures by the full amount of the taxes paid. The idea that taxes equal to public expenditure can create employment only to the extent that they reduce saving Haavelmo finds incorrect. Wallich's argument, which hinges on government taking income, part of which otherwise would have been saved, and spending it in its entirety, Haavelmo believes to be both incorrect and dangerous. The "argument that the government spends income that otherwise would have been partly saved is dangerous as it might lead to the false belief that the

---

[87] Trygve Haavelmo, "Multiplier Effects of a Balanced Budget," *Econometrica*, Vol. 13 (1945), pp. 313–14.

[88] *Ibid.*, pp. 314–18.

higher the propensity to save for the public the larger the effect of the fiscal policy discussed."[89]

Haavelmo's article led to a number of comments and elaboration of specific points. Haberler suggested that the formal precision of the argument should not deceive us into believing that tax-financed expenditures are as powerful an anti-depression measure as deficit-financed expenditures.[90] To this Haavelmo readily agreed. "Since the multiplier effect of each dollar of tax is only equal to 1, there can . . . be no disagreement . . . on the point that deficit spending, usually, would be much more effective in increasing total income." The point that the initial spending does not have to be financed by borrowing to obtain the type of income expansion under discussion was reiterated. The force that drives gross income up when there is a rise in public expenditures on goods and services balanced by increased taxes is "the over-all increase in the marginal propensity to spend, resulting from the government's propensity to spend being equal to unity."[91]

If the latter proposition is essentially correct, it may be important for an economy in which there are important lags in public facilities—highways, schools, and the like. It suggests that, with employment and utilization of resources below optimum levels, unemployed labor and idle resources can be used to provide needed goods and services, without changing the net surplus or deficit position of the government at given income levels. At any given time both tax-financed and debt-financed public outlays for goods and services are reflected in the national income. With unused resources available, either method of financing will result in a higher national income. The two methods of financing differ in that one is more stimulative than the other.

[89] *Ibid.*, pp. 312–14.
[90] G. Haberler, "Multiplier Effects of a Balanced Budget: Some Monetary Implications of Mr. Haavelmo's Paper," *Econometrica*, Vol. 14 (1946), p. 149.
[91] *Ibid.*, p. 158.

Later several analysts questioned whether a tax-financed rise in public expenditures could cause an equal increase in national income. The view that such an increase in expenditures has a multiplier of 1 in all or most cases was said to be unrealistic. Ralph Turvey took the position that the theorem that a balanced budget increase has a multiplier of unity is a very special case. His analysis suggests that both the objects of additional expenditures and the subjects of taxation would have to be selected with great care if a multiplier approximating unity is to be attained in practice.[92]

Baumol and Peston carried the analysis a step further. They argued that there is very little assurance that unity is even a rough approximation to the multiplier associated with any balanced budget expenditure program a government may be expected to undertake. In their opinion a constant multiplier is unrealistic. There is "no reason to believe that the magnitude of the balanced budget multiplier will remain unchanged with changing time and circumstances." The expansionist effect of a balanced tax-expenditure rise in the budget will tend to be reduced during periods of low national income and increased in more prosperous times.[93]

In a comment on the Baumol-Peston analysis, Alvin Hansen pointed out that when the notion that a tax-financed increase in government outlays was expansionist was first hit upon, the exact magnitude of the expansionist effect was not the primary matter under discussion. Moreover, in developing models characterized by a unit balanced budget multiplier, Haavelmo and others based this outcome on certain

[92] Ralph Turvey, "Some Notes on Multiplier Theory," *American Economic Review*, Vol. 43 (1953), pp. 275, 284–86.

[93] William J. Baumol and Maurice H. Peston, "More on the Multiplier Effects of a Balanced Budget," *American Economic Review*, Vol. 45 (1955), pp. 140 ff. John G. Gurley criticized the analyses of a balanced tax-expenditure rise in the budget on the ground that this and the other two methods (loan finance and tax reduction) of closing a deflationary gap discussed in the literature stopped short of a general analysis of the routes to full employment. "Fiscal Policies for Full Employment: A Diagrammatic Analysis," *Journal of Political Economy*, Vol. 60 (1952), pp. 525ff.

rigid assumptions. They "did not assert that in the actual world we can count on a balanced budget multiplier of one." That is to say, a multiplier of one is attainable in practice, only if the formal conditions specified by the several authors are met. In other circumstances matched increments of taxes and public expenditures are likely, if not certain, to have some expansionist effect.[94]

[94] Hansen, "More on the Multiplier Effects of a Balanced Budget: Comment," *American Economic Review*, Vol. 46 (1956), p. 157. The balanced budget theorem "makes clear (1) that matched increments of taxes and factor-purchase expenditures are very likely, if not certain, to have an expansionary effect, and (2) that this effect will vary with consumption propensities and with government expenditure leakages via imports, purchases of capital assets, and the like." Walter W. Heller, "CED's Stabilizing Budget Policy After Ten Years," *American Economic Review*, Vol. 47 (1957), p. 638.

CHAPTER VII

Fiscal Policy and Economic Stabilization

THE ANALYSIS IN THE PRECEDING CHAPTER has shown that fiscal policy assumed a new role after World War II. In marked contrast with the prewar years when overcoming the depression was the major objective, the primary purpose of fiscal policy was to assist in keeping the economy operating at or near full employment. The usefulness of fiscal-policy measures now depended on whether they helped to stabilize income and employment at high levels. In this environment the type of fiscal policy that would best serve the goal of economic stabilization became a matter of great importance.

During the war years economists and others concerned with an orderly transition to a peacetime economy assumed that the federal government would pursue an active fiscal policy after the war. If both compensatory public spending and tax adjustments to stimulate purchasing power should be resorted to, the reliance placed on discretionary fiscal measures presumably might be far greater than at any time during the depression. When pessimistic economic forecasts for the immediate postwar period proved wide of the mark, a reaction in fiscal and budget thinking set in. For a period of several years there was increasing emphasis on automaticity in fiscal policy.[1]

---

[1] The erroneous and inadequate forecasts were not the only reason for the rising popularity of the automatic approach. Heller mentions three additional reasons: (1) the size of the postwar budget made automatic flexibility quantitatively more

Automatic Stabilizers and the Stabilizing Budget

Automatic stabilizers are elements of public expenditures and revenues that operate to increase or decrease output or spending power and that are set in motion by a decline or rise in economic activity, without the necessity of formal action for the purpose of effecting such increases or decreases.[2] When income rises, the automatic stabilizers come into play and tend to widen the margin between total income and disposable income, thereby retarding the rise in disposable income. Conversely, when consumer and other demands decline and a downward trend in national income sets in, they tend to narrow this margin and lessen the rate of decline in disposable income. The automatic stabilizers reduce the range of fluctuations—they do not fully offset them.

Disposable income or spending power is influenced by automatic changes in both public expenditures and taxes. Unemployment compensation payments are the principal category of expenditure that increases or decreases automatically as output falls or rises. At the same time a change in the volume of employment operates to lower or raise the pay roll base on which unemployment compensation and old-age contributions or taxes are levied. On the revenue side, the personal income tax is a leading automatic stabilizer.[3]

important than in the prewar years; (2) a shift of emphasis from secular stagnation to the problem of cyclical fluctuations, which gave a higher priority to flexibility and reversibility in policy; and (3) "the attractions of a budgetary policy based on automaticity and marginal budget balancing as a pragmatic middle ground on which a consensus of otherwise widely divergent groups might be reached." Walter W. Heller, "CED's Stabilizing Budget Policy After Ten Years," *American Economic Review*, Vol. 47 (1957), p. 635.

[2] Automatic stabilizers are sometimes referred to as "built-in stabilizers" or embraced within the term "built-in flexibility."

[3] For a comprehensive discussion of the "built-in flexibility" of the individual income tax, see Joseph A. Pechman, "Yield of the Individual Income Tax During a Recession," in *Policies to Combat Depression* (1956), pp. 123 ff.

The progressive feature of this tax enhances the magnitude of its stabilizing effect. When incomes rise, income taxes payable rise more than proportionately and disposable income less than proportionately. Conversely, as incomes decline, income taxes decline more than proportionately and disposable income less than proportionately.[4] The corporate income tax acts as a powerful automatic stabilizer. When changes in the level of economic activity occur, business profits—and the base for this tax—rise and fall far more sharply than the national income.

The idea of automatic stabilization is at the heart of the stabilizing budget policy proposed by the Committee for Economic Development. The underlying principle was developed by this organization into a full-fledged theory of budget policy. This policy is stated as follows: "Set tax rates to balance the budget and provide a surplus for debt retirement at an agreed high level of employment and national income. Having set these rates, leave them alone unless there is some major change in national policy or condition of national life."[5] Fluctuations in national income do not call for changes in tax rates, or in the volume of expenditures except for the automatic response of some expenditure items such as unemployment compensation payments. Certain expenditures such as those for public works may be advanced or held back to meet changing economic conditions within the limits of the over-all expenditure program. Surpluses would not be

[4] The personal exemptions are an important factor influencing the progressivity and therefore the stabilizing effect of the personal income tax. In the lower-income ranges the exemptions are the dominant element determining the effective rate on personal incomes. The pay-as-you-go system adopted during World War II resulted in a much more rapid response of personal income tax collections to changes in national income. The time lag was eliminated or greatly reduced, thereby enhancing the automaticity of the effect. The pay-as-you-go system did not in itself effect any change in tax liabilities in relation to the income on which they are based.

[5] Committee for Economic Development, *Taxes and the Budget: A Program for Prosperity in a Free Economy* (November 1947), p. 22. The policy recommendations of the committee are framed with reference to the cash or cash-consolidated budget. All cash transactions between the government and the public are included. See p. 322.

used to increase expenditures, but would become available for debt retirement.[6]

The automatic changes in tax collections and expenditures with fluctuations in the national income, it is said, are precisely what is required if fiscal policy is to aid economic stability. As the national income rises, tax collections will rise, taking more and more from the available income of the public. Expenditures under programs such as unemployment compensation will fall. "This process will restrain increases of demand and curb inflationary pressure." Similarly, the automatic decline of tax revenue acts to check a downward movement. "When production and income drop, tax collections will fall too. Income after taxes will decline less than income before taxes. This will help to sustain production and employment. The stabilizing effect will be reinforced by an increase in unemployment compensation and other payments."[7]

In its initial proposal the committee recommended that tax rates be set sufficiently high to yield a surplus of about $3 billion at a national income corresponding to employment of about 96 per cent of the labor force. With the labor force at the 1947 level, this surplus would be attained with unemployment at about 2.5 millions, and the budget would be balanced with unemployment at approximately 4 to 4.5 millions.[8] In a popular version released several years later, the committee was less specific; the stabilizing budget policy "would produce surpluses in good years to retire debt created in bad years."[9] In 1954 the committee did not stress the desirability of achieving a surplus and aimed merely at a

[6] During mild recessions the Committee for Economic Development would rely strongly on monetary policy. The role of monetary policy is discussed in *Jobs and Markets* (1946), pp. 85 ff; *Monetary and Fiscal Policy for Greater Economic Stability* (1948); *Flexible Monetary Policy: What It Is and How It Works* (1953); and *Anti-Recession Policy for 1958* (March 1958), p. 13.

[7] *Taxes and the Budget: A Program for Prosperity in a Free Economy*, p. 27.

[8] *Ibid.*, p. 32.

[9] Committee for Economic Development, *The Stabilizing Budget Policy: What It Is and How It Works* (July 1950), p. 11.

balanced cash budget at high levels of employment. The
higher revenue requirements which obtained, it was believed, made this change in emphasis desirable.[10] Under
stable conditions tax rates might remain fixed for long periods.
It is recognized, however, that the automatic responses of
tax revenues and expenditures might not be sufficient to
cope with a severe depression. With this thought in mind,
the committee stated that under the stabilizing budget policy
"tax rates would remain unchanged unless the depression became particularly serious."[11]

The stabilizing budget plan combines the qualities of
simplicity and automaticity of response. The committee emphasizes that it "does not depend for its stabilizing effect
upon an impossible accuracy in forecasting economic fluctuations or an impossible speed in making fiscal decisions and
taking fiscal action."[12] Surpluses and deficits generated by
inflationary and deflationary deviations from high employment would be welcome as stabilizing influences, but tax
rates would not be altered to magnify these surpluses and
deficits as an offset to moderate economic fluctuations.[13] A
major advantage claimed is that the operation of the plan is
entirely free of human control. There is no administrative or
timing problem of any kind. When a change in the economic

[10] Committee for Economic Development, *Taxes, National Security and Economic
Growth* (January 1954), pp. 11–12. The committee did not abandon the idea of
achieving a surplus. It merely gave up this goal for the period in which certain conditions prevailed.

[11] *The Stabilizing Budget Policy: What It Is and How It Works*, p. 9. In line with
this policy, in March 1958 the Committee for Economic Development recommended
a temporary reduction in personal income taxes of one fifth or approximately $7 bil-
lion as soon as the economic situation "becomes clearly worse" than in 1949 and
1954. *Anti-Recession Policy for 1958*, A Statement by the Program Committee of
the Committee for Economic Development, pp. 8, 19–21.

[12] *Taxes and the Budget: A Program for Prosperity in a Free Economy*, pp. 28–29.

[13] Heller, "CED's Stabilizing Budget Policy Ten Years After," *American Economic Review*, p. 636. CED policy "rests on the assumption that human frailties and
institutional deficiencies—reflected in imperfections and errors of forecasting, slow-
moving executive and legislative processes in taxation, and a tendency of human
beings to be timid, unpredictable, and biased towards inflation—make it necessary
to use automatic rather than discretionary fiscal changes in national stabilization
policy." *Ibid.*, p. 637.

trend occurs, the response follows immediately and is always in the right direction.

The monetary and fiscal framework for economic stability suggested by Milton Friedman combines automaticity in the operation of the fiscal system with sweeping changes in the monetary and credit system. The monetary and banking system would be reformed so as to eliminate both the private creation or destruction of money and discretionary control of the quantity of money by central bank authority. The monetary functions of the banking system would be limited mainly to the provision of depositary facilities, clearing of checks, and the like. The chief function of the monetary authorities would be the creation of money to meet government deficits, and the retirement of money when the government is running a surplus.[14]

The federal government would adopt a policy of determining the volume of government expenditures on goods and services entirely on the basis of the community's desire, need, and willingness to pay for public services. Changes in the level of expenditure on goods and services would be made solely in response to alterations in the relative value attached by the community to public services and private consumption; such expenditures should not be changed in response to changes in economic activity. In addition, there would be a predetermined program of transfer expenditures, consisting of "a statement of the conditions and terms under which relief and assistance and other transfers will be granted." This program would be changed only in response to alterations in

[14] Milton Friedman, "A Monetary and Fiscal Framework for Economic Stability," *American Economic Review*, Vol. 38 (1948), p. 247. What would be involved in the proposed reform is summarized, as follows: "The private creation of money can perhaps best be eliminated by adopting the 100 per cent reserve proposal, thereby separating the depositary from the lending function of the banking system. The adoption of 100 per cent reserves would also reduce the discretionary powers of the reserve system by eliminating rediscounting and existing powers over reserve requirements. To complete the elimination of the major weapons of discretionary authority, the existing powers to engage in open market operations and the existing direct controls over stock market and consumer credit should be abolished."

the kind and level of transfer payments the community feels it should and can afford to make.[15] Though the program would not be changed in response to cyclical fluctuations, expenditures would vary automatically over the cycle. They would tend to be high when unemployment is high and low when unemployment is low.

Federal revenues would be obtained from a progressive tax system, with major reliance on the personal income tax. As much of the tax bill as possible should be collected at the source. Rates and exemptions would be set in the light of the expected yield at a level of income corresponding to reasonably full employment at a predetermined price level. The budget principle might be either that the hypothetical yield should balance government expenditure, including transfer payments (at the hypothetical level of income) or that it should lead to a deficit sufficient to provide some specified secular increase in the quantity of money. The tax structure would not be changed in response to cyclical fluctuations, but tax receipts would vary automatically. "Changes in the tax structure should reflect changes in the level of public services or transfer payments the community chooses to have. A decision to undertake additional public expenditures should be accompanied by a revenue measure increasing taxes."[16]

Under this proposal federal expenditures "would be financed entirely by either tax revenues or the creation of money"—that is, the issue of non-interest-bearing securities.

[15] *Ibid.*, p. 248. Transfer expenditures include payments for interest, veterans' benefits, agriculture aids, relief, social security benefits, and the like, for which the government does not obtain currently produced goods or services in exchange. They are treated essentially as taxes with a minus sign. "The Problem of Economic Stability, A Committee Report," *American Economic Review*, Vol. 40 (1950), p. 513.

[16] Friedman, "A Monetary and Fiscal Policy for Economic Stability," *American Economic Review*, pp. 248–49. The federal government would keep two budgets: (1) the stable budget in which all figures refer to the hypothetical income; and (2) the actual budget. "The principle of balancing outlays and receipts at a hypothetical income level would be substituted for the principle of balancing actual outlays and receipts." *Ibid.*, pp. 249–50.

"Deficits or surpluses in the government budget would be reflected dollar for dollar in changes in the quantity of money; and, conversely, the quantity of money would change only as a consequence of deficits or surpluses."[17]

In considering this and similar proposals, a key question is whether an economy operating within the suggested framework would tend to adjust automatically to an optimum level of activity. If when the economy is out of equilibrium in either direction it moves toward full employment and stable prices, it may be sufficient to moderate fluctuations through the working of automatic fiscal and monetary changes, thereby facilitating the corrective process. On the other hand, if because of existing institutional imperfections and fortuitous developments—such as a sharp change in the cold-war climate—a tendency toward stable equilibrium is not discernible, discretionary action may be essential.

Friedman's position was questioned by Paul A. Samuelson, among others. He agreed with Friedman that a rational use of resources requires that governmental expenditures on goods and services should be determined solely on the basis of the community's "desire, need, and willingness to pay" for these services, and that they should be changed only in response to changes in the relative value the community attaches to private and public services. But this principle, according to Samuelson, does not imply that public expenditures on goods and services should not be changed when economic activity changes. The real social cost of using resources does not remain constant. It may be entirely rational to increase public expenditures during a depression, because the real social cost of using resources that otherwise would be unused is zero *provided* any alternative private uses government might be able to stimulate have a marginal

---

[17] *Ibid.*, pp. 250–51. In his analysis Friedman uses "tax revenues" as the equivalent of current revenues. It will be understood that federal revenues include a variety of fees, charges, and miscellaneous income, in addition to taxes.

value less than that of the additional public expenditure.[18]

A rational and competent public expenditure policy for a democracy is necessarily based on a number of criteria. Such a policy requires that some consideration be given to economy. For this reason alone economists may be justified in disagreeing with proposals to hold public expenditures on goods and services constant, regardless of the state of economic activity. Since the real social cost of employing unused resources is zero, "it may be rational to expand public expenditures in depression even within a formula for expenditures determined solely by 'desire, need, and willingness to pay.' For willingness to pay must certainly increase as cost falls toward zero."[19]

The objectivity and clarity with which the issues raised by automaticity in fiscal policy have been presented have received the commendation of economists and laymen alike. The influence of the stabilizing budget proposal, together with the discussion of the underlying issues, has been enormous. The ideas embraced by "automatic stabilizers" and "the stabilizing budget" have become firmly embedded in professional, business, and official thought with respect to fiscal and budgetary policies.

For almost two decades automatic stabilization has been stressed by economists in discussions of stabilization policy.

---

[18] Samuelson, "Principles and Rules in Modern Fiscal Policy: A Neo-Classical Reformulation," in *Money, Trade, and Economic Growth: In Honor of John Henry Williams* (1951), pp. 157 ff; "Full Employment versus Progress and Other Economic Goals," in *Income Stabilization for a Developing Democracy*, Max F. Millikan, ed. (1953), pp. 560–61.

[19] Robert A. Dahl and Charles E. Lindblom, "Variation in Public Expenditure," in *Income Stabilization for a Developing Democracy*, pp. 354–61. For the reasons here mentioned public expenditures varied with a view to stabilizing the economy have an independent justification in terms of their value relative to their costs. This is in essence the same justification that was advanced in earlier discussions of countercyclical public works. The economic cost as well as the monetary cost of public works, it was emphasized, would be lower if they were expanded during a recession and contracted during boom periods. See, for example, Otto T. Mallery, "The Long-Range Planning of Public Works," in *Business Cycles and Unemployment* (1923), pp. 231–32.

In a statement transmitted in 1949 to the Joint Committee on the Economic Report, sixteen economists stated that "the existing automatic flexibility makes an important contribution" to economic stability. But sole reliance cannot be placed on this device. It is only "a first line of defense; more must be done to cope with serious economic fluctuations."[20] A subcommittee of the Committee on Public Issues of the American Economic Association reached a similar conclusion: "Most economists approve the greatest possible use of automatic stabilizers, but do not consider it prudent to rely solely on them. Hence they favor use of additional stabilizing measures if unemployment or inflation pass certain points."[21]

The stabilizing budget proposal and automaticity in fiscal policy have had a profound influence on the thinking of the business community. Polls conducted by *Fortune* magazine indicate that in 1949 more than half of those responding regarded automatic stabilization as a valid approach to fiscal policy. The 25,000 business executives polled were confronted with the choices that government might make with regard to fiscal policy in a recession. A balanced budget or a moderate surplus prior to the beginning of the recession was assumed. The executives were asked whether (1) they would raise taxes and try to balance the budget; (2) leave taxes alone and let the deficit grow; or (3) cut taxes in order to make fiscal policy an active device for strengthening business incentives and expanding purchasing power.[22]

[20] "Federal Expenditure and Revenue Policy for Economic Stability," *American Economic Review*, Vol. 39 (1949), p. 1268. Formula flexibility was recommended as a subject for further exploration. Under formula flexibility Congress would enact laws providing, for example, for tax reductions and upward revisions of expenditure programs if unemployment exceeds a specified figure, or production falls below a certain level. This supplement to automatic stabilization would be a sort of half-way measure between automatic stabilization in a strict sense and discretionary action by the Chief Executive or an agency clothed with full authority.

[21] "The Problem of Economic Instability, A Committee Report," *American Economic Review*, Vol. 40, p. 522.

[22] "The Education of the Businessman," *Fortune*, Vol. 40 (August 1949), p. 48; also in *Readings in Economics from Fortune*, R. E. Mulcahy, ed. (1954), p. 81.

A majority of 53 per cent was reported as favoring the second choice, or the automatic stabilizing budget policy. Perhaps more surprising, no less than 26 per cent favored the third choice—cutting taxes and accepting a larger deficit. Only 16 per cent chose the orthodox course of raising taxes and trying to maintain a balanced budget. Commenting on the latter figure, the editors of *Fortune* state that the "first choice, that of orthodoxy, would surely have won something close to a unanimous vote in 1930." They conclude that a "liberalizing process has been at work that increases the chances of fending off depressions in the future; or of preventing recessions from turning into depressions."[23]

A majority of the business executives polled no longer equate an annually balanced federal budget with fiscal soundness. This poll suggests that in the event of a sharp recession, a concerted effort to increase tax revenues for the purpose of maintaining a balanced budget would be construed by most executives as a perverse approach to fiscal policy. Rather than being dependent on a balanced budget, favorable action on decisions that would help bring about a recovery might depend on official acceptance of modern fiscal-policy ideas in the formulation of budget policy. The turn-about in business thinking is nowhere better illustrated than in pronouncements concerning the income tax. Until the mid-1930's the tendency of income tax revenues to decline sharply, or more than proportionately, with changes in national income was regarded as a major disadvantage of this form of taxation. With the more recent emphasis on automatic stabilization, this "disadvantage" has become a virtue.

Automatic stabilization has attained the status of a principle or guide for fiscal policy. For example, the first of three "economic principles" formulated by the Joint Economic Committee in 1956 is: Federal tax policy "should recognize that the level of tax revenues in relation to the

[23] *Ibid.*

amount of government expenditures has an important bearing on the level of economic activity. This would tend to result in federal surpluses and debt retirement during prosperous and boom periods and deficits during recessions and depressions." The second principle is even more pertinent: "Tax policy should improve the automatic stabilization potential built into the federal revenue system." This committee looks with satisfaction on the "built-in features" of the present revenue structure, though it recognizes that they cannot fully counteract fluctuations in economic activity.[24]

The committee stated that "increasing the capacity of the Federal revenue system to provide automatic stabilization is an important factor in Federal tax policy." Enhancing the built-in flexibility of the revenue system, in the committee's view, requires mainly strengthening the individual and corporate income taxes. "The stabilizing capacity of income taxes depends primarily on (1) the size of the tax base relative to the actual income of individual and corporate taxpayers, (2) the responsiveness of the items of income which comprise the tax bases to changes in levels of economic activity, and (3) the degree of effective progression in the rate structure applied to the tax base."[25]

There is also a wide interest in increasing expenditure flexibility. Because of the preponderance of military expenditures, federal expenditures in the postwar period have been less subject to deliberate countercyclical variation than in the 1930's. Moreover, foreign aid expenditures are not likely to move countercyclically, except perhaps in the event of extreme adversity. Realism requires that one recognize that built-in flexibility in public expenditures is rather limited, apart from unemployment compensation payments. Relief payments respond to some extent to changes in employment and gross national product, but fully automatic increases are possible only within the limits of available ap-

[24] *Federal Tax Policy for Economic Growth and Stability*, S. Rept. 1310, 84 Cong. 2 sess., pp. 2–4.
[25] *Ibid.*, pp. 4–5.

propriations. Public works can be speeded up or contracted, subject to the same restriction. Agricultural benefits do not follow a clear countercyclical pattern, and the bulk of veterans' aids do not fluctuate with changes in employment.

In appraising the possibilities of greater expenditure flexibility, it is well to keep in mind that in the period since World War II federal expenditures have been decidedly unstable. Federal spending has been the least stable of the major components of final demand for goods and services. In several instances such as the Korean War federal expenditures contributed to over-all instability. Until 1954 postwar fluctuations in federal spending were largely accidental.[26] The comparative stability since 1954 cannot be construed as a permanent change in pattern. The unsettled international situation would seem to preclude such an interpretation.

Recent experience in no way invalidates the conception of built-in expenditure flexibility or the desirability of making federal and other public expenditures more flexible. It merely suggests that the problem of attaining a stable economy is complicated by developments such as the outbreak of the Korean War, together with the cessation of hostilities a few years later.

Rules and Discretionary Action in Fiscal Policy

The discussion of the automatic stabilizers and the stabilizing budget raised in dramatic fashion the issue of rules versus discretionary action in budget and fiscal policy. When the stabilizing budget proposal was first presented, the Committee for Economic Development was sharply critical of a

[26] Bert G. Hickman, "Federal Spending and the Stability of the Postwar Economy," in *Federal Expenditure Policy for Economic Growth and Stability*, Papers Submitted by Panelists Appearing Before the Subcommittee on Fiscal Policy, Joint Economic Committee, 85 Cong. 1 sess. (1957), pp. 357 ff.

managed compensatory fiscal system. Dependence on accurate forecasting of business fluctuations, it was said, "is even greater for the compensatory budget than for the annually balanced budget. If forecasting is inaccurate, the compensatory budget could easily increase fluctuations rather than moderate them." Neither the balanced budget principle nor the compensatory system is conducive to economy. The former allows a growth of public expenditures in boom times—the latter assumes an expansion in bad times. "The really frightening possibility is that we shall oscillate between adherence to the annual balance principle in prosperity and belief in compensatory spending in depression. This could only mean an endless ascent to higher and higher government spending, both in prosperity and depression."[27]

A rule such as the stabilizing budget—or a balanced budget at high employment—is thought to be essential for budgetary discipline. The pressures on Congress for increased expenditures both for present functions and for new activities are enormous. In the absence of an operating rule or other formula, it is said, the problem of enforcing even a semblance of discipline might be almost insurmountable. Traditionally, this has been a principal argument in support of the annually balanced budget. Unless Congress is compelled to raise revenues equal to expenditures, it is contended, a reckless approach to appropriations will ensue and responsible management of the finances may become impossible.

The only rule that currently commands fairly general acceptance is that the federal budget should be balanced at high employment. This of course is a principal facet of the stabilizing budget proposal. Realistically viewed, this rule is perhaps more accurately regarded as a modification of an old rule than as a new one. Nevertheless, rigid adherence to this rule might in some instances be inconsistent with the stabilization objective. One can imagine a high-employment economy in which a developing imbalance between current saving

[27] Committee for Economic Development, *Taxes and the Budget: A Program for Prosperity in a Free Economy*, pp. 21, 30.

and private investment might require siphoning a larger portion of money savings to the public sector. If state and local needs did not take up the slack, federal borrowings might be desirable.

Thus far the search for a rule that will be a satisfactory guide for formulating budget policy in a stabilization context has not been especially successful. The reason is perhaps obvious. The goal of public economic or stabilization policy is a balanced economy operating at high-level employment. Perhaps no rule concerning the state of the federal accounts that might be formulated will be satisfactory in all circumstances. One can agree that "the prospective state of the nation's economic budget should . . . serve as the criterion for budgetary policy."[28] But this standard defies reduction to a single rule of budgetary conduct that will be adequate as a guide to budget formulation and implementation in a political environment.[29]

Until more experience has been gained, it is natural that there should be some distrust of discretionary action. The belief that political considerations will often be compelling has not been dispelled, and there are those who feel that discretionary action might frequently mean wrong action. It is the nature of discretionary action that the possibility of incorrect action can never be ruled out completely. Yet is there not reason to believe that in fiscal and economic matters we have attained a degree of sophistication where the contributions of discretionary action to stabilization policy will far exceed the offsets chargeable to erroneous decisions? If this question cannot be answered in the affirmative, there is little hope that either an adequate fiscal policy or an effective stabilization policy can be devised.

To be effective, both fiscal policy and public economic policy must be flexible. The problems that confront those

[28] Arthur Smithies, *The Budgetary Process in the United States* (1955), p. 442.

[29] "A workable rule of budget policy has to resolve a great difficulty. The budget at the same time serves a political and an economic purpose, and these purposes are often in apparent conflict with each other." Gerhard Colm, *The Federal Budget and the National Economy* (1955), p. 36.

responsible for stabilization policy have different causes and often require different treatment. It follows that "no detailed blueprint of specific actions can be responsibly laid down in advance of the event." Preventive action, together with prompt and vigorous action as changing conditions may require, is the essence of a stabilization program. Automatic stabilizers cannot be counted on to do more than restrain either an upward or a downward tendency of the economy. The idea that the government can wait until some price index or unemployment figure reaches a specified magnitude does not constitute a sound approach to an effective stabilization policy. It overlooks the need for constant vigilance and preventive action.[30]

Where does this leave us with respect to the question of rules versus discretionary action in fiscal policy? In the first place, the question should probably not be put in this manner. The choice is not between alternative approaches—rules or no rules. On careful examination, the difference between those who favor adherence to a budget rule and those who emphasize discretionary action is one of degree. Thus under the stabilizing budget policy tax rates would be let alone unless there is some major change in national policy or condition of national life. Under adverse economic conditions, tax rates would remain unchanged unless the recession or depression became particularly serious. On the other hand, those who favor a more active fiscal policy do not take the position that reliance must necessarily be placed exclusively on discretionary action. They recognize the merits of automatic or quasi-automatic devices. At the same time, they feel that all such devices should be "carefully watched and judiciously interfered with," as occasion may require.[31]

[30] *Economic Report of the President* (Jan. 28, 1954), pp. 111–14.

[31] "At the practical level there is much to be said for various quasi-automatic devices provided they are carefully watched and judiciously interfered with. Administrative convenience, quickness of action, minimization of manpower and other advantages can be pointed to." Samuelson, "Principles and Rules in Modern Fiscal Policy: A Neo-Classical Reformulation," in *Money, Trade, and Economic Growth: In Honor of John Henry Williams*, p. 165.

One should be careful not to overemphasize the debate concerning rules and discretionary action. With the passing of time, the apparent cleavage will doubtless appear to have been a minor yet interesting phenomenon in the evolution of fiscal policy. The only point at issue relates to the extent to which reliance can or should be placed on rules and discretionary action in charting an appropriate fiscal policy for the future. In the nature of the case, this question is one on which complete unanimity of opinion will probably never prevail.

Fiscal Policy and the Budgetary Process

From its inception the administrative difficulties encountered in implementing modern fiscal policy have been stressed by those who questioned its feasibility. No federal agency, it was said, was charged with the duty of co-ordinating policies concerning public expenditures and taxation with the requirements of the total economy. The federal government was not organized in such a manner that fiscal policy could be made operative and effective.[32] Improvements in both organization and procedures since World War II have made these criticisms seem less cogent. For example, the creation of the Council of Economic Advisers and the Joint Economic Committee was essential if the goals of fiscal and economic policy were to be realized. In addition, legislative and executive improvements have helped make the budget a more effective instrument.

Fiscal policy, together with other phases of economic policy, has enhanced the importance of the federal budget as an instrument of executive management. Expansion of

[32] See, for example, Charles C. Abbott, "Administration of Fiscal Policy," *Harvard Business Review*, Vol. 23 (1944–1945), pp. 46 ff. and the observation by Beardsley Ruml cited at the beginning of this article.

responsibilities in the economic sphere has pointed up the inadequacy of traditional budget principles such as comprehensiveness, unity, and periodicity or annuality, which were formulated with legislative control in mind.[33] The federal concern with economic stabilization has directed attention to budget principles designed from the point of view of the chief executive.

In 1945 Harold D. Smith, Director of the Bureau of the Budget, discussed with great clarity eight budget principles as seen from the viewpoint of executive management. When the Employment Act of 1946 was approved, it automatically elevated these principles to a position of greater prominence. The first principle is *executive budget programming*. The key idea is that the budget reflects the program of the President, and, when enacted, it becomes the work program of the government.[34] In developing this program the stabilization objective is necessarily kept in mind. The requirements of fiscal policy and related phases of stabilization policy have given executive budget programming a new dimension.

A second principle is *executive budget responsibility*. An appropriation ordinarily authorizes rather than directs an agency to spend money. "The chief executive . . . has the responsibility of seeing that the agency programs are brought into accord with legislative intent and are executed with the greatest possible economy."[35] In areas such as public works "legislative intent" embodies not only the conditions specified in the appropriation measures and other enabling legislation, but also the goals set forth in the declaration of policy in the Employment Act of 1946.

A third principle is *executive budget discretion*. Appropriations should be made for "broadly defined functions of an agency . . . in harmony with legislative determination of the

[33] Other principles mentioned in the literature include clarity, publicity, accuracy, detailed specification, prior authorization, and exclusiveness. Harold D. Smith, *The Management of Your Government* (1945), pp. 83–85; Jesse Burkhead, *Government Budgeting* (1956), pp. 106–07.

[34] Smith, *The Management of Your Government*, pp. 87–90.

[35] *Ibid.*

current objectives of government." The executive branch should be allowed to determine "the precise means of operation to achieve the purposes set forth by the law." This principle ties in closely with *flexibility in timing,* a principle of the highest importance for economic stabilization.

The budget should contain provisions that permit immediate adjustment to changing economic conditions with which fiscal policy must cope. Flexibility in timing can, for example, be accomplished if the legislature appropriates funds for certain construction and developmental programs for an extended period, say, of five years. Timing of the program could then be modified by the executive in accord with economic necessities.[36]

Another principle is *budget reporting.* Preparation of the budget, legislative action, and budget execution must be based on full financial and operating reports flowing up from the administrative units of the government. "Budgeting without such reporting would be blind and arbitrary." Closely related is the principle of *adequate budget "tools".* A properly staffed budget organization under the direct supervision of the chief executive is a prime essential. In addition, he should have the authority to make monthly or quarterly allotments of appropriations and to set up reserves out of appropriations.[37] Both powers are obviously of great potential importance in connection with the stabilization goal.

The remaining principles suggested by Smith are *multiple procedures in budgeting* and *two-way organization.* Modern government includes different types of operations, which require varying procedures for effective management. The "methods of budgeting may vary for different types of governmental activities." Concerning two-way organization Smith states:

Although budget preparation and budget execution must be directed by the chief executive, efficient budgeting requires the active cooperation of each agency and its major units. . . . Budgeting is not only a central function, but a process that should permeate

[36] *Ibid.,* pp. 92–93.
[37] *Ibid.,* p. 91.

the entire administrative structure. Traffic between the central office and the agency offices responsible for budgeting and programming should move on a two-way rather than a one-way street.[38]

A number of improvements have been made in the budget since World War II. Thus the Government Corporation Control Act of 1945 established budget controls over government corporations and adopted the concept of "business-type" budgets for corporations wholly owned by the government.[39] Some of the recommendations for budget reform made by the Hoover Commission were made effective by the Budget and Accounting Procedures Act of 1950. Among the provisions of this act is the requirement that the budget set forth the "functions and activities of the Government."[40] This was intended to be a step towards adoption of a program or performance budget. The commission defined a program or performance budget as "a budget based on functions, activities, and projects . . . which would focus attention upon the general character and relative importance of the work to be done, or upon the service to be rendered, rather than upon the things to be acquired, such as personal service, supplies, equipment, and so on."[41] Another development was the clarification of the responsibilities of the Bureau of the Budget by the General Appropriation Act for 1951. This act specified the procedures the Bureau should follow in setting up apportionments and reserves.[42]

---

[38] *Ibid.*, pp. 92–93.

[39] 59 Stat. 597; Colm, *The Federal Budget and the National Economy*, p. 21.

[40] 64 Stat. 832.

[41] *Budgeting and Accounting*, Report to the Congress by the Commission on Organization of the Executive Branch of the Government, H. Doc. 84, 81 Cong. 1 sess., p. 8. Commenting on the intention to move toward a program or performance budget, Colm states: "Beginning in 1949 with the budget estimate for 1951 the budget document moved toward the presentation of the appropriation requests in terms of the program budget in line with the Hoover Commission recommendations. However, a program budget requires more than a mere reshuffling of budget items. It requires an approach in which programming and budgeting are like the two sides of one coin. In this respect only a modest start has been made." *The Federal Budget and the National Economy*, p. 22.

[42] 64 Stat. 765.

In the executive branch the outstanding achievement is the attainment of greater flexibility in the approach to the budget and the economy.[43] Official pronouncements concerning budget and fiscal policy reflect a breadth of outlook that was unheard of less than three decades ago. Reviewing the period since 1921 Colm states: "The Budget Message developed from a brief statement of the government's financial position and policy into a broad state document presenting an outline of what the government hopes to achieve and particularly of the relationship between budgetary and economic policy."[44] Since the Employment Act of 1946 the economic report must be read in conjunction with the budget message, if one is to obtain the full significance of this development. The economic role of the federal government is stressed in the economic report, and the budget message is concerned mainly with functions and programs.

In stressing this favorable development, there is no intention of minimizing organizational and structural defects that at times seem to stand in the way of an effective fiscal policy. Prominent among these is the existing distribution of fiscal policy and stabilization activities among a variety of agencies and offices. For example, under our system of government revenue proposals and the initiation of revenue legislation are regarded as prerogatives of the Treasury Department and the Committee on Ways and Means of the House of Representatives. The budget message usually includes only general statements concerning tax policy. From an economic standpoint, it may be highly desirable to know the views of the President and his economic advisers concerning the kinds of taxes that should be increased, reduced, or newly enacted.[45] A consequence of this proliferation is

[43] The change in outlook here referred to was considered in detail in Chapters 5 and 6.

[44] Colm, *The Federal Budget and the National Economy*, pp. 23–24.

[45] Smithies, *The Budgetary Process in the United States*, p. 201. Since 1946 the economic reports have included numerous references to tax policy; but there has been little mention of what might be termed the "specifics" of taxation.

that co-ordination in the interest of a common objective is made more difficult.

On the expenditure side of the budget, responsibilities are even more widely diffused. Attainment of flexibility in public works expenditures requires the co-ordination of the activities of numerous agencies—the Corps of Engineers, the Bureau of Public Roads, the Bureau of Reclamation, and the General Services Administration, among others. The office of public works planning in the executive office endeavors to co-ordinate federal policies in this area, and is also concerned with the integration of federal, state, and local policies. The Council of Economic Advisers and the Bureau of the Budget are necessarily interested in public works activities on a continuing basis.[46]

A logical corollary of flexibility in fiscal policy is flexibility in programming. Progress here has not been outstanding, in part because of the limited areas in which a substantial degree of flexibility is possible. No stand-by appropriation for public works for use in the event of a serious recession has been approved, though a measure of flexibility is possible within the limits of current appropriations. For the most part, suggestions that would increase expenditure flexibility have not progressed beyond the discussion stage.[47] Similarly, little has been done to improve revenue flexibility, beyond approving the degree of flexibility attained through the built-in stabilizers.

[46] When fiscal and monetary policy are considered jointly, the Board of Governors of the Federal Reserve System, an agency that is not directly responsible to the President, assumes a major role. Moreover, fiscal policy and in much less degree monetary policy may be subject to the whims of Congress. Fiscal policy must of course be ironed out within whatever debt limit the Congress may see fit to impose.

[47] Five years ago Gerhard Colm suggested the desirability of a three-point program that would mean greater expenditure flexibility: (1) the formulation of a five-year program of developmental government investments; (2) flexible grants-in-aid; and (3) the provision of some contingency expenditures in the operating budget. Fiscal Policy and the Federal Budget," in *Income Stabilization for a Developing Democracy*, p. 258.

The Influence of the "New Economics"

To the reader well versed in modern economics, the influence of economic theory on the ideas embraced within the term "fiscal policy," is no doubt so obvious that a résumé may seem superfluous. The present summary may be helpful for those who are unfamiliar with or only slightly acquainted with the evolution of economic thought during the past few decades.

From the time that the table "The Government's Budget and the Nation's Budget" was included in the budget message (January 1945), there was no longer any doubt concerning the influence of the "new economics" on fiscal and budget policy. This table in itself, as has been pointed out, did not imply adherence to any economic theory.[48] Nevertheless, it suggested that the major sectors of the economy must mesh with reasonable effectiveness if high level national income and a prosperous economy are to obtain. The table and the accompanying discussion considered together were equivalent to "an official recognition of the essentially Keynesian proposition that the federal budget should be used to contribute to the larger context of the total national economy."[49]

The legislative history of the Employment Act of 1946, together with a comparison of the bills approved by the Senate and House with the act as approved, might seem to suggest that at this juncture the "new economics" was not a major influence. That the new approaches were not mentioned in the act was at least in part a concession to political realities.[50]

---

[48] See p. 243.

[49] Stephen K. Bailey, *Congress Makes a Law* (1950), p. 25.

[50] John R. Fredland states: "In this respect the Act may be regarded as a more sophisticated piece of legislation than the original bill or the senate-passed measure. But the Keynesian content with respect to policy is implicit, rather than explicit." "Keynesian Ideas as Reflected in Domestic Fiscal and Monetary Policies of the United States, 1945–1953," pp. 96–97. (An unpublished Ph.D. thesis at The American University, dated Sept. 24, 1956.)

Considerable antipathy toward Keynes' prescription for economic stability existed during the late 1930's, and it carried over into the war period. "Keynesian economics" was linked with "collectivism" by those who opposed any expansion of the role of government. In extreme cases it was asserted that if public policy were based on the new economics, the federal government would soon control the entire economy. Sight was lost of the fact that neither Keynes nor the great majority of the "new economists" regarded governmental intervention in the economy as a desirable goal in itself. Their objective was economic stability at a high level of employment, and a considerable incursion of governmental activity was regarded as necessary if this goal were to be attained.

The real test, as Fredland states, "is in the type of thinking and writing and legislative practice that the Employment Act would foster." When one reads the budget messages, the economic reports of the President, the reports and studies of the Joint Economic Committee, and other official documents for the years 1946–1958, the answer is immediately at hand. Numerous sections or portions of these documents may be said "to be rooted in a 'Keynesian' complex of ideas, at least as the term 'Keynesian' is popularly understood, in that their very existence is based on the assumption that *if need be* the government can intervene successfully in maintaining employment."[51]

Perhaps the most important of the modern conceptions is that the federal government has a major responsibility for the nation's economic welfare. When President Truman said that the government must assume the ultimate responsibility for the economic health of the nation, and that there is no other agency that can, he was expressing a truth that had become apparent by the mid-1930's. Recognition of its essential accuracy was a necessary step in the evolution of the idea that the government has a positive and complementary

[51] *Ibid.*, pp. 97–99.

role to play in the economy. When Stuart Chase stated in 1932 that under adverse conditions governmental expenditures "may have a balance-wheel function," he was advancing an idea that was far from original. Numerous advocates of countercyclical public works and adequate relief payments during the depression of the 1930's and in earlier depressions had said or implied as much. The contribution of Keynesian economics is that the balancing expenditures of government take their place as a component of total spending and aggregate effective demand in a theoretical system that commands professional respect.

In modern fiscal theory a countercyclical or anti-depression expenditure program is not an end in itself. The same applies to an anti-recession tax cut designed to increase consumer purchasing power and public investment. Their merit stems from their value in holding economic fluctuations and unemployment within tolerable limits. The expectation that appropriate action will be taken may in itself be helpful in minimizing fluctuations. Thus when the 1953–1954 recession set in, President Eisenhower was reported as saying that he wished to refrain from any suggestion that the government was unable to act positively to strengthen the economy. It was the President's position that timely action would forestall the need for drastic action later.[52]

A second and related conception is that public budgets, and particularly that of the central government, are a vital element in the economy. Their significance is primarily economic rather than financial; governmental demands for goods and services account for a substantial portion of aggregate demand. The money costs of government are subordinated to real costs—the goods and services required by and allocated to government for the performance of its functions. On first thought this may seem to be merely a matter of emphasis. But it is something more. With the development of modern economics, the idea that government should

[52] Robert J. Donovan, *Eisenhower: The Inside Story* (1956), pp. 209, 213, 215, 219.

be viewed primarily as a financial burden on the economy ceased to be tenable. Government came to be regarded as a sector of the economy, one that both complements and supplements private economic activity.

The economic approach to governmental budgets does not ignore the financial or money-raising aspects of public finance. Economic theory does not hold that the money costs of government are of no consequence or that their apportionment is a matter of indifference. On the contrary, it is recognized that the allotment of money costs through the tax system, together with the allocation of a portion of the money savings of the community into public capital formation, has important economic effects. Theorists and others who view public expenditures from the standpoint of their effects on the national economy do not deny the merits of the money-cost approach. What they do deny is that governmental budgets and activities can be studied solely from the viewpoint of the individual, the household, or the firm.

The modern idea is that a high level of public expenditures may constitute a bulwark against a serious recession. This was the view of the President and other officials, as well as of economists, at the time of the 1953–1954 decline. The same thought has been expressed with respect to the recession that set in during the summer and fall of 1957. For example, Secretary Sinclair Weeks stated that because of the size of the federal budget a severe and fairly long recession seemed unlikely.[53] This point of view is diametrically opposite to the accepted creed of only a few decades ago. Until the mid-1930's large or rising public budgets in time of peace were widely regarded as impediments to economic growth, and even as a depression-making factor. A corollary of the modern view is that changes in budget levels may be a major determinant of economic trends.

Public expenditures and fiscal policy have an important role to play in the economy, according to modern economics.

[53] *New York Times* (Jan. 2, 1958), p. 1.

This role is viewed as a complementary or balancing one. The Keynesian school holds that changes in investment do not automatically follow changes in the amounts saved at given levels of income. When disequilibrium occurs in an advanced and complex economy, forces do not necessarily come into play that will restore the balance at or near full employment. When it is admitted that a portion of productive resources may not be utilized by private business, "we must also admit the possibility of the State claiming these resources through means other than taxation. . . . We must also admit that an increase of the outlay of the State beyond its revenue can increase the national income. The notion that a balanced budget is desirable in all circumstances falls to the ground as soon as we abandon the classical assumption of automatic full employment."[54]

If private investment falls off and saving in excess of demand at desired levels of income appears imminent, the Keynesian fiscal policy recommendation is increased public expenditures, a reduction in taxes, or both. Conversely, when private investment demands rise sharply, a reduction in public outlays or an increase of taxes or both may be necessary to maintain economic balance.[55] The contribution of modern economic and fiscal theory is that public expenditures and governmental activities have attained a new dignity. The nineteenth century conception that virtually all public activities requiring the allocation of resources to government impinge on the private sector, thereby impeding economic growth and lowering the level of living, has become obsolete.[56]

[54] E. F. Schumacher, "Public Finance—Its Relation to Full Employment," *The Economics of Full Employment*, Pt. 4, Oxford University Institute of Statistics (1945), p. 89.

[55] The complementary nature of private and public investment has been recognized by both postwar Presidents. (See pp. 244–47, 249, 251–52.) Keynesian theory recognizes that in many circumstances the contribution of fiscal policy will be enhanced if appropriate action is also taken in the monetary field. That is, fiscal policy and monetary policy are viewed as complementary.

[56] Lest this statement leave an erroneous impression, the change in outlook toward governmental activities was not solely a development of the 1930's and later

Though the new ideas have had a pervasive influence, fiscal and economic policy has not been couched exclusively in Keynesian terminology. A key thought running through the official documents of the postwar years is that government should maintain a favorable environment for the enterprise or private sector of the economy. Historically, this conception is at least as old as the federal government. In the present century it was stressed by Theodore Roosevelt, and later it was a leading premise underlying the Harding-Coolidge drive for economy. There is, of course, nothing inconsistent in the emphasis on a favorable environment and the "new economics."

A closely related concept that occasionally finds expression is that the largest possible share of the people's income should be left in their hands to meet their private wants. Stated differently, a low level of taxation is deemed in the public interest. This idea is deeply rooted in the orthodoxy of conservatism, which is implied in much of earlier classical economics. It is a corollary of the view that public expenditures represent undesirable consumption and impede the growth of capital. In contrast, modern economics envisions government as an agency providing essential services that develops in harmony with a thriving private sector. A low level of taxation is not the optimum under all conditions.

The Public View on Modern Fiscal Policy

Since 1940 or 1941 the public has become increasingly familiar with modern fiscal-policy ideas. To a considerable

---

decades. Keynes' *General Theory* and other facets of modern economics gave a sharp upward thrust to a trend of ideas that at times seemed to be almost submerged. The roots of some of these ideas go back to the nineteenth century. See, for example, the discussion of the views of Henry Carter Adams and Richard T. Ely in Chapter 3.

extent, this development was an outgrowth of personal observation. While the war lasted, it was obvious that government demands for goods and services were a highly important component of aggregate demand. The meshing of private and public activities in carrying the war effort to a successful conclusion was impressive. It was apparent that if aggregate demand could be kept large enough, there need be no large-scale unemployment after the war. To the layman as well as the economist, the wartime experience suggested that the possibilities of complementary public and private efforts in dealing with peacetime economic fluctuations should be fully explored.[57]

Numerous business and professional leaders who a decade earlier believed a balanced peacetime budget was essential for recovery changed their position during the 1940's. Early in 1944 a leading New York bank stated that annual budget balancing in time of economic adversity should no longer be the primary goal of public policy.

Everyone recognizes the obligation to extend help to the needy in periods of unemployment, despite differences of opinion as to whether this should be a federal or local responsibility. Most people likewise recognize the need for government support in tiding over key situations, where time is needed to make adjustments in orderly fashion and where breakdowns might have serious and widespread repercussions. . . . In financing depression spending, few economists and experts are now such financial purists as to insist that the costs be met entirely out of taxes, and to disapprove some measure of borrowing and credit expansion as a means of mitigating deflationary pressures. [58]

In the educational process by which a new approach to

---

[57] It is not implied that the criteria of wartime economics and finance are applicable in time of peace. "In war, we spend money and run into debt, not because we can 'afford' to in any ordinary sense, but because—compared with the supremely important objective of winning the war—almost nothing else matters." *National City Bank Letter* (January 1944), p. 11.

[58] *Ibid.* The limitations of compensatory public expenditures were also discussed in this article. The only point we wish to make is that this publication denied the validity of the annually balanced budget rationale under adverse economic conditions.

budget policy came to be accepted, the work of the Committee for Economic Development established in 1942 was outstanding. The committee indicted the annually balanced budget policy on the grounds of its perverseness. It requires that tax rates and expenditure programs be changed at times and in directions most harmful to high employment and stable prices. This policy "does not in the long run promote government economy." A fiscal system predicated on an annually balanced budget "dissipates the potentially large surpluses of good times and strives vainly for balance in bad times." In a fluctuating economy such a program will not result in debt reduction. A balanced budget program "requires a degree of accuracy in forecasting fluctuations in business activity that has not been achieved in the past and that is not possible now." It involves irregular and unpredictable variations of tax rates, with unsettling effects on business and personal planning.[59]

This criticism by an influential business group was an important milestone in the process by which the hold of the traditional balanced budget rationale was lessened. The wide dissemination of the policy statements of the committee helped gain approval of the idea that the annually balanced budget rule was outmoded. These statements were prepared in consultation with competent economists. To a considerable extent, they reflected the thinking of the economics profession. Public acceptance of the indictment of the balanced budget was in a sense a vindication of the work of those economists who had endeavored to come to grips with the chief problem of the peacetime economy—harmful business fluctuations. Through their efforts fiscal policy was taken

[59] *Taxes and the Budget: A Program for Prosperity in a Free Economy*, pp. 20–21. An additional disadvantage is that in an era when national defense considerations are paramount, compression of expenditures to attain budgetary balance under adverse economic conditions might involve unwarranted risks. "The need for government-expenditure programs does not run parallel to business activity. There is no conceivable argument for having less defense in times of depression than in times of boom." Smithies, *The Budgetary Process in the United States*, p. 439.

out of "the enclosure where it was bounded by the Treasury's income and outgo sheets and forced . . . to live in the whole economy, with the wholly praiseworthy aim of making our economy a happier and more prosperous one."[60]

From the time the Employment Act was signed (February 1946), it appeared that the logic of events would probably impel the government to move toward compensatory finance, whether it wanted to or not. Underlying this legislation, as well as innumerable official pronouncements of the past twelve years, is the belief that free man can shape social instruments to his own purposes. Though at the time the public was perhaps not aware of all the implications of this legislation, it was apparent to most informed citizens that over a period of years public full employment or stabilization policy and an annually balanced budget policy were irreconcilable.[61]

An overwhelming majority of the people have come to believe that a smoothly functioning economy is a prime essential for national well-being. They believe that fiscal policy should be concerned with balancing the nation's economic budget. The "vast majority of Americans agree that the government should continue to accept an over-all responsibility for the satisfactory operation of the national economy," and that it should continue to accept responsibility for relief when necessary. They do not believe that this responsibility implies governmental control and domination of the entire economy. With some exceptions, they believe that the oft-repeated assertion that we are evolving toward some form of collectivism is a delusion.[62]

It is not possible to determine the precise point in time when the idea that government should pursue an active fiscal policy and employ compensatory fiscal principles as a component of stabilization policy became the majority view.

[60] Alzada Comstock, "Fiscal Policy," *The Forum*, Vol. 110 (August 1948), p. 69.
[61] Leo Barnes, "How Dangerous is the Public Debt," *Atlantic Monthly*, Vol. 177 (February 1946), p. 95.
[62] Frederick Lewis Allen, "The Unsystematic American System," *Harper's Magazine*, Vol. 204 (June 1952), pp. 24 –25.

There is reason to believe, however, that this date may have preceded the approval of the Employment Act of 1946. In any case the wartime experience immediately following the great depression had a tremendous impact on accepted thought. Yet it would be erroneous to assume that acceptance of modern fiscal-policy ideas is all but universal.

An influential minority continue to regard any departure from a balanced peacetime federal budget with serious misgivings. They feel that adherence to the balanced budget prescription is essential if extravagance in public expenditure is to be avoided. Only a few years ago an amendment to the Constitution outlawing federal deficits in time of peace was proposed in the expectation that it might enforce an annually balanced budget. A commentator sympathetic to this proposal stated that for twenty years "Uncle Sam has been floating around in a sea of red ink." The federal government owes $275 billion, a sum so big it is virtually impossible to visualize. There will be no end to reckless spending and the crushing national debt until the Bridges-Byrd amendment puts a stop to "running the government on red ink in time of peace." Their amendment "will restrain reckless men engaged in the dark enterprise of spending this great, rich, once free republic into bankruptcy."[63]

To this minority federal expenditures are unconscionably high. It is said that if public expenditures are continued at recent levels, they will destroy the enterprise economy and our liberties. In at least one instance federal spending, together with the taxes required, has been likened to the bubonic plague.[64] According to this philosophy, the private

---

[63] John T. Flynn, "Bridges and Byrd vs. the 'Good' Public Debt," *American Mercury*, Vol. 79 (October 1954), pp. 51–55.

[64] Lane D. Webber, "Bubonic Budgets: Government Spending Can Be Fatal," *Vital Speeches*, Vol. 15 (Dec. 15, 1948), pp. 150–53. "High in the horrors of history ranks the bubonic plague. . . . It is usually fatal. . . . Once started it quickly becomes epidemic." In our society the people, through their chosen representatives "determine and dictate the kind and extent of government they want." The trouble arises because of human "rodents," who "disease themselves with the philosophy of

sector and the public sector of the economy are largely anti-thetical, though a minimum of governmental activities is re-garded as essential. The more extreme versions give the im-pression that a state of near belligerency exists. The "free enterprise system" on which our liberties depend "is being dealt savage blows," and if the trend is too long continued will be destroyed by excessive federal spending and excessive taxation, together with other excesses.[65]

A rise in public spending because of a recession or depres-sion is anathema to those who continue to espouse a philoso-phy of extreme individualism. In the spring of 1949, and again in 1958, planning to cope with the recession that might re-quire an increase in federal spending was regarded with dis-favor. To those who hold that federal spending has reached ruinous proportions and that the federal finances are in a de-plorable state, the federal debt is a matter for grave concern. They give no credence to the view that we might somehow be able to live with a debt of the present size. The only choice is between paying off the debt and repudiation. The idea that the federal debt is in the nature of a mortgage continues to be advanced in support of the thesis that the present federal debt burden is intolerable. "Where is the finely drawn line between freedom and slavery when, under the present defi-cit, every baby born in this country has a $1,675 first-mort-gage tag hanging around its neck?"[66] One is reminded of the Spencer-Sumner thesis that taxes measure the degree of slavery, which enjoyed considerable popularity during the latter part of the nineteenth century.

The principle that national growth tends to minimize the burden of public debts is not mentioned by those who assert

---

the 'isms'," who believe that government can and should do all things for all people. The fellow-traveling elements of society also play a role in bringing on an "epidemic of government spending for paternalism" and "the bubble of bubonic budgets."

[65] Harry F. Byrd, "Are We Headed Toward Collectivism?" *New York Times* (Dec. 18, 1949), sec. 6, p. 7.

[66] Barry M. Goldwater, An Address in the United States Senate, April 8, 1957, *Congressional Record*, Vol. 103, Pt. 4, p. 5260.

that the federal debt will cause an "economic collapse." Apparently the only hope, according to this view, is a statutory debt limit not too much above the outstanding federal debt. In some instances this limit, which has been changed repeatedly by legislative enactment, has been discussed as though it were equivalent to the extreme limit of the credit power of the federal government. For example: "Were this country normal, which it is not, the exceeding of the legal debt limit would have caused a furor and made headlines. There was nothing resembling a furor last fall when the limit of our credit was reached. A bemused and well-regimented public said nothing."[67]

We have managed to live with a federal debt in the range of $250–$280 billion for well over a decade, and there is almost universal agreement that a rigid program of debt retirement should not be attempted. A magnitude such as $280 billion is meaningful, only when it is related to other phenomena and appraised in relation to growth. The annual interest charge on the federal debt represents a smaller percentage of the budget than in 1940. In relation to the national income, the interest requirement is approximately three fourths as large as in 1946. In the circumstances, identification of the federal debt with a continuing crisis and eventual disaster seems a peculiar phenomenon. Yet it is understandable. According to a philosophy that gained ascendency during the nineteenth century, a permanent or continuing public debt, together with the redistributive effect of the annual interest charge, was unthinkable and should not be tolerated. A moral issue was thought to be involved. In the pronouncements that stress the intolerable level of the present federal debt, the dominant note seems to be that a public debt, even though the bulk of it was incurred in the defense of the nation, is evil and immoral.

---

[67] "Are We Going to Borrow Ourselves into Prosperity?" a signed editorial by Wilfley Scobey, *Saturday Evening Post*, Vol. 226 (Feb. 6, 1954), p. 12.

CHAPTER VIII

Concluding Statement

THROUGHOUT THE GREATER PART OF OUR HISTORY, peacetime budget and fiscal policy was predicated on the belief that the federal budget should be balanced annually. The desire for financial stability was one of the forces that led to the Constitutional Convention of 1787 and the establishment of the new nation. Because of the vicissitudes of the preceding years, acceptance of the balanced budget rationale was regarded by Hamilton and other leading statesmen as necessary for sound finance. If the public credit was to be securely established, it was essential that adequate provision be made for the service of the outstanding debt. The policy most widely favored called not only for a balanced peacetime budget, but for the rapid elimination of the public debt as well. A policy of debt reduction was thought to be conducive to a strong federal credit.

In the thinking of the late eighteenth and nineteenth centuries, a public debt was regarded as undesirable for economic reasons. Elimination of the outstanding debt, it was said, would liberate the public resources and lighten the burden on the working classes. A revenue system based mainly on customs duties supplemented at times by internal excises was obviously regressive. At the same time, the debt was held mainly by the well-to-do, on whom the burden of taxation was comparatively light. As a consequence, the payment of

interest involved a redistribution of income from the poorer
to the more prosperous classes.

The principal economic reason advanced in support of the
balanced budget was that an increase in public debt involves
a draft on funds or savings that otherwise would be available
for private capital expansion. Public borrowing, it was argued, slows economic progress because it impinges on the
growth of capital. On the same line of reasoning, it was held
that the retirement of public debt freed capital for productive
uses. With the development of the wages-fund doctrine, the
principal economic arguments were in effect packaged into a
unified anti-public-borrowing philosophy. Public borrowings,
it was reasoned, reduced the wages fund, thereby lowering
the wage level and placing the incidence of loans directly on
the workers. Because of the regressive revenue system, a dis-
proportionately large portion of the burden of debt service
was borne by the working classes. Since only small amounts
of government obligations were held by the lower-income
groups, redistribution of income in favor of those with higher
incomes was inevitable.

The acceptability of a policy centered on the balanced
budget philosophy was enhanced by the moral connotation of
indebtedness. In both official and popular pronouncements it
was frequently asserted that a public debt is an evil or is immoral. Not even the economists were entirely free of this belief. A government that habitually does not raise revenues
that will cover its expenses, it was said, is likely to become an
extravagant and irresponsible government. Curiously, a similar line of reasoning was used later—especially during the
1880's—to condemn surpluses that seemed unmanageable.
Both a dearth and an excess of revenues were thought to be
conducive to extravagance and irresponsibility.

The idea that adequate provision for debt service is conducive to a strong public credit is as valid today as it was
during the formative years. There are few who would deny
that, other things being equal, a reduction in indebtedness

may strengthen the public credit. The principal change in recent decades is that debt reduction in itself no longer enjoys a high priority. The modern view is that the retirement of public debt is not an independent objective—one that should be pursued under all peacetime conditions. Debt reduction is deemed appropriate only when the economy is buoyant, and especially when inflationary forces are operative.

With the passing of time, the economic arguments summarized above ceased to be meaningful. Of these, the view that public borrowing lowers wages because it impinges on the wages fund was discredited well before the turn of the century. When it came to be recognized that the wages-fund doctrine was based on incorrect premises, this phase of the argument against public debts was no longer tenable. ·

The belief that public borrowing in an advanced country such as the United States necessarily retards growth by impinging on the supply of capital is best described as archaic. With the change from a capital-importing to a capital-exporting nation, the idea that it is not possible to have too much saving lost whatever validity it may have formerly possessed. Sophisticated observers have long stressed the importance of balanced growth, with consumption and capital formation interacting on each other. It is true that in many circumstances public and private borrowers compete for available funds. But the point to be emphasized is that public borrowing may be as justifiable as private borrowing. In modern economics public and private investment are viewed as complementary.

The notion that the retirement of a national debt necessarily and under all conditions frees capital in like amount for productive purposes has even less validity. Assuming a constant cash or working balance, surplus revenues are a prerequisite for debt reduction. The collection of revenues in excess of the amounts needed to balance the budget impinges both on consumption and on saving; consumption and saving are lower by indeterminate amounts. When the surplus is used to retire public debt held by individuals and financial institutions, government in effect acts as an intermediary in the transfer of funds from taxpayers to holders of government obligations. The latter, it may be assumed, will find appropriate reinvestment outlets for the bulk of their funds. The net addition to the funds becoming available for investment resulting from debt retirements would equal the full amount of retirements, only if no part of the surplus revenues impinged on saving and no portion of the funds received by bondholders were used for consumption. Given the present federal tax structure and the current distribution of debt holdings, these conditions are not likely to be fulfilled.[1]

With the adoption of the modern progressive income tax and the wider distribution of debt holdings, it could no longer be claimed that the federal debt imposes a disproportionate burden on the lower-income classes. This argument hinged in part on the fact that customs duties and excises are regressive, and partly on the fact that the debt was held primarily by the well-to-do classes. When the federal revenue system ceased to be regressive, the redistribution and excessive burden arguments lost their force. The servicing of the federal debt continues to operate to redistribute income. But the progressive tax structure and the wide distribution of government obligations among all classes of society, together with savings institutions, pension funds, and the like, suggest that redistribution in favor of the well-to-do classes is a phenomenon of the past.

Beliefs and attitudes with respect to the public debt can only be appraised in the light of conditions in the era in which they were held. With the exception of the discredited wages-fund theory, the economic reasons offered in support of the position that public borrowing should be kept at a minimum

---

[1] When a government surplus is used to retire debt held by commercial banks, there is a contraction of bank credit. Assets and liabilities of the banking system are reduced by the same amounts.

and that a reasonably rapid retirement of public debt is desirable often possessed validity in the environment in which they were advanced. The fact that they had a time-and-place significance does not detract from their merit. Indeed, taking into account the postulates of classical economics and traditional attitudes toward the role of government, it is difficult to visualize how an alternative line of reasoning might have gained enough support to have had any impact on prevailing conceptions. Orthodox finance was the logical corollary of orthodox economics.

From the beginning of our national history, ideas in public finance have been influenced by the unfolding of events. At the outset acceptance of the balanced budget philosophy was facilitated by the adverse financial experience during the Revolutionary War and under the Articles of Confederation. There was an awareness that the public credit is a valuable resource, especially in an emergency. The experience of the preceding fifteen years suggested to Hamilton and others that the preservation of the public credit depended on the consolidation of existing indebtedness and the provision of adequate revenues for debt service. The thought that the interests of the new nation would be best served if Hamilton's ideas were adopted was soon translated into policy.

A number of illustrations of how the events of the nineteenth century influenced the germination of ideas, which in turn had an impact on public policy, might be cited. One will suffice. The federal debt at the close of the Civil War, in the opinion of some, was so large that extreme measures were called for. Advocacy of repudiation was by no means uncommon. As reputable an economist as Henry C. Carey took the position that it was foolhardy to try to pay both the principal and interest in gold or its equivalent. But to President Grant and others the size of the debt was neither forbidding nor a bar to progress. In their view, the key factor was that we were a young and growing nation with a future almost beyond comprehension. Official policy should not be predicated on the assumption that extremely rapid reduction of the federal debt was essential; the claims of tax reduction should also be considered. Under the policy of gradual reduction, the burden of the debt was met in part through economic growth. As stated by Simon N. Patten a half century later, the Civil War debt was paid by "the great inventions of the epoch."

Developments in public finance and economics since 1930 afford a striking example of the interaction between events, ideas, and public policy. In the early years of the great depression a concerted effort was made by the President and the leadership of both parties in Congress to adhere to the balanced budget philosophy. Yet a balanced federal budget was almost impossible to attain—the annually balanced budget dogma in effect gave way to necessity. Alternatives were soon suggested, and within a few years what came to be known as compensatory fiscal theory gained numerous adherents. Acceptance of the compensatory rationale and other facets of modern fiscal policy was facilitated by the development of Keynesian economic theory. Though in this instance practice preceded theory, taking into account the entire period since 1933, theory and policy have interacted on each other. To say that fiscal policy in turn has influenced events is perhaps superfluous.

The change in outlook on fiscal and budgetary matters that has occurred since 1930 is best described as revolutionary. Government is no longer regarded primarily as a financial burden, except perhaps by a small minority. The expenditures of government have come to be viewed as a vital component of aggregate effective demand. Perhaps most important is the modern idea that budget and debt policies should be formulated and adjusted in the light of the total economic situation. The balancing or stabilizing role of governmental fiscal operations is widely recognized.

For a quarter of a century no federal administration has

taken the position that an annually balanced budget represents the ultimate in financial soundness in all circumstances. The almost obsessive belief in the balanced budget that influenced public policy during the early years of the great depression has practically vanished. Habits of thought that in the past have militated against needed emergency action have not disappeared. But those who hold that government should assume a completely passive role have dwindled to a point at which they are a minority.

It is not our view that the balanced budget philosophy is without influence.[2] Thus, in January 1957 President Eisenhower equated a balanced budget with fiscal integrity.[3] In December 1958—about a month before the release of the budget for 1960—the importance of balancing the budget was stressed by the President.[4] In the circumstances, it would be idle to claim that the balanced budget idea is no longer meaningful. The point to be emphasized is that on these occasions the President gave a high priority to a balanced budget under the conditions which it was assumed would prevail in the near future. His observations do not imply rigid adherence to annual balance under all peacetime conditions. At no time has he claimed that bringing the budget into balance was the essential first step in overcoming a recession.

The idea that the federal government has a positive role to play in the economy is accepted by influential elements in all segments of society. We have come to realize that substantial unemployment is not an inevitable social evil, but can be alleviated by governmental action. Virtually all sections of

---

[2] "In economics . . . all doctrines live on persistently. No new theories ever completely supplant the old." Gunnar Myrdal, *The Political Element in the Development of Economic Theory* (English edition, 1953), p. XIV.

[3] *Budget of the United States Government for the Fiscal Year Ending June 30, 1958,* pp. M.5, M.23.

[4] *Washington Post* (Dec. 23, 1958), p. 1.

the community believe that the government should, if necessary, lead and organize action to deal with unemployment.[5]
The evolution of the idea that in dealing with economic adversity the federal government should assume a major responsibility was spurred by the events of the 1930's. Through
force of circumstances unemployment became a problem of
high national importance, and emergency measures were
planned in national terms. In turn, the severity of the depression directed attention to the imperative need for an effective
stabilization policy.[6]

Perhaps in no other sector has the change in attitude been
so pronounced as in the business community. In the business
creed government often seems to be viewed negatively, as a
restraint on the individual, and restraints in general are
suspect. But the managerial group take a broader view. They
"approve government fiscal policy designed to mitigate cyclical fluctuations even if this policy includes deficit spending,
which is strongly condemned by the classical version of the
creed."[7] With the management group mainly in mind, the
editors of *Fortune* say that it is now almost universally accepted that in the event of a serious depression government
"must undertake very large counter cyclical spending programs."[8]

It has come to be recognized that the federal government
"has a special responsibility to use its powers to curb both
inflationary and depressive tendencies of the economy."[9] In
discharging this responsibility, fiscal policy will play a vary-

[5] These observations apply to other countries as well as the United States. See, for
example, R. I. Downing, "Is An Economic Policy Possible?" *Public Administration*,
Vol. 15 (1956), pp. 273 ff. This publication is the Journal of the Australian regional
groups of the Royal Institute of Public Administration.
[6] "Whenever the people come to think nationally about any question they usually
transfer the control of that question to the national government." Carl Becker, *The
United States: An Experiment in Democracy* (1920), p. 102.
[7] F. X. Sutton, S. E. Harris, Carl Kaysen, and James Tobin, *The American
Business Creed* (1956), pp. 186, 189–90.
[8] Editors of *Fortune* with the collaboration of Russell Davenport, *U.S.A. The
Permanent Revolution* (1951), pp. 203–04.
[9] *Economic Report of the President* (January 1954), p. 54.

ing but often prominent role. Faced with an economic decline, there is no possibility that a balanced federal budget will enjoy the highest priority. For the indefinite future, any counterpart of the almost frantic groping for a balanced budget that characterized the period 1931–1933 is neither probable nor possible.

The modern conception is that the only sound fiscal policy is a flexible one. This is a logical extension of the idea that a free society is a flexible society—one willing to experiment and "seeking to adjust its conditions to its changing needs." A free society "enthrones no dogma."[10] In fiscal matters, as in other areas, it avoids rigidities by refusing to be bound over an extended period by any theory or doctrine. A free society welcomes new ideas, in the expectation that they may prove superior to accepted or received doctrine. Such a society will seek useful elements in all theories and ideas that may be advanced. It will accord to none the attribute of immutability.

[10] Robert M. MacIver, "Government and the Goals of Economic Activity," in A. Dudley Ward, ed., *Goals of Economic Life* (1953), p. 202. This volume was prepared by a study group authorized by the Federal Council of Churches.

APPENDIX

The Federal Budgetary Record

THE BUDGETARY RECORD of the federal government is in some respects an extraordinary one. During the long period from 1789 to 1930 peacetime budgets usually showed an excess of receipts over expenditures.[1] When deficits were incurred, they were generally rather small. The federal government operated under a reasonably effective budget system only during the last decade of this 140-year span. On the other hand, since 1930 peacetime deficits have been the rule rather than the exception. The federal accounts showed a surplus in only five of the 22 years classified as peacetime years. In this period the mechanics of budgeting were perfected to a degree perhaps not thought attainable at the inception of the executive budget system.[2]

THE PERIOD 1789–1916. It is apparent from the discussion in this study that in the long period before the adoption of the executive budget system, the budgetary procedures of the federal government were not well organized. Two principal factors influenced the peacetime fiscal record during the first century and a quarter of our national history. First, there was a fairly steady flow of customs revenues into the federal Treasury.[3] Marked declines in customs

---

[1] In official and popular usage a balanced federal budget has meant one with a surplus of receipts over expenditures. This usage has been followed even when receipts exceeded expenditures by a wide margin. Prospectively a precisely balanced budget is perhaps not an unrealistic concept. But it is highly improbable that the accounts for any completed fiscal year will balance exactly.

[2] The apparent paradox here suggested should not be misinterpreted. It is scarcely conceivable that, with much higher budget levels and heavier taxes, the federal government would have long continued to operate under the antiquated procedures employed before World War I.

[3] In the 112 peacetime years covered by the table on page 315, revenues from customs exceeded internal revenue in all but 12. Of these years, only three were prior to 1900: 1867, 1868, and 1894. Moreover, internal revenue exceeded customs in only

revenues occurred only during the more severe depressions. Second, peacetime expenditure requirements were generally so moderate that raising the necessary revenues did not present a serious problem. In the absence of direct federal taxes, there was little awareness of federal tax burdens.

Though the size of peacetime surpluses and deficits was largely fortuitous, the predominance of surpluses was not entirely accidental. For the most part, federal officials and the public regarded revenues in excess of expenditures as desirable. This was especially true whenever federal debt was outstanding. Debt reduction assumed a surplus of revenues and, as emphasized in this study, public opinion strongly approved the use of surpluses for debt retirement. The normal peacetime expectation was revenues at least equal to expenditures, including operating costs, capital outlays, and interest. In the absence of effective budgeting, attitudes toward the public debt served to some extent as a unifying element in federal financial operations.

A surplus was reported for 82 of the 112 years before World War I classified as peacetime years. In 16 years revenues exceeded expenditures by over 50 per cent, and in 27 years revenues exceeded expenditures by amounts ranging from 25 to 50 per cent of expenditures. On the other hand, peacetime deficits were incurred in only 30 years. In only 6 fiscal periods did the deficit amount to more than one fourth of expenditures. The peacetime budgetary record of the federal government from 1789–1791, the first fiscal period under the Constitution, to 1916 is summarized in the table on page 315.

The preponderance of peacetime surpluses becomes more meaningful when considered in connection with the federal debt. Until the great depression of the 1930's sharp increases in the federal debt were incurred only during war periods. Pressures for debt reduction were strongest immediately after these wartime increases.

The federal debt outstanding in 1791, following the assumption and funding legislation, was approximately $75 million,[4] and at the beginning of the nineteenth century it was $83 million. By 1812 the

---

five of the fourteen years prior to 1900 classified as war periods: 1864, 1865, 1866, 1898, and 1899. *Annual Report of the Secretary of the Treasury on the State of the Finances for the Fiscal Year Ended June 30, 1956*, pp. 318–20.

[4] It would be incorrect to say that the debt was this large at the beginning of Washington's first administration. The assumption and funding proposals were not approved until August 1790. See p. 11.

Federal Peacetime Surpluses and Deficits Compared with Total Expenditures, Fiscal Years 1791–1916[a]

Fiscal Years	Number of Years Revenues Exceeded Expenditures by				Number of Years Revenues were Less than Expenditures by		
	1–10%	10–25%	25–50%	Over 50%	1–10%	10–25%	25–50%
1791–1811...	4	1	6	5	—	4	1
1816–1846[b]..	2	3	8	9	3	3	3[b]
1849–1860...	3	3	2	—	—	2	2
1867–1897...	8	6	11	2	3	1	—
1900–1916...	6	3	—	—	7	1	—
	23	16	27	16	13	11	6

[a] Based on data in *Annual Report of the Secretary of the Treasury on the State of the Finances for the Fiscal Year Ended June 30, 1956*, pp. 318–21. The first fiscal period began in 1789 and ended in 1791.

[b] Includes the half-year period January 1 to June 30, 1843.

debt had been reduced to $45 million. The combined deficits for the four years 1812–1815, which embraced the War of 1812, amounted to $68 million, as may be seen in the table on page 316. For the first time the federal debt exceeded $100 million. Total debt as of January 1, 1816 was over $127 million.[5] In the two decades following the War of 1812 the debt was reduced rapidly. Complete elimination of the federal debt was achieved by January 1835. A steady flow of customs revenues, usually in excess of budget needs, was the major factor in accomplishing this result.[6]

The War with Mexico in 1846–1848 was scarcely a disruptive influence on the nation's finances. The largest deficit was incurred in the fiscal year 1847—about $31 million. The net increase in debt caused by this war was slightly over $40 million.[7]

[5] Considerably more money had been borrowed than was needed. The Treasury operated temporarily with what for the time was an extraordinarily large cash balance. Davis R. Dewey, *Financial History of the United States* (1931), pp. 113, 125, 142, 165.

[6] Receipts from the sale of public lands were also of considerable importance. Delayed receipts on account of the internal revenue taxes imposed during the war were of some importance during the period 1816–1820.

[7] The deficit for the fiscal year ended June 30, 1849 is not here counted as a war-period deficit. The War with Mexico ended officially with the Treaty of Guadalupe Hidalgo signed on February 2, 1848. For the first few years after the War the federal debt was in the range of $60–$70 million.

Federal Receipts, Expenditures, and Deficits
During War Periods[a]

(In millions of dollars)

Fiscal Year	Receipts	Expenditures	Deficit	Deficit as Percentage of Expenditures
		I. WAR OF 1812		
1812............	9.8	20.3	10.5	51.7
1813............	14.4	31.7	17.3	54.6
1814............	11.2	34.7	23.5	67.7
1815............	15.7	32.7	17.0	52.0
		II. WAR WITH MEXICO		
1847............	26.5	57.3	30.8	53.8
1848............	35.8	45.4	9.6	21.1
		III. THE CIVIL WAR		
1861............	41.5	66.5	25.0	37.6
1862............	52.0	474.8	422.8	89.0
1863............	112.7	714.7	602.0	84.2
1864............	264.6	865.3	600.7	69.4
1865............	333.7	1,297.5	963.8	74.3
1866............	558.0	520.8	37.2[b]	7.1[b]
		IV. THE SPANISH-AMERICAN WAR		
1898............	405.3	443.3	38.0	8.6
1899............	516.0	605.1	89.1	14.7

[a] Source: *Annual Report of the Secretary of the Treasury on the State of the Finances for the Fiscal Year Ended June 30, 1956*, pp. 318–21.
[b] Surplus.

The combined deficits for the Civil War period amounted to approximately $2.6 billion. In several years the proportion of expenditures covered by revenues was extremely small, as may be seen in the table above. This war brought the federal debt to an entirely new level. The reported debt in 1866 was almost $2.8 billion, compared with less than $100 million in 1860. The debt was sharply reduced during the next three decades; in 1893 it reached a low of $961 million.

The Spanish-American War, together with the unsatisfactory economic conditions during the 1890's, resulted in a fairly sharp increase in the debt. Total federal debt rose to over $1.4 billion in 1899. Only moderate reductions were made during the next 17 years; for 1916 the comparable figure was a little over $1.2 billion.

WORLD WAR I AND THE POSTWAR DECADE. During World War I federal expenditures and debt reached entirely new levels. The combined deficits for the three-year period ended June 30, 1919 exceeded $23 billion. Expenditures for 1919 amounted to $18.5 billion, an enormous figure by previous standards. For 1918 and 1919 less than 30 per cent of expenditures were covered by revenues. The federal debt on June 30, 1919 was over $25 billion.

Federal Receipts, Expenditures, and Deficits
World War I[a]

(In millions of dollars)

Fiscal Year	Receipts	Expenditures	Deficit	Deficit as Percentage of Expenditures
1917.............	1,124	1,977	853	*43.1*
1918.............	3,665	12,697	9,032	*71.1*
1919.............	5,152	18,515	13,363	*72.2*

ᵃ Source: *Annual Report of the Secretary of the Treasury on the State of the Finances for the Fiscal Year Ended June 30, 1956*, pp. 320–21.

The decade of the 1920's was a period of large surpluses, as may be seen in the table on page 318. The size of the surpluses was in part a consequence of planned debt reduction. Following the war, reduction in the size of the debt was deemed imperative. With this objective in mind, a sinking fund was established in accordance with a provision in the Victory Liberty Loan Act of 1919.[8] In order to make the sinking fund an effective debt reduction device, the required allocations were included in budget expenditures for 1921

[8] 40 Stat. 1311. It was provided that during each fiscal year there should be placed in the sinking fund a credit amounting to (1) 2½ per cent of the aggregate amount of Liberty Bonds and Victory Notes outstanding on July 1, 1920, less an amount equal to the par amount of any obligations of foreign governments held by the United States on July 1, 1920, plus (2) the interest which would have been payable during the fiscal year for which the appropriation is made on the bonds purchased, redeemed, or paid out of the sinking fund during such year or in previous years.

Federal Receipts, Expenditures, and Surpluses
Fiscal Years 1920–1930[a]

(*In millions of dollars*)

Fiscal Year	Receipts[b]	Expenditures[b]	Surplus	Surplus as Percentage of Expenditures
1920............	6,648	6,357	291	4.6
1921............	5,571	5,062	509	10.1
1922............	4,026	3,290	736	22.4
1923............	3,853	3,140	713	22.7
1924............	3,864	2,901	963	33.2
1925............	3,609	2,892	717	24.8
1926............	3,753	2,888	865	29.9
1927............	3,992	2,836	1,156	40.8
1928............	3,872	2,933	939	32.0
1929............	3,821	3,086	735	23.8
1930............	4,020	3,282	738	22.5

[a] Source: *Annual Reports of the Secretary of the Treasury on the State of the Finances for the Fiscal Years Ended June 30, 1920–1930.*
[b] Tax refunds are excluded from both receipts and expenditures.

and later years. For the decade ended in 1930 retirements through the sinking fund amounted to almost $3.2 billion. Other debt retirements chargeable against ordinary receipts—mainly principal and interest on the debts of foreign nations paid in United States obligations—were over $1.6 billion. During this decade over $4.8 billion of debt retirements were included in the budget.[9]

Yet a substantial surplus over and above these retirements was reported for each year. For the ten-year period additional debt retirements from surplus also amounted to about $3.2 billion. Total retirements for the decade were slightly over $8 billion, or about one third of the debt outstanding on July 1, 1920.[10]

[9] The expenditure totals in the table above do not include statutory debt retirements. Inclusion of debt retirements in budget expenditures involves double counting over a period of time. Thus, expenditures financed from borrowings were included in the budget totals during World War I; inclusion of statutory debt retirements in expenditures during the 1920's in effect duplicated the same expenditures.

[10] Data derived from the *Annual Reports of the Secretary of the Treasury on the State of the Finances.* The figures here cited do not include retirements of almost $1.2 billion for the fiscal year 1920; about three fourths of this reduction was achieved by drawing down the cash or general fund balance of the Treasury.

THE DEPRESSION OF THE 1930's. Though the downswing marking the beginning of the great depression began in 1929, the federal accounts did not show a deficit until 1931. The beginning of deficit finance may be placed at the first quarter of the calendar year 1931—the third quarter of the fiscal year 1931.[11] The deficit of $462 million for the fiscal year 1931 was far in excess of any peacetime deficit previously incurred.

The combined deficits for the decade 1931–1940 amounted to over $28 billion. As a consequence, the federal debt rose to approximately $43 billion. The figures for the deficits expressed as a percentage of expenditures shown in the table below are of interest. In four of the ten years, less than half of expenditures were covered

Federal Receipts, Expenditures, and Deficits
Fiscal Years 1931–1940[a]

(In millions of dollars)

Fiscal Year	Net Receipts[b]	Expenditures[c]	Deficit	Deficit as Percentage of Expenditures
1931............	3,115	3,577	462	12.9
1932............	1,924	4,659	2,735	58.7
1933............	2,021	4,623	2,602	56.3
1934............	3,064	6,694	3,630	54.2
1935............	3,730	6,521	2,791	42.8
1936............	4,069	8,494	4,425	52.1
1937............	4,979	7,756	2,777	35.9
1938............	5,615	6,792	1,177	17.3
1939............	4,996	8,858	3,862	43.6
1940............	5,144	9,062	3,918	43.2

[a] Source: *Annual Report of the Secretary of the Treasury on the State of the Finances for the Fiscal Year Ended June 30, 1956*, pp. 322–23.

[b] Excludes refunds of receipts and receipts transferred or credited to the federal old-age and survivors insurance trust fund and the railroad retirement account.

[c] Excludes refunds of receipts and amounts appropriated to the railroad retirement account.

[11] The lag between income tax collections and the incomes on which the taxes were based was the major reason for the delayed effect on federal revenues. Income tax collections for the first half of the fiscal year 1931 (July–December 1930) were based mainly on personal and corporate incomes for the calendar year 1929. For further discussion, see p. 144.

by receipts, and in four additional years the deficit amounted to over one fourth of expenditures.

WORLD WAR II. Federal expenditures for the six fiscal years embracing the World War II period amounted to over $380 billion.[12] Of this amount, less than half was covered by revenues. The combined deficits for the six years amounted to $211 billion. The proportion of expenditures covered by borrowings was substantially less than during the Civil War and World War I.

Federal Receipts, Expenditures, and Deficits
World War II[a]

(In millions of dollars)

Fiscal Year	Net Receipts[b]	Expenditures[c]	Deficit	Deficit as Percentage of Expenditures
1941............	7,103	13,262	6,159	46.4
1942............	12,555	34,045	21,490	63.1
1943............	21,987	79,407	57,420	72.3
1944............	43,635	95,058	51,423	54.1
1945............	44,475	98,416	53,941	54.8
1946............	39,771	60,447	20,676	34.2

a Source: *Annual Report of the Secretary of the Treasury on the State of the Finances for the Fiscal Year Ended June 30, 1956*, pp. 322–23.

b Excludes refunds of receipts and receipts transferred or credited to the federal old-age and survivors trust fund and the railroad retirement account.

c Excludes refunds of receipts and amounts appropriated to the railroad retirement account.

THE PERIOD 1947–1958. In common with earlier war and postwar periods, World War II was followed by much higher peacetime expenditure and debt levels. Deficits were incurred in seven of the eleven years 1947–1958, as may be seen in the table on page 321. These ranged from about four per cent of expenditures to almost 13 per cent. The largest surplus was over $8.4 billion for 1948, an amount equal to approximately one fourth of expenditures. Expenditures reached their postwar low in 1948—$33 billion. For the

---

[12] Both the fiscal years 1941 and 1946 are here classified as wartime years. Serious defense preparation began with the German invasion of the Low Countries in May 1940, or shortly before the close of the fiscal year 1940. The Japanese phase of the War ended in the early part of the fiscal year 1946.

seven years 1952–1958, expenditures were in the range of $65 to $75 billion.

As a consequence of the large deficits incurred during World War II, the gross federal debt reached a peak of $269 billion at the end of the fiscal year 1946 (June 30, 1946). During the fiscal year 1947 the debt was reduced by over $11 billion to approximately $258 billion, mainly by drawing down the general fund balance. Since 1947 the changes in the outstanding debt have been moderate, with a fairly pronounced upward trend from 1951 to 1955. The gross debt on June 30, 1958 amounted to $276 billion.[13]

Federal Receipts, Expenditures, and Deficit or Surplus
Fiscal Years 1947–1958[a]

(In millions of dollars)

Fiscal Year	Net Receipts[b]	Expenditures[c]	Deficit or Surplus (+)	Deficit or Surplus (+) as Percentage of Expenditures
1947............	39,786	39,032	+ 754	+ 1.9
1948............	41,488	33,069	+8,419	+25.5
1949............	37,696	39,507	1,811	4.6
1950............	36,495	39,617	3,122	7.9
1951............	47,568	44,058	+3,510	+ 8.0
1952............	61,391	65,408	4,017	6.1
1953............	64,825	74,274	9,449	12.7
1954............	64,655	67,772	3,117	4.6
1955............	60,390	64,570	4,180	6.5
1956............	68,165	66,539	+1,626	+ 2.4
1957............	71,029	69,433	+1,596	+ 2.3
1958[d]............	69,083	71,896	2,813	3.9

[a] Source: *Annual Report of the Secretary of the Treasury on the State of the Finances for the Fiscal Year Ended June 30, 1957,* pp. 338–39.

[b] Excludes refunds of receipts and receipts transferred and credited to the federal old-age and survivors insurance trust fund and the railroad retirement account.

[c] Excludes refunds of receipts and amounts appropriated to the railroad retirement account.

[d] Preliminary figures from the *Treasury Bulletin* (August 1958), p. 1.

[13] The effect of major wars on the federal budget is well illustrated by the postwar figures. In each year of the period since the end of World War II interest payments alone exceeded federal expenditures for all purposes in the early 1930's.

The data for receipts, expenditures, and deficits or surpluses thus far presented in this summary relate to the administrative budget. The figures in the several tables are from the Treasury's historical series. In recent years the so-called cash or cash-consolidated budget has been widely used by economists and statisticians in their analyses of the relations between the federal government and the economy. The merits of the cash-basis figures for economic analysis are unquestioned. Our sole reason for not using this basis in the table on page 321 covering the period 1947–1958 is that in a historical study a fairly uniform statistical series should be used.[14]

In the early years of the great depression there was increasing interest in the financial relations between the public and the government. The distinction between total budget expenditures and the cost of government, realistically viewed, loomed less important. The interest of economists and other analysts came to be centered on what was called the federal net contribution to purchasing power, or net income-creating expenditures. The budget aggregates were unsatisfactory for the purpose of showing the flow of funds to and from the public. In deriving figures for the "net contribution," budget expenditures such as the transfer to the civil service retirement and disability fund, interest on federal obligations credited to trust funds, and subscriptions to the capital stock of government corporations were excluded. These expenditures did not result in any cash outgo from the Treasury. Receipts that took the form of intragovernmental transfers were also excluded.[15]

---

[14] Discussions of the federal budget at times seem to suggest that receipts and expenditures include only current income and current operating costs. The federal budget is in no sense comparable to an income statement of a corporation. This was made clear in W. F. Willoughby's analysis of current receipts and current operating costs for the period 1921–1930. (*Financial Condition and Operations of the National Government 1921–1930*, 1931, pp. 117 ff.) This study demonstrated the importance of distinguishing among operating costs, capital outlays, investments, and debt service. The difference between budget expenditures and current costs of operation is now appreciably larger than during the years covered by Willoughby's study.

[15] During the 1930's Martin Krost and Lauchlin Currie of the division of research and statistics of the Federal Reserve Board helped to develop the procedures that led to the present-day concept of the cash or cash-consolidated budget. Memoranda on file in the library of the Board of Governors of the Federal Reserve System include: (1) "The Measurement of the Net Contribution of the Federal Government to National Buying Power" by Martin Krost (Aug. 16, 1938); and (2) "Explanation of Method of Compiling Net Contribution," by Currie and Krost (Feb. 10, 1939). This work was initiated well before the dates of these memoranda.

Federal Receipts From the Public and Payments to the Public
Fiscal Years 1948–1958[a]

(In millions of dollars)

Fiscal Year	Receipts	Payments	Deficit or Surplus (+)
1948........	45,357	36,493	+8,864
1949........	41,576	40,570	+1,006
1950........	40,940	43,147	2,207
1951........	53,390	45,797	+7,593
1952........	68,013	67,964	+ 49
1953........	71,499	76,773	5,274
1954........	71,627	71,860	232
1955........	67,836	70,538	2,702
1956........	77,088	72,617	+4,471
1957........	82,106	80,007	+2,099
1958[b].......	81,855	83,328	1,473

[a] Source: *Budget of the United States Government for the Fiscal Year Ending June 30, 1959*, p. 879.
[b] Preliminary figures from the *Treasury Bulletin* (August 1958), p. 17.

When the Social Security Act was approved in 1935, the difference between the administrative budget and the cash or cash-consolidated budget became of far greater importance. Budget receipts and expenditures exclude the transactions of the old-age and survivors insurance trust fund and the unemployment trust fund, together with numerous other trust funds and deposit accounts. In recent years receipts from the public credited to these funds and payments to the public charged thereto have run well into the billions.[16] The rise in the level of social security contributions and benefits, together with the creation of the highway trust fund, has widened the margin between the administrative budget and the cash budget.[17]

[16] For the fiscal year 1957 receipts credited to trust and deposit accounts were $14.4 billion and expenditures were $13 billion. *Budget of the United States Government for the Fiscal Year Ending June 30, 1959*, p. 827. The bulk of these amounts was reflected in receipts from and payments to the public.
[17] A detailed explanation of the difference between the two bases is beyond the scope of the present study. For a complete explanation see Special Analysis A, "Federal Government Receipts from and Payments to the Public," *Budget of the United States Government for the Fiscal Year Ending June 30, 1959*, p. 879. See also Gerhard Colm, *The Federal Budget and the National Economy* (1955), pp. 75–76.

Federal receipts, expenditures, and deficits or surpluses are shown on a cash basis in the table on page 323 for the period 1948–1958. Since cash expenditures from trust and other funds greatly exceed the non-cash expenditures included in the administrative budget, the budget level on the cash basis is well above that for the administrative budget. For 1958 the difference was over $11 billion. Similar comparisons for other years may be made by referring to the tables on pages 321 and 323.

INDEX

Index